REINVENTING
TALENT
MANAGEMENT

REINVENTING
TALENT
MANAGEMENT

How to Maximize Performance
in the New Marketplace

William A. Schiemann

WILEY

John Wiley & Sons, Inc.

For general information on our other products and services or for technical support, please contact our Customer Care Department within the United States at (800) 762–2974, outside the United States at (317) 572–3993 or fax (317) 572–4002.

Wiley also publishes its books in a variety of electronic formats. Some content that appears in print may not be available in electronic books. For more information about Wiley products, visit our web site at www.wiley.com.

Library of Congress Cataloging-in-Publication Data

Schiemann, William.
   Reinventing talent management : how to maximize performance in the new marketplace / William Schiemann.
      p. cm.
   Includes bibliographical references.
   ISBN 978-0-470-45226-4 (cloth)
   1. Personnel management. 2. Ability. 3. Performance. I. Title.
   HF5549.S224 2009
   658.3'14–dc22   2009008839

Printed in the United States of America

10 9 8 7 6 5 4 3 2 1

To Valeria, Wotan, and my family for their unconditional love and to the Metrus team for their extraordinary support.

Contents

Foreword

"Our people are our most important asset"

This is the management mantra I have heard during my career of more than 30 years in the field of human resource management. But where this phrase was once rattled off by executives and managers as trite and meaningless rhetoric (because they never really meant or acted on it), today it's quite different. Today, this phrase is uttered in hushed and fearful tones by executives and managers acknowledging and contemplating the challenges of delivering value within their organization through people. In short, the rhetoric has been taken over by the reality.

As business and organizational leaders have confronted this new reality, they have looked for new ways to better understand, measure, and manage this important asset. While they may understand intuitively the importance of their talent strategies to organizational success, they yearn for a model that allows them to conceptualize, measure their progress, and leverage this asset to add greater value.

For many, the push for a new model arose in the context of rapid growth and change in their organizations or industries. How do we get a handle on the value of the growing enterprise when so much of it is related to the talent we find, keep, or lose? But the value of such a model becomes even more important during significant economic turmoil. How can we fully value our organizations in a chaotic environment when we can't really assess the equity we've built through our talent management? How do we make decisions regarding our very survival when we don't fully appreciate whether or not we can execute new strategies with the talent we have, and don't fully appreciate the talent we'll need?

With this book, Dr. Schiemann has provided such a model. The book represents a fresh approach to talent management by presenting a fresh concept in the People Equity framework.

Based on sound research, insight and experience garnered from more than 70 academics, C-suite executives, practitioners, and talent Thought Leaders, Bill has provided information, tools and ideas for challenging old ways of thinking. And thankfully, yours doesn't have to be a huge organization to apply them. In short, the People Equity framework provides the human resource management field with a model similar to what Process Reengineering, the Balanced Scorecard, and Six Sigma did for other elements of the business.

In a global economy with periods of booms and bust, Bill's People Equity framework is a welcome addition to the knowledge we'll all need to survive and thrive.

—**Susan R. Meisinger, SPHR, JD**
Retired CEO, Society for Human
Resource Management

Preface

I am writing this book for three reasons:

1. Many companies are leaving a lot of value on the table—unfocused activities, wasted labor resources, skill mismatches, service shortfalls, underused technology, low innovation, and disengaged workers—all because they don't have an adequate understanding of the full set of factors that drive peak performance in this newly emerging market. In the past, organizations could afford "human spillage" as one executive put it and still succeed in the marketplace; those firms are in the process of being weeded out of the market as you are reading this. Those who can leverage their talent better than their competition will have a significant advantage.

2. Few organizations are measuring their talent management effectiveness well. Measures are woefully inadequate in this nascent field. At the local level, managers often lead by intuition or by time-tested experimentation. However, few have gauges—like the fuel gauge on your automobile dashboard—telling them how full or empty their human capital is. Unfortunately, "empty" is discovered only after there is a talent drain or customers go elsewhere.

3. Talent management is not just a business issue; it's also a societal issue— How will society engage talented people in organizational life? How will organizations attract and retain these talented people in a world of increasing competition for the 'right' talent? What is it about organizational life that can be not only financially rewarding, but also fulfilling?

This book is equally applicable to both large and small organizations, for profit or not, regulated or unregulated, local or global, public or private, service or manufacturing. Why? Talent is a core ingredient to all of these organizations—a necessity for success. For example, while you may think of an organization such as the Girl Scouts as simply an important local developmental experience for your daughter, the Girl Scouts is also an organization that employs over 9,500 people, has 109 boards of directors for regional councils, and has over 900,000 volunteers, all supporting over 2.5 million Girl Scouts. What may have appeared to the casual observer as a local community group is also a major business with all the attendant challenges that large organizations encounter: managing a global and local brand, finding the best talent, managing values, acculturating it, developing skills, optimizing talent, and retaining the best talent. And the Girl Scouts must do that with employees, part-timers, volunteers, and parental oversight; that is, they cannot command the direction, the values, the work ethic—no, they must set a direction and then engage those stakeholders in the mission.

The Girl Scouts are not alone. When you stop to think about it, there are thousands of other organizations that face the same challenges, whether they are large or small—finding, growing, and retaining the best talent that will be a good match for their particular organization. And conversely, it is in the best interest of the individual to seek, find, evaluate, engage, and stay with an organization that is enabling that person to increase his value—to grow monetarily, intellectually, socially, and emotionally.

The Economic Crisis

When we began the research for this book, many of the people we interviewed were focused on the emerging talent shortage taking place in a number of industries, functions, and geographies. As the book was being finished, the market had drastically changed because of the economic recession in many parts of the world. And yet, the most successful organizations that we studied were still intently focused on doing a better job in managing talent. Why? As you will discover throughout the book, these organizations have come to realize that talent management is a key competitive advantage regardless of the economy. In fact, for many of these firms, this lesson was driven home even more effectively during prior recessions. For some, it truly meant survival.

For others, it meant positioning to become dominant leaders in the next growth wave. When economies rebound in the next few years, the fight for the 'right' talent will be ferocious—not just challenging or tough, but ferocious! No, short-term economics will not determine the winners; they will be determined by their ongoing ability to manage talent more effectively than their competition does.

With Baby Boomers and their knowledge and values departing (albeit at a slower rate than anticipated before the economic downturn of late 2008), a new set of workers with different values, skills, and expectations will replace them, creating new challenges.

The book is intended for a variety of audiences:

- Anyone who has responsible for leading people. The principles discussed will significantly help managers of people be more effective in achieving their goals through more effective management of people.
- Finance professionals, such as chief financial officers and controllers, who are being called upon to measure human capital, and the value it contributes.
- Those who are responsible for strategic planning and execution. The principles and approaches of this book will provide invaluable help in developing people strategies and integrating them into the overall business strategy.
- Anyone interested in or responsible for succession planning and leadership development. The elements of this book provide insight into why high potential leaders falter, and methods for assessing and improving leadership effectiveness.
- Anyone who is teaching or is a student of human resources or related disciplines, such as organizational behavior, productivity and performance, organizational psychology, and labor relations.

I hope that the People Equity model will provide readers with new ways to think about talent management, and about the factors that enhance it. I have provided some ideas and tools to enable readers to apply the new thinking to their own organization. There are also references throughout the book to additional information and tools, which can be found at rein ventingtalentmanagement.com. Finally, I hope that the concept of true value creation through organization talent is one that will help companies work through difficult environments and emerge stronger than ever.

Acknowledgments

I began writing this book during an economic boom and completed the task as companies around the world continued to battle the effects of a severe economic downturn. As market conditions deteriorated, the central People Equity concept of this book was put to a severe test. I am indebted to the diverse pool of contributors whom you will encounter in the pages that follow for their insights in helping me shape and reshape the core set of ideas presented in *Reinventing Talent Management*. Those ideas have taken on greater force and value for managing talent regardless of the vagaries of economic cycles.

While I take sole responsibility for the content of this work, it would not have been possible without the support from so many wise and insightful people who care deeply about this subject.

First, I want to thank the many human capital thought leaders—over 70 executive, academic and association leaders—who have added rich cases, insightful research findings, and a wealth of practical applications. In addition to them, I would also like to thank those who reviewed and provided numerous valuable suggestions to earlier drafts of the book, particularly the major contributions of John Boudreau, Wayne Cascio, Judy Clark, Edward Gubman, Peter Hom, Mark Huselid, Robert Liden, Jeffrey Marcus, Richard Reilly, Joseph Rosse, Dean Spitzer and Howard Winkler.

Emily Smith and Lena Ogan contributed many hours of research support that yielded countless great cases and information included in this book. Cristina Matos-Kober, Bret Weinshank, and Jerry Seibert were invaluable in providing research and database information from the Metrus Institute that helped to quantify many of the issues discussed in the book. I owe enormous gratitude to Susan Bershad, John Lingle, and Brian Morgan for their insightful input to the book's concepts and ideas. I'm also indebted to my editor, Lauren Lynch, for her early support of the concept and her valuable insights.

And finally, this book would not have been possible without the enormous dedication of three people. The first, Peter Tobia, has served as both the godfather of editing and my publicist and literary agent for longer than either of us can remember. The second, Colette Tarsan, has been the organizing force that has kept me on track through the long days (and nights) of planning, interviewing, writing, and editing of the book. She worked tirelessly to ensure the success of this project, and I owe her a huge debt of gratitude. And finally, to my wife Valeria, who has given me unwavering support, taking on some of my roles at the office, providing innovative ideas for the organization of the book, and motivating me to stretch to new heights during the toughest hours of writing. This group has been my lifeline for the past year. I can't thank each of you enough!

SECTION I

New Rules in a Changing World

This book is about the lifeblood of organizations: people and value creation. I have been particularly attracted to this subject because of its profound effect on the quality of life for individuals, organizations, and even civilizations. Countries have risen and fallen based on value delivered. We have witnessed marginal organizations, including some great brands, being eliminated in the recent economic recession, and individuals have either been displaced or are thriving in new roles based on their value contribution. Whether you think about it daily or not, most of us go through life engaging in activities that create more or less value for ourselves and others. We go to school to increase our personal knowledge and our potential value to institutions of various types. We join social groups to become more socially adept—or valuable—to those groups and to satisfy our own social needs. We join sports teams to grow physically and to become better team members. And we go to work to find value of various types: monetary, social, intellectual, artistic, competencies, increased self-worth, and so forth.

Organizations, like living organisms, are also value-producing entities. A symbiosis between organizations and people has existed since early time: Organizations depend on the effectiveness of their people to create value in the market while at the same time people depend on organizations not only for their wages, but to increase their sense of self-worth. Given the time that most people spend with their work organizations, these organizations can't help but be a major influence on their employees' identity, sense of fulfillment, and overall satisfaction.

For much of the twentieth century, this relationship was understood and predictable. But over the last decade or more, this individual–organization relationship is changing due to economic, cultural, technological, and political forces that require new ways of thinking about talent. Certainly the most recent recession has laid open many false assumptions about leaders, values, and the world of work. Copycat, vanilla approaches to talent management created many mediocre firms that were talent-depleted or bankrupt. Many were simply trying to follow the "best practices" formulas of the apparently successful firms without fully understanding the connections with their own unique strategy. Some of those are now gone because of gaps in their ability to attract top performers, their approaches to productivity, or their ability to retain the best performers. Their middling approach to talent management was adequate in booming markets when all boats were rising, but it has been fatal in a major market downturn or in environments with serious competition. I have seen this in the betrayed, blank faces of employees in organizational ghost towns.

And yet in other organizations, I find bright-eyed, exuberant, and engaged employees. The difference is both in value creation and the match between individuals and organizations with the means to accomplish that. Firms that have already positioned their talent for tough competition; created hungrier, more engaged and talented people; and developed winning cultures that enabled them to grow even closer during the downturn have been the most successful. Those organizations have moved beyond the placards, wallet cards, and banners to vibrant talent-driven cultures.

Value creation requires people who focus on agreed-upon goals, who bring knowledge and skills that will enable the organization to satisfy its customers, and who are willing to put in whatever it takes to help the organization succeed. What are the ingredients that enable this to happen? What is it that outstanding organizational leaders are doing to attract and retain superior performers who are willing to work tirelessly for the organization? What systems and tools are in their talent arsenals that enable them to leverage their human capital investments far better than most? And, how do individuals best grow their personal value by affiliating with the right kinds of organizations?

We know how to address these issues—and we can no longer waste the valuable resource represented in our talent. At the Metrus Institute, we have witnessed a wide performance spectrum and have discovered some underlying factors that differentiate the winners from all others. There is no magic bullet, but there are proven principles. Some of the principles have been around for a long time; others are new, based on emerging challenges in the new marketplace.

The newly emerging concept of People Equity described in the pages that follow is a useful framework for strategy makers and talent implementers alike. This framework will:

- Guide understanding of what optimizes workforce performance and capacity, and hence the return on talent investments
- Help senior leaders align talent with their business strategy, ensuring that sufficient talent exists in the right configurations to compete in the marketplace
- Enable talent leaders to do a better job of attracting, selecting, and retaining the best talent
- Enable Human Resources professionals to be more successful in building and executing their talent-related programs and processes, thereby enabling them to justify human capital investments more effectively
- Provide a structured set of tools that senior leaders can use to assess their current and potential leadership talent, and enable them to target resources to close leadership talent gaps

- Provide a playbook for managers to grow and develop as leaders of people, giving them the key success ingredients in managing their employees
- Give employees and team members a better sense of how personal and organizational value dovetails, and what they need to do differently to become fulfilled in their roles in a variety of organizations

Organizational Darwinism will favor workforces that are highly aligned and efficient in executing strategy, that have the right capabilities to meet customer expectations, and that are highly engaged in the mission of the organization. Having a highly productive culture is no guarantee of success, but the reverse is a guarantee of failure.

Let's explore the possibilities . . .

1

The Talent Challenge

"While some businesses skated by with mediocre talent management in the past, they will no longer be able to do so, given the fiercely competitive world ahead."
—Susan Meisinger, retired CEO, Society for Human Resource Management

T hink about any important goal in your life—getting an A in an important course, seeing your child graduate, completing a successful journey, getting that promotion, learning a new language, mastering a favorite hobby, even getting your golf handicap to levels that your friends envy. Why do some people seem to breeze through these life hurdles while others struggle? Is there some secret that they possess, or are they just lucky?

Early mentors in my life filled me with insights that at first mystified me, and later settled in at a more profound level. One lesson that I remember well was from a relative who frequently reminded me that "The harder he worked, the luckier he got." That was generally true, but he had so many setbacks that I began to question his advice. Why was it that he could never hit the mark despite all the hard work?

My father-in-law was famous for reminding a smug 20-something, "It's not only what you know, but who you know!" Wait a minute, I had more education than he did and I thought information was power! It sounded too political and unfair to a purist coming out of school, but I began to appreciate his wisdom when I struggled with getting my right answers accepted in my first major corporate experience. But even with his extensive network, he seemed to struggle to achieve some aspirations. Why was that?

And my graduate adviser was quick to tell me, "Work smart and not hard!" Wow, was I wasting that much time? What was he really telling me? Was he implying that I was not competent enough to earn my doctorate? I began to realize that I was spending too much time on interesting classes and research activities, but perhaps low- or no-value activities in pursuit of a key goal—my dissertation.

And finally, my parents saw the importance of creating value with advice such as "Make a difference!" It sounded like a noble thing, but little did I realize that it was *the* primary idea that would enable me to achieve success along the way.

Each of these admonitions (and I'm sure that you have many similar examples) intertwined throughout much of my life as I struggled to uncover the ingredients of success in college, in my academic career, in my life in a corporate behemoth that employed nearly one million employees, in a firm that I started over 20 years ago, and in my personal hobbies and aspirations. I began to realize that there were underlying factors that drive success.

But were these my own instincts? My own formula? As I examined the world informally, I began to recognize that these were not unique to me, but seemed to apply to others as well. In observing people who were successful and comparing them to those who were less so, I realized that you cannot control all of the factors in life that lead to success versus failure, but that there seemed to be some important ways in which you can stack the deck in your favor to increase the odds. As I began watching, studying, and later scientifically researching successes and failures across the globe—in sports, in business, in life—I came to realize that those who are successful increase their odds of succeeding by leveraging certain success factors, whether knowingly or unwittingly.

This book is about stacking the deck, and about growing value, both personally and in organizations as they realize the value contribution of people to organizational success. And it is not only about exploring what has guided others to success, but also about how those underlying success factors will become even more important in a world that is dramatically changing. In short, it is about making a difference!

Let's take a look at two situations. While the names have been changed for confidentiality, the stories are based on real firms. We will begin with a smaller organization because many of the underlying issues are multiplied across the many smaller units of larger global organizations, frequently becoming lost in its complexity.

Bob's Service Star

Imagine you own a small business like Bob, and you generate $500,000 a year in sales. For the past five years, you have cleared $50,000 annually. Not bad for a small business. After asking a few questions, and doing a few calculations, what if you were told that you might have earned $100,000, or double your existing profit. I'm sure that you would want to know what could make such a difference. And when you were told that much of that gain is in your people, you might step back and say, "Wait, I manage my people as tightly as anybody, and I don't see how that would be possible!" And what if you further heard that, based on your answers to a few of my questions, you have a good chance of being out of business in five years? You would almost assuredly laugh and say, "You don't know my business as well as I do." You are right that no one can know the intricacies of your business as well as you do, but armed with a few questions about your business, a look at recent research and best practices, and an understanding of emerging trends, even an outsider could have a good chance of being correct.

Recent research conducted by the Metrus Institute in partnership with the American Society of Quality tells us that:

- Firms that receive high scores in managing their human capital are more than twice as likely to be in the top one-third of their industry in financial performance, compared to those who manage labor poorly. If the average small business is earning a 10 percent profit, recent research and best practice information suggests it could be earning as much as twice that.

- Firms in the top 25 percent on key people practices are losing far fewer of their top performers—8 percent on average compared to 18 percent in low people-practice businesses. For Bob's service business, which has 16 employees, with an employee replacement cost (finding, training, and getting them to peak productivity) of $12,000 per employee and a turnover rate of 50 percent, turnover costs are $96,000 per year. By adjusting some key people practices resulting in higher employee engagement, turnover costs could be cut in half— bringing $48,000 more to the bottom line!

- Quality provided to customers is substantially higher with highly engaged and capable people who are aligned with their customers. Companies in the top quarter of firms on those people factors have over twice the chance of being in the top third in quality among their competitors. As the competition gets tougher, top quality firms are retaining and growing their customers far better; low quality firms are seeing significantly reduced financial results or dropping out.

  Bob's Service Star is losing 20 percent of its customers each year— over half because they are looking for higher quality. Assuming that this 20 percent of the customers represent 20 percent of the revenue, then $100,000 of revenue must be replaced each year. By bringing the right talent, information, and resources to customers at the moment of truth in service delivery, that replacement number can be cut in half. In other words, the company earns $50,000 by having employees with the right service mentality.

- Typically, 15 to 30 percent of an employee's time is wasted in low- or no-value activities (for example, low priority e-mail, meetings without actions, socializing, phone calls, peripheral projects), because of mis- alignments of one type or another—employees don't understand your goals or policies, their values are not in concert with the organization's, or they get themselves involved in activities that are not as meaningful or productive. As my academic adviser suggested, they may be working hard, but not smart.

  Highly aligned businesses can often bring that unproductive time below 10 percent. This recapture of employees' time yields $40,000 of bottom line savings in found labor time to redeploy on additional custom- ers, new products or services, or to scale back labor costs.

- Market trends will have an adverse impact on Bob's Service Star. First, if Bob's region follows national demographic projections, Bob will have to cope with a substantially different labor force, one with a different availability and mix of skills and interests. Howard Winkler of Southern

Company has struggled with this issue in the Southeast, for example. He notes that there has been a great deal of commotion concerning the shortage of engineers, but in many locales around the world, basic skilled trades are not in great supply—plumbers, electricians, welders, machinists, and yes, even, auto mechanics.

During recessionary periods, there will be greater competition to secure customers, meaning that Bob will face competitors, (some new and often with lower costs), that will drive prices down. Second, some competitors, such as the dealerships that compete with Bob's, may well be outsourcing a portion of their backroom work (for example, diagnostics or advisory services) to India, Latin America, China, or other lower-labor-cost locations. This will not only create pricing pressures, but could also increase the standards for quality or speed to compete effectively.

During the next economic expansion, organizations like Bob's will likely face double jeopardy. First, misaligned or disengaged employees who stayed put during the recession may be eager to leave, leading to a further strain on the existing talent pool. Many organizations will go from talent feast to talent famine. Second, because of the global demographics and skills mix, the world will face a talent vacuum in many of the most desirable and critical skill areas. Organizations that are not well positioned are apt to be stripped of top talent without much warning.

This combination of trends has the potential to create the perfect storm—for Bob and for millions of other business leaders, small and large. The prediction that Bob and other firms might be out of business may not be wacky after all.

Large Corporations Face Perhaps Even Greater Challenges

We started with an example that resonates with many of you—a local small business of the sort that employs millions of workers across the globe. Large corporations, however, employ nearly half the population in many industrialized countries.

If the statistics presented here are applied to large corporations, the impact is dramatic. Imagine the success of a $3 billion firm that could be 5 to 15 percent more profitable and more sustainable in the future. That's a lot of money to the bottom line!

Let's take a look at GlobalCompute, a global technology giant. Martha Werthing[1] had been a successful business executive who rose through the finance ranks, taking on key operational assignments, and finally assuming the leadership of a major Fortune 500 firm. She was a charismatic speaker who talked brashly about her competitors and was fearless of their might and reputation.

She fought hard to restructure the organization to acquire missing core competencies. Internally, she challenged her global leadership team to take on important competitive battles. She articulated a clear future strategy for the business and could bring even the most cynical managers to tears with her vision of bringing the competition to its knees.

But execution is often the Achilles heel of strategy, even when it is clear and compelling. Given the speed with which GlobalCompute's formidable competitors moved, the challenge was implementing precise market plans that depended on speed, innovation, new products and capabilities, and a highly effective internal team. While employees left her town meetings ready to take the hill, they soon bogged down on defining the hill, battling internal customers over who was right, jockeying for power, and struggling to find an identity. The company was simply not agile enough to beat the competition to the punch. While her vision was initially compelling, people quickly reverted to their historical patterns of behavior and functional silos. The misalignments were deeply embedded in the *how* not the *what*.

Moreover, the company's capabilities were falling short of market expectations. Products were late to market, inconsistent in quality, had features that did not meet market promises, and were delivered by a disconnected sales force. No one took action to address historical values and structures that were now only obstacles to the new business plans. Without a deeper base of understanding and trust that would help create the alignment needed to execute, her beginning-of-the-week words of wisdom were only faint echoes on Friday morning.

Employees knew and trusted their earlier world; they knew what to expect and how to operate in the old ways. Many were still very much committed to the old vision and values, believing that "this too shall pass." And even those who wanted to embrace the new vision didn't know how.

Not surprisingly, the new strategy went nowhere, and Martha Werthing was asked to resign. She left behind a highly talented, but siloed and demoralized culture. Rather than creating a more committed and engaged workforce, an atmosphere of cynicism, a distrust of leadership, and frustration torpedoed the goals and brought the house down.

Werthing was considered near the top of her competitive class, and yet she failed. She was astute at the 50,000-foot level, but couldn't align and mobilize people to execute the business strategy. She had a deep understanding of the business dynamics of her industry, but could not surmount the people challenges, which proved fatal to strategy execution. She failed when:

- People—including her board and executive suite—were not *aligned* with her vision. The organization could not succeed as a house divided.
- She miscalculated her ability to bring the right *capabilities* to the marketplace—great skills and technology alone were not enough. Talent needed to be calibrated to the vision, brand, technology, and resources in a way that customers valued.
- She struggled to hold the initial *engagement* of many of her people in the vision, which could not survive executive in-fighting, functional silos, poor follow-through on commitments, rapidly changing strategies, low communications transparency, and lack of input and involvement of employees.

Werthing's situation is not unique. She and many senior leaders like her fail to successfully address the make-or-break talent factors that determine the profitability and growth of today's organizations. Many of the old rules no longer apply. And the new rules must be applied differently in various organizations and cultures.

Reinventing Talent Management will demonstrate the need to adopt fresh thinking to managing talent in organizations of every size and type. Our conclusions are based on an examination of the new talent marketplace and the role it plays in shaping organizational growth and survival. The talent marketplace is the playing field for determining who gets what talent and how well it is being used within and outside of the organization. Externally, it is represented by global and local forces that influence an organization's ability to obtain and keep the talent it needs to be successful. Internally, it is the vibrant day-to-day dynamics that enable some organizations to have the right talent in the right place to achieve business goals better than the competition can. This often means talent that creates more satisfied customers, is more skilled, has stronger leaders, actively recruits new talent, is innovative, is loyal, and is more productive—in short, the talent has been optimized.

In support of my conclusions, I will share with you important information based on research conducted with thousands of organizations, case studies of businesses that are succeeding and failing, interviews with over 70 talent thought leaders from academia, industry, government, and talent-related professional associations, and emerging trends that will determine who will win now and well into the future, regardless of the vagaries of economic cycles and boom-or-bust market conditions.

I will present a tested framework that has practical implications for how to more effectively manage talent in this new marketplace. From it, we will draw clear implications for making decisions and allocating resources in the many aspects of talent management—from finding it, to developing it, to keeping it. The framework also provides a clear template for measuring talent, allocating limited resources, and making important talent decisions.

Finally, you will find throughout the book many recommended actions and best practice ideas for board directors, C-suite executives, managers, and human resources professionals, based on our research, best practice cases across a variety of organizations, and the practical suggestions of talent leaders in high-performing organizations.

Let us begin with a look at the talent marketplace.

Ten Trends That Will Change Your Future

1. *Global competition.* It is an economic truism that the pattern of supply and demand has a decisive effect on the destiny of nations, markets, and companies. With global barriers coming down and technological reach expanding, there are far more suppliers offering more products than customers can consume. While this is Economics 101, the scope of the change is far greater than most are ready for; many businesses large and small are about to be jolted by new and varied competitive faces.

Just look at the local bookstore in the face of Amazon. Look at Blockbuster in the face of Netflix. Look at United in the face of Southwest. Look at Yahoo in the face of Google. Look at Sears and Kmart in the face of Wal-Mart. Look at GM in the face of Toyota, which recently took the crown as the world's biggest automaker after 77 years of GM dominance.[2]

Sears is a great example of an organization that broke the competitive barrier with a catalog that transformed shopping over a century ago, only to be out transformed by big box stores like Wal-Mart. Survival of most organizations will depend on their ability to deliver *unique value* they can provide and sustain in a marketplace characterized by new forms of competition and a far greater number of competitors.

2. *A change in labor supply and demand.* In 2005, the United States passed a watershed moment in its history: For the first time in modern history, its labor supply and demand curves crossed.[3] In aggregate, there were an insufficient number of people to fill the number of jobs that were required to fuel current needs, not to mention future growth. The recession that began in December 2007 certainly put many people back on the street temporarily, alleviating the enormous talent stress that was escalating in early 2008, but that does not mean that the right talent is available where it is needed, which is addressed shortly.

Some look to Asia as a source of labor. This, too, is deceptive, because of the huge variability of skills across countries like China and India—many unskilled agrarian workers and a paucity of managerial and professional talent. Think of China as a global black hole that sucks in skilled talent from India, Korea, Southeast Asia, Eastern Europe, and even the United States to meet the needs generated by its rapid growth. During a recent visit, this author found great shortages of skilled managers—especially in middle management ranks. According to demographers and futurists, only India, among the major talent pools, will continue to be a net exporter of talent through 2020.

3. *Uneven distribution of talent.* Look for niche shortages. In labor-challenged locations such as Hawaii, jobs such as nursing and industries like high tech and energy have been struggling to find the right talent for many years. While the recession that began in 2008 will provide some labor capacity relief, it will not do so everywhere or evenly. And when the next spurt of growth occurs, these niches are likely to be the first ones stressed.

During the competitive growth period before the most recent recession, Hawaii was approaching 2.0 percent unemployment—numbers the economists would consider full employment because of job changes, displacements, and so forth. While their unemployment numbers have been rising, they remain about 2 to 3 percentage points below that of the mainland United States. Many skills are still in short supply.

Some professions, like nursing, scientists, and engineers have experienced worldwide shortages.

Houston is an example of a combination of industry and profession scarcity. In 2001, with the fall of Enron and low energy prices, it was a pocket of unemployment; in 2008, it was a pocket of talent drain as the demand for all forms of energy had skyrocketed at the same time that many engineers and energy professionals were in the process of retiring. Demographers tell us that over 30 percent of the professional talent in that industry—engineers, geologists, and the like—are expected to retire in the next several years. Rather than 401(k)s that have eroded in the market meltdown, many members of this group have generous defined-benefit pensions, meaning that they will still get guaranteed annuities that will allow them to retire comfortably. A major challenge for leaders in oil and gas, assuming the cost of energy rises, is enticing knowledgeable would-be retirees to stay with the organization in some capacity. Organizations such as Chevron have developed incentive packages to encourage their experienced knowledge workers to either stay on or return after retiring with an attractive alternative compensation arrangement.

Some emerging industries, like green technology, are seeking scarce skills in fields like wind and solar power, bioecology, marine food harvesting, and clean energy.

In other regions, like parts of the Midwestern United States and Western Europe, or in traditional manufacturing jobs, talent is readily available. But even in these places, many workers who have been displaced by the recent recession will be unable to assume existing jobs or emerging jobs in the next growth period because they will not have the necessary skills or the ability to relocate to where those jobs are. This, in effect, is unavailable labor.

4. *Managing diverse workforces in diverse places.* When I attended engineering college, I had my first encounter with Indian, Chinese, and Iranian students from what seemed like mysterious and exotic locations. I learned about iguzi stew and cooked squid, not bad alternatives to the mystery meat of the university cafeteria of the time. While I thought the religious habits of Hindus, Sikhs, Moslems, and Buddhists strange and different, I began to appreciate over time the great differences across the globe that were only beginning to impinge on my narrow Midwestern world view. While I had only one African-American student on my dorm floor in the middle of a city that was statistically over one-third black, as I write this today, I note the election of the first African-American president of the United States of America who hails from that same city.

"People managers will need to acquire a new global perspective, one never previously imagined," says Robert Hoffman, Executive Director of Organizational Development at Novartis Pharmaceutical Corporation, who has witnessed similar trends at global businesses in which he has worked. "Talent will increasingly be managed globally, requiring strong and broad skills, coupled with appropriate sensitivities to different religious practices, ethnic backgrounds, lifestyles, modes of learning, and expectations of what work is."

Other well-documented demographic trends also will change substantially the look and behavior of our workforce. Generational differences are a specific form of diversity that will challenge current and future leaders. Baby Boomers will be retiring in increasing numbers, and as they do, they are being replaced by workers with vastly different work values, lifestyle preferences, and skills. "The new generation of people we are hiring today are smarter than ever," says Dick Clark, controller for Monsanto, and he raises an important question: "How do we adapt ourselves in order to better lead them?" Managing this new generation in a way that creates high people engagement, retention, and strong customer loyalty perhaps will require different approaches. Generation X-ers and Millennials (Generation Y-ers) may come with different technological skills, communication and learning styles, work preferences, and values.

5. *Skill and mind shifts.* As Daniel Pink argues convincingly in *A Whole New Mind*,[4] individuals and organizations alike need to think about new competitive success factors, as technical, accounting, programming, legal, and other skilled jobs are being automated or deployed to lower-cost locations, and critical remaining ones will need to be staffed and managed

in different ways. He and others state that the emerging job opportunities will include roles and tasks that are not capable of being reengineered or outsourced abroad—tasks requiring innovation, artistry, complex decision making, in-person services, and so forth. If Pink is correct, the twenty-first century MFA (Master of Fine Arts) may supplant the MBA of the twentieth century, in which case many countries will have a glut of MBAs coupled with a severe shortage of artistic professionals—artists, designers, creators; they simply aren't in the pipeline.

6. *Technology.* "Technology is changing the way we work and how fast we work," says David Ulrich of the University of Michigan, when we interviewed him for the book. Leif Meneke, vice president of talent and leadership for the Americas at Deutsche Bank said, "Technology and systems now enable people to manage human capital in far more effective ways. We have eliminated the routine and trivial task and focus more on real people issues." Over the past decade, much of this has been through the development of better human resources databases that allow organizations for the first time to connect demographic information with performance data, customer ratings, benefit preferences, safety, and a host of other important information. Mining these data and performing decision analyses is still emerging as a major effectiveness opportunity.

The use of Internet and intranet technologies for things such as employee surveys, which can now be connected to database information such as performance and potential ratings, has not only reduced process time, but it has enabled organizations to instantly reach colleagues, suppliers, and other stakeholders around the globe.

There are also exciting new technologies being used to transform talent management and organizational performance. IBM, for example, demonstrated the use of virtual technology to conduct routine and high impact activities around the globe, ranging from job interviews to orientation sessions to focus groups to training. Participants used avatars representing themselves to travel (without lost baggage) through a virtual world, learning and building new relationships with people in faraway places that would be impossible or very expensive in the past.

Another promising new area of technological applications is the use of networking theory, mapping, and applications. For example, it is now possible to cost effectively map knowledge and social relationships that are critical to getting the work done. This has profound implications for replacing retiring or departing gatekeepers, social influencers, or those who connect groups. Organizations such as Yahoo and Oracle are tapping into social and professional networks such as MySpace or LinkedIn and using Twitter to get quick feedback on how the job interview was perceived by the applicant.

The implications for the talent leader is that many of these techniques will provide more profound information enabling faster, more effective decisions using fewer resources—a competitive advantage for those who can leverage technology the best.

7. *Leadership succession gaps.* In a recent survey of over 500 global C-suite executives conducted by the SHRM Foundation, one of the top stay-awake-at-night issues for senior leaders is finding sufficient leadership talent. This was rated as urgent both today and for the future. Even a quick check with the talent leaders' panel that we interviewed for the book during the market freefall of 2008 surprisingly reaffirmed a continuing concern about succession. In fact, many thought that the recession would force many of their current top leaders to retire, creating a vacuum of ready leadership talent to fill the void. Many organizations are already suffering from a lack of top leadership talent, and this gap will only increase in the upcoming years. Those who mismanage these smaller talent pools will be forced to buy highly priced external talent, with higher failure rates—estimated as high as four out of five hires at senior levels! The heightened level of competition for talent will be a great advantage for free agents, but will prove increasingly cost prohibitive for organizations and their shareholders.

8. *The cost of talent mistakes is growing.* As strategic talent becomes scarcer in many industries and jobs, and as human capital becomes a larger portion of overall corporate assets in many industries, the cost of talent mistakes will increasingly take its toll on the bottom line. Knowledge organizations such as IBM or service businesses such as UPS realize that their profits lie in how well they can manage talent. Organizational managers will need to be more precise in defining their most strategic talent needs and more effective in acquiring them. Today, many recruiting, screening, and selection processes are crude at best. Such imprecision will become inordinately expensive in the coming years. "And talent is not captive," notes Wayne Cascio, a leading researcher and educator with the University of Colorado at Denver and recent chairman of the SHRM Foundation. The quality of onboarding, training, developing, and coaching talent will be crucial to retaining it.

9. *Paucity of human capital measures.* While most management teams know exactly how much equipment, inventory, and space they own, few have good measures of their talent gains and losses. In the average service organization today, 80 to 95 percent of total real assets—those invested in people—never appear on the balance sheet.[5] And when measures do exist for an organization's talent, they are often tactical and rearview metrics that do not adequately capture the value of the workforce. For example, top talent turnover is a lagging indicator in many organizations, which

puts them at a competitive disadvantage compared to organizations that have good leading indicators of talent. Organizations with good predictors of turnover can address critical causes before top talent is out the door.

10. *Low readiness for change.* While some firms are building models to project needed workforce size, few are prepared for the talent gaps (and in some cases gluts) that are around the corner, and fewer still have carefully determined which jobs are strategically critical. Among those who understand and accept the flood of changes that are ahead of them, few have sufficient plans, measures, or processes in place to reach higher ground in time. Huge numbers of employees will soon be displaced, so there is little time to prepare for the inevitable transition.

A quick look at the auto industry should give pause to anyone contemplating the future. The United States is accumulating hundreds of thousands of displaced autoworkers who are unable to work in new-demand jobs, or are unable to find employment paying comparable wages to the jobs they left. This situation has been driven by several generations of auto industry leaders, union leadership, and workers who expected things to continue as they had in the past. They failed to prepare for a future that was right in front of their eyes.

Use the exercise provided in the Appendix or online at **www .reinventingtalentmanagement.com** for a discussion of these trends and their implications for your organization.

The Perfect Storm

Martha Werthing was a victim of a combination of these factors, in particular trying to force a strategy into diverse cultures without appropriate attention to traditional values, transparency and inclusion, team values, effective human capital measurement, readiness for change, and leadership succession. Bob was flying blind with dealerships encroaching on his traditional turf because he had been assuming that the old rules still applied—blind employer loyalty, ample talent when needed, customers with the same expectations, and traditional performance standards. The mix of these trends creates the ingredients for a perfect storm. This talent tsunami will soon be coming to a company near you. Are you prepared?

With such significant people challenges facing organizational leaders, I was surprised to find few approaches available to help leaders measure—and manage—the overall value and future potential of their workforces. Figure 1.1 provides a sample of what we found in our review of the field—a grab bag of concepts and definitions that were often overlapping, poorly executed, and having no clear framework for integrating them. While concepts like

FIGURE 1.1 Traditional People Metrics

leadership, innovation, or employee satisfaction are clearly important, it is hard for organizational leaders to know when, where, and how to address these to maximize their return on human capital investments.

In contrast, models exist for capturing value for shareholders and the external market. For shareholders, *financial equity* provides a way to look at the overall financial health of the organization, largely determined by capital markets. For customers, concepts such as *customer equity*[6] or *market-perceived value*[7] have been offered as meaningful ways to understand and measure the value of customers to an organization. These customer concepts have been quite effective in capturing the overall value of a strong brand, good products, and positive customer relationships in improving overall shareholder value.

Unfortunately, there has been no parallel concept for the human side of an enterprise. While the concept of *human capital* comes closest, it suffers from lack of common definition, level of analysis, and measurement, which is discussed further in subsequent chapters.

In the search for a parallel human resources value concept, we began by first going back to basics. How do people create value for organizations and their customers? How can we measure the value of that contribution and potential? How can that value be enhanced?

We have studied scores of successful and unsuccessful organizations over the past decade, examined research related to employee value creation, and interviewed hundreds of talent leaders to find answers to these questions.

A Promising New Path

This search identified three overarching factors that when managed well consistently lead to success: *Alignment, Capabilities*, and *Engagement* (ACE). While we elaborate on the definitions and power of these three components in

Chapter 2, you might think about Alignment as the extent to which organizationally everyone is synchronously rowing in the same direction. Capabilities include the organization's talent, information, and resources needed to increase customer value. Engagement is the energy, or motivation, of employees to help the organization achieve its objectives. These three factors are directly related[8] to key business outcomes such as employee retention, product and service quality, customer or client loyalty, internal stakeholder satisfaction, and financial performance.[9]

While these three concepts have existed in various forms for many years, they have been mired in multiple definitions and never formally integrated into a framework for understanding the human value creation process and measuring the levels of that contribution. We believe we have taken a step toward accomplishing this and have called this framework *People Equity*.[10]

As a descriptive term, People Equity has several advantages over the term *human capital*. First, investors, board members, and senior executives are conditioned to think in terms of financial and market equity, and more recently, customer equity, as positives that are central to their interests. Capital is too often thought of as a cost or resource to be constrained. Second, in many earlier human capital uses, a disproportionate emphasis was placed on competencies, thereby missing other important elements that compose the overall value of people to the organization and its shareholders.

This book is about stacking the deck in your favor—about growing value both personally and organizationally. It's about making a difference. Both Martha Werthing at GlobalCompute and Bob at Bob's Service Star would have been better positioned by improved understanding of the talent marketplace and the trends we have described and by applying the People Equity framework to their respective organizations.

Our journey begins with how you can use the People Equity framework and principles to optimize people and performance, beginning with understanding the concept of People Equity better—how it relates to organizational success and how you can control it (Chapters 2 and 3). We turn our attention next to how People Equity is measured and used to make critical resource investment decisions (Section II). In Section III, we devote a chapter each to Alignment, Capabilities, and Engagement—the three ingredients to optimizing talent and organizational performance. Section IV is devoted to specific applications of People Equity in the overall talent life cycle: acquiring, acculturating, developing, and retaining the right talent. You will find many case studies and best practice applications throughout the book, as well as practical tools to begin applying these concepts successfully.

2

People Equity: What It Is and Why It Matters

"We spend all our time on people. The day we screw up the people thing, this company is over."
—Jack Welch, former GE CEO turned management guru[1]

People Equity: So What?

"People are our greatest asset," says Kenneth Chenault, the CEO of American Express[2]—a comment echoed by numerous corporate leaders over the years. Yet, as Ed Lawler states in his recent book, *Talent: Making People Your Competitive Advantage*,[3] delivery on this promise is rarely executed well.

When I ask audiences the "What's your most important asset" question, usually tongue in cheek, snickering and groaning follow quickly. When I ask why the reaction, the response is typically: "We don't ever seem to live up to those words!" When I probe further, they tell me:

- "Management says that food safety and customer satisfaction is most important, but someone should tell it to my boss, who believes cutting costs and doing things faster are more important," says an employee of a global quick serve restaurant chain.
- "We say customer satisfaction is Number One, but then we cancel service and business acumen training that are intended to increase our customers' satisfaction," laments a human resources professional in a regional bank.
- "We talk about employee loyalty, but we just humiliated an employee who we walked to the door during a dismissal. What did that say to everyone else about people being our most important resource?" offered a middle manager from a global pharmaceutical firm.

These three statements are just a slice of the typical comments demonstrating why it is not enough to say we understand that people are important. Intentions must be converted to blueprints for action at the storefront or shop floor level—the level where real behaviors make or break a business. It is here where major gaps are most likely to occur, ones that reduce customer and employee loyalty, increase turnover, and reduce profitability.

Our quest was to understand which factors were really important in helping connect the boardroom with the knowledge, service, or production worker. This meant understanding the dynamics of what connects employee behavior, organizational goals, and customers. More specifically, it means understanding why:

- Executives' words and intentions often do not jibe with reality.
- Employees' priorities are often different from those of their leaders.

- Employees get turned off by their organizations—why they start at 100 percent Engagement and often slip to 50 percent or less.
- Customers are frequently disappointed at the moment of truth in their interactions with vendors and their employees.

By understanding these issues and by examining them in both successful and unsuccessful organizations, we sought to identify controllable factors that leaders and employees could leverage for greater value to all major stakeholders: employees who could enjoy longer and more fulfilling employment; employers who could grow their businesses faster and more profitably; customers who would have far better buying experiences; and communities that would thrive with healthy businesses adding to their local economies.

While we have examined thousands of organizations and hundreds of success factors cited by gurus, corporate leaders, middle managers, community advocates, labor leaders, and average employees, we found no silver bullet. While concepts such as Empowerment or Re-engineering have extended our organizational thinking, they have been viewed too often as panaceas.

What we did discover were three factors that appeared to explain more than 80 percent of the gaps we had found in performance: Alignment, Capabilities, and Engagement. These factors, taken in combination, explained why many disconnects occur and why the employee laments discussed earlier are felt. For example,

1. The different priorities and messaging of senior leaders versus local restaurant managers in the food and safety example are a clear case of mis-Alignment that undermines employee clarity regarding priorities.
2. The slash and burn of training targeted to improve customer service was a clear case of a decision that reduces Capabilities to serve the customer.
3. The disrespectful treatment of a dismissed employee was a clear case of an action that is likely to decrease employee loyalty or Engagement.

As we experimented with the three factors of Alignment, Capabilities, and Engagement across many different organizational scenarios, we found that they helped explain why organizational and individual performance was often not optimal. But this insight, in turn, raised further questions, which are outlined in Figure 2.1.

We address these questions through the remainder of the book, beginning with the definitional and relevance questions in this chapter, followed by information on the Drivers of People Equity, measurement, resource

FIGURE 2.1   People Equity Questions

- What are these three People Equity factors? What role do they play?
- Do these three factors truly have a decisive impact on business and personal success? If so, in what ways?
- Are the three factors of People Equity predictable and controllable? What are the drivers or levers of control?
- If these factors are important, are they measurable and do they predict important personal and business outcomes?
- How can People Equity and its three components help in making talent investment decisions?
- How can leaders and employees use People Equity to optimize performance?
- How can People Equity inform design and delivery of key aspects of the talent management life cycle: acquiring, acculturating, developing, and retaining the right talent for your strategy?

allocation, optimizing talent, and then a look at some of the key stages of the talent management life cycle.

People Equity: Three Pieces to the Puzzle

In reviewing 50 years of organizational research and 20 years of client research and case experience across thousands of organizations in almost every industry, it became clear that despite the "We are really different" refrain that we've come to expect from most executives that we encounter, there appeared to be three common people factors that repeatedly influenced their business success. More specifically, these three human capital factors—Alignment, Capabilities, and Engagement—not only drive overall workforce performance, but also other very important business outcomes as well, including customer satisfaction, quality, and financial performance.

The three key elements of People Equity are depicted in Figure 2.2. *We refer to this People Equity platform as the ACE (Alignment, Capabilities, and Engagement) model.* When any one component is deficient, performance suffers. For example, it is possible to have short-term Engaged employees, but if they are misaligned with the organization's goals, they are unlikely to meet business targets. Let's take a look at each of the factors.

FIGURE 2.2 Key Elements of People Equity

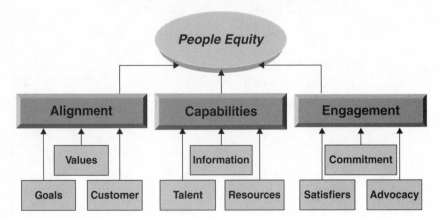

Alignment

When I was growing up, *Alignment* was associated with what your automobile needed when its wheels wobbled. But in reality, Alignment is part of our lives every day.

Let's take a familiar example for most parents, who often act like they live in Garrison Keillor's Lake Wobegon, where all of the children are above average. Assume that your gifted child loves geography. She studied hard during much of the weekend (remember, she is engaged in her subject), but when she took the test and we learn the results, we're shocked to discover that she failed. You later learn from one of your daughter's friends that the exam focused on Europe, not Africa, as your daughter had assumed—whoops! It's a common case of student-teacher misalignment. Easily corrected? You bet. But she still keeps the failing grade for her performance.

The same might also be true for a restaurant manager being transferred to a new territory if he uses prior assumptions about customers and employees. When those assumptions do not jibe with those of the customer, sales plummet.

In the organizational context, vertical Alignment is the extent to which employees are connected to or have a line of sight to the business strategy and goals. Values Alignment includes the connectedness of employees' behaviors with organizational values. Horizontal Alignment is the extent to which work units are effectively aligned with one another to deliver high value products or services to customers. Just as with the automobile, high Alignment means less organizational wobble or drag.

Capabilities

Capabilities capture the extent to which the organization effectively develops talent, information, and resources to increase customer value.

- A bank that I worked with several years ago had an exciting new strategy that had emerged from customer and bank employee focus groups: Consolidate customer contacts to one loan officer in each branch. For customers, this would make relationships with the bank easier; for the bank, it offered opportunities to cross-sell products. After extensive training of loan officers and much hoopla, the initial rollout fizzled. Customers actually threatened to leave, as did red-in-the-face loan officers. An important part of the Capabilities dimension is Information, which, in the bank's case, was an embarrassing gap. When customers came in to a branch, the IT system would not allow loan officers access to information on bank relationships that were initiated at other branches. Customers wanting to discuss small business loans, equity lines of credit, mortgages, or other business with an officer could not do so without taking a time-wasting detour into the past. Having high Capabilities requires having not only the right talent or skills—the usual suspects when things go awry—but also the right information and resources at the moment of truth for the customer.

While there are many definitions of Capabilities floating about, we settled on a definition that is customer-centric: The extent to which the organization effectively creates talent, information, and resources *to grow customer value*. Furthermore, this definition addresses not only the idea of talent, which many human resources professionals and business leaders think about first, but also the other critical components—information and resources—that are needed to meet customers' needs and expectations. Why customer needs and expectations? Because this is the value driver for most organizations.

We also prefer this definition because it can be applied inside the organization as well. Everyone has a customer[4] for her services, whether she interfaces with the external customer or indirectly provides products and services for someone who does. When you as a customer think about a moment of truth—getting that rental car when you need it, having your computer problem solved by someone on a help line, or securing that important tool for a home project from a local retail store—you want a perfect experience. That is, you want to expend the least effort necessary to solve your problem or need.

When things go wrong at that moment of truth, whether it is weak talent (knowledge, skills, and abilities) of the people you deal with, missing information, or insufficient resources—you will be disappointed, which can lead to your departure or at least reduced buying in the future.

While customers are the primary area of impact of strong Capabilities, productivity is also affected. Lower skilled workers, with poor resources or inadequate information are handicapped in their ability to produce higher volumes of quality outputs.

Engagement

Engagement goes beyond employee satisfaction with or commitment to one's job or organization. It includes the level of advocacy on the part of employees for their organizations as great places to work, purchase from, and even invest in.

Engagement is a more recent evolution of earlier employee satisfaction and commitment research. In general, the literature has evolved from job satisfaction and morale to employee commitment to workforce Engagement, which implies the highest level of connectedness to the organization. The acid test of Engagement is the extent to which employees are willing to go beyond the minimum requirements of their role to provide additional energy or to advocate for their organization to others as a great place in which to work or invest.

Early studies on employee satisfaction revealed that satisfied employees were adding more value than others to organizations through improved performance, higher customer satisfaction, or lower turnover costs. To this early work was then added the concept of job commitment, and most recently Engagement, which has linked the concept to a wide array of business outcomes, such as higher discretionary effort, faster performance, higher quality, and reduced turnover. It has also been linked to personal outcomes, including reduced stress and conflict, better health, and greater fulfillment. In the past decade, Engagement has become embedded as an important element of a healthy workforce. But as we shall see, Engagement alone is not enough to drive top performance.

When the three factors of People Equity are at maximum strength, people work at peak performance, often with the most personal fulfillment. For example, in the tough, quick-serve restaurant business with its high employee turnover, Jack in the Box found that when its 30,000 employees had high ACE scores, their employees demonstrated higher discretionary effort and had lower intentions to leave, their customers were more satisfied, and their restaurants were more profitable.

With these three critical elements defined, we set about trying to understand and then test:

- Why these concepts seem to be so powerful in driving business and personal success

- How these three concepts work in concert with important talent management situations—the acquisition, development, optimization, and retention of talent
- How we could measure and manage these ACE factors in a framework that would enable us to allocate and target scarce organizational resources more effectively

Reality Testing People Equity Impact

For part of that testing, for example, we teamed with *Quality Progress* and the American Society for Quality for a major study, enlisting respondents from more than 2,000 organizations.[5] The results were revealing.

- Organizations with higher People Equity scores were almost twice as likely to be at the top of their industry in financial performance. Figure 2.3 shows that if an organization is in the top quartile on People Equity, it will have a 65 percent chance of being in the top third of its industry in financial performance, compared to only 37 percent for low People Equity organizations.
- High People Equity organizations are nearly four times more likely to have higher quality. Figure 2.3 also shows that organizations in the top quartile on People Equity have a 71 percent chance of being in the top

FIGURE 2.3 People Equity Impact on Quality and Financial Performance

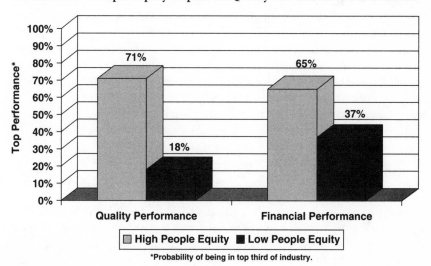

FIGURE 2.4 People Equity Impact on Turnover

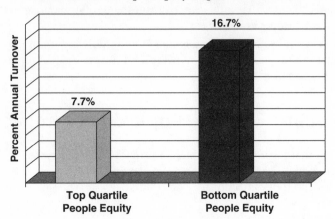

third of their industry in quality compared to only 18 percent for those whose employees are in the bottom quartile on People Equity.
- High People Equity organizations will lose fewer people—many fewer. Firms in the top quartile (Figure 2.4) on People Equity lost only 7.7 percent of their employees compared to more than 16.7 percent for those that were low in People Equity. For the average-sized manufacturing firm in our study, this represented a nearly $19 million cost advantage that high People Equity organizations enjoyed over low People Equity firms. People Equity has significant bottom-line implications.

In a second study with *Quality Progress* and the American Society for Quality with over 1,200 respondents conducted by Seibert and Lingle,[6] the researchers found that People Equity was also an important driver of internal customer service among more than 12 different functions that serve other internal stakeholders. Functions such as information technology, human resources, finance, manufacturing, law, and procurement, among others, that had employees with higher Alignment, Capabilities, and Engagement scores received significantly better value ratings from their internal customers.

- The majority of high People Equity companies achieved the very top internal service ratings, while the majority of low People Equity companies (61 percent) received the lowest ratings.
- A strong service culture is associated with good internal service; no surprise there. But when combined with a high level of People Equity, the results were dramatic: nearly 70 percent of such companies got the top internal service ratings. On the other hand, a strong service culture is not

enough if People Equity is low. Only 26 percent of companies with a strong service culture, but low People Equity, achieved the top ratings— powerful evidence of the unique contribution People Equity makes.

Growing Shareholder Value and People Equity

Based on what we have learned about People Equity and how it relates to other important organizational drivers and results, we constructed the model shown in Figure 2.5.

People Equity provides a bridge between important human capital investments and shareholder equity because it captures the value creation of people and the role that people play in executing the business strategy.

Like other business assets, People Equity creates revenue and profit. It also has potential future value that is either enhanced or decreased over time.

The People Equity–Financial Connection

People Equity is related to Shareholder Value and financial performance, typically through its effect on other key elements. For example, financial performance is typically higher when productivity is high and top performers

FIGURE 2.5 People Equity Is Key Driver of Shareholder Equity

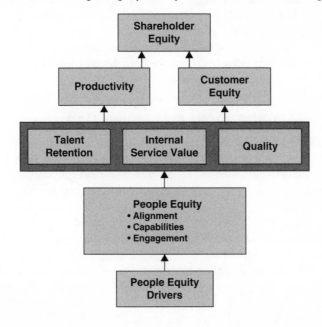

FIGURE 2.6 Veterans Administration Example

VETERANS MEDICAL CENTERS: EFFECTS OF WORK CLIMATE ON
BUSINESS RESULTS THROUGH EMPLOYEE SATISFACTION

| One Standard Deviation Increase in WORK CLIMATE (from mean 2.89 to 3.02) | → | Increase in EMPLOYEE SATISFACTION (from mean 3.24 to 3.36) | → | REDUCTION IN COST OF $128.38 Per Unique Patient or -$400,300,000 Across ALL MEDICAL CENTERS |

From Rita Kowalski, Conference Board Performance Measurement
Conference, May 2003.

stay with the organization. High productivity is achieved by having appropriately skilled and motivated employees who are riveted on the most
important activities that generate value for a particular organization.

A good example of this was found in the U.S. Veterans Administration.
Feuss and his colleagues[7] found that, among Veterans Administration
employees, higher Engagement (and work climate) scores translated to higher
numbers of claims being processed and $400 million dollars in increased
productivity (Figure 2.6). Productivity is often a result of improvements in
speed or quality of performance.

While a great deal of Shareholder Value can be generated through
enhanced productivity and quality alone, the biggest payoff for most organizations is through their customers, as we shall see.

The People Equity–Customer Connection

From a customer perspective, Rust and his colleagues[8] identified three factors
that drive overall customer value: Brand value, Relationship and Retention
value, and Product and Service value. The role that people play varies by
organization, but it is clear that employees can play a role in all three areas.

Brand

Think about how top-notch service employees epitomize the brand at
Nordstrom's—a top service retailer in the United States. This is a function
of hiring and training great service people coupled with a strong customer
value philosophy and strong service processes. I had an opportunity to observe
customer service quality at Nordstrom's shoe department while my wife was

making a purchase. She was immediately assigned a service person, asked to sit and relax as her attendant brought shoes, and invited to stay relaxed as the attendant went away and processed the sale. Buying shoes without the usual hassle! I came away impressed by both their process and their talent.

Other brands have created distinct niches that have loyal followers: Wal-Mart for price; Apple for innovation; McDonald's for consistency anywhere in the world; Starbucks as an alternate-to-the-office meeting place. Each of these brands depends strongly on their employees to operate in a fashion that is consistent with the brand image.

Relationship and Retention Value

Arguably, the most important role that employees play in the customer loyalty equation is in building great relationships. Think about those tellers at your bank that have built long-term relationships with customers. In many organizations, the longevity of its best people is one of the most important factors in keeping customers loyal. Customers like to deal with good people they know.

A while ago I moved to a new area, developed car trouble, and found myself looking for an auto shop that I could trust. I found Repairs Unlimited, a mom-and-pop auto shop that seemed to have the right formula—a dad and his two sons who had been in business for years, with a loyal customer following. As I began dealing with Repairs Unlimited, I was impressed by the fact that the staff took a personal interest in me. They remembered my name, the history of my cars, always provided good explanations for work needed, and looked for the best value in repairs—not ones that would net them the highest margin. When one of the sons, Dave, took over the business, he continued and even enhanced that service, always finding ways to fit me in at the last minute, taking the time to search for the best parts, and recommending alternatives when he could not solve my problem. His style epitomized the Macy's Santa in *Miracle on 34th Street*. And it worked—I have been returning to Repairs Unlimited for nearly 30 years.

Product and Service Value

Talent also has an immense impact on product and service value. In service businesses, employees are the product. Accountants, lawyers, financial advisers, management consultants, and the like embed value in the service they bring to clients. Even in tangible product businesses, employees operate in so many interface roles with customers: sales and customer representatives, billing and account inquiries, product technicians and troubleshooters, and many others.

Furthermore, external customers are simply the end of a long chain of value, much of which is managed invisibly to the customer, at least when all goes right! For example, for your flight to arrive on time with your baggage intact, many different employee groups—not just the ones you customarily see such as gate agents and flight attendants—have played a significant role.

The folks dealing with logistics play a major role in arrival satisfaction, but they are, for the most part, invisible. Pilots, baggage handlers, flight schedulers, cleaning crews, and maintenance all play important roles in your satisfaction with the flight. If you arrive after a perfect flight experience—on time, right destination, good service, and safely—but baggage is delayed inordinately long, the entire experience is shattered as a result. Everything must come together at the moment of truth.

This internal chain is heavily influenced by People Equity. If your gate agent cannot get support from engaged and competent logistics or cleaning crews, the gate agent cannot get the plane out on time. Even if your pilot is doing her best to get you to the destination on time, but she cannot get good routing from the logistical people or upon arrival cannot get ground crews and gate support to quickly park and deplane, you will have a bad experience. Alignment, Capabilities, and Engagement must also be managed across job or functional silos for the customer to have a great experience.

The People Equity–Performance Connection

While there are many customer and financial consequences of having high or low People Equity, there are also human resource consequences. One of the biggest is the loss of high performers. In the ASQ study described earlier, the impact of being in the top versus the bottom quartile of People Equity equated to $19 million in employee churn costs for the average-sized manufacturing firm in the study—not exactly chump change.

People Equity is also related to productivity. Numerous studies over the years have shown the link between Alignment factors such as clear goals and productivity. And clearly, productivity is a major driver of financial performance for most businesses.

This should bring us to an inescapable conclusion that People Equity—and its constituents Alignment, Capabilities, and Engagement—is a critical link in the value chain for any organization in which people play a key role in its overall delivery of value.

The Impact of Low People Equity

Table 2.1 summarizes the business outcomes of low Alignment, Capabilities, and Engagement. This summary is based on a variety of research and case studies over the past 30 years. While a case could be made that Engagement or Capabilities, for example, affect many of the business consequences in the other columns, the intent of this chart is to show where the dominant impact is. Each ACE dimension seems to drive some outcomes more than others:

Table 2.1

The Business Impact of Low Alignment, Capabilities, and Engagement

Low Alignment	Low Capabilities	Low Engagement
• Confusing brand promise	• Unable to meet customer requirements	• Low external or internal customer satisfaction due to disengaged workers
• Many urgent but not important activities	• High rework	• Low productivity due to mediocre energy
• Non-competitive costs due to misdirected energy, talent	• High warranty or guarantee claims because of product deficiencies	• Top talent loss when market conditions permit
• Burnout or talent loss—working hard, but not smart	• Overstaffing to meet standards or customer requirements	• Dead wood: Unmarketable employees retire in place
• Overstaffing, to compensate for time lost on low value activities	• Low customer relationship scores, lower customer retention	• Low referrals of new talent from existing workforce
• Low teamwork, high conflict across interdependent units	• Employee/ Supervisory burnout, turnover because of performance shortfalls with customers	• Cynical or apathetic culture

- Alignment often predicts goal attainment, productivity, and financial performance most directly.
- Capabilities often have the strongest connection to customer outcomes such as customer loyalty or retention.
- Engagement is typically the strongest predictor of employee turnover and discretionary effort at work.

People Equity Profiles

While we have seen the advantages and consequences of strong or weak levels of A, C, or E, in reality, these profiles do not occur in isolation. When you combine the three ACE dimensions, there are eight major profiles.[9] Table 2.2 shows a summary of these People Equity profiles into which organizations

Table 2.2
People Equity Profiles

Alignment	Capabilities	Engagement	Profile
⬆	⬆	⬆	Superior Performance
⬇	⬇	⬆	Cheerleader
⬆	⬇	⬆	Under-Equipped
⬇	⬆	⬆	Strategic Disconnect
⬆	⬆	⬇	Under-Achiever
⬆	⬇	⬇	Indifferent
⬇	⬆	⬇	Talent Waste
⬇	⬇	⬇	Performance Laggard

and their subunits fall. Which one describes your overall organization? Your unit? The profiles are helpful in understanding organizational and managerial strengths and vulnerabilities.

While labels can be dangerous when used improperly, they can provide a quick read on the human capital health of a particular unit. For example, the Cheerleaders may be highly engaged in the success of the organization in the short term, but out of touch with critical requirements, such as its brand promise. They may also lack the Capabilities required to deliver on committed goals.

The Under-Equipped profile occurs when the organization has created a highly Aligned workforce that is at least temporarily Engaged, but unable to satisfy the customer because of missing skills, information, or resources. At Wegman's, a touted "Best Places to Work" grocery store, I met a clerk who was desperately trying to help me find some soup. Despite her best intentions and lots of time chasing down colleagues, she could not locate the item. She confessed that she had similar trouble three times during the same day. Clearly, there was a Capabilities gap—both in her knowledge and in the store's system for finding goods. (P.S. The store actually had the soup, but nobody could find it.)

Don't expect the Under-Equipped to come in singing the company song. It is difficult to be smiley-faced and enthusiastic when you are clear on what you are suppose to do and want to do it, but lack the capability to perform well and please customers.

The Strategic Disconnect is a frequent and particularly insidious profile, because it is not as detectable to the casual observer as are some of the other profiles. The workforce, unit, or individual is Engaged and has the right Capabilities, but the organization has not created a clear line of sight to the strategy or brand promise, resulting in wasted resources that devote far too much time to low or no value-added activities. Employees with this profile think they are working on high-priority tasks, when in fact they are not. "We are working hard," they typically say, but others counter that they are not working smart. Lack of rewards and positive recognition eventually sinks in to alert employees in this group that something is wrong. The question is, will they see the light in time?

An important note is warranted here. The first four profiles in Table 2.2 are all high on Engagement, but only the Suprior Performer scores highly on all three ACE factors. This is important because in recent years, Engagement has been viewed as a silver bullet of employee management. Without high Alignment and Capabilities, Engagement alone is insufficient. Furthermore, Engagement will wane over time without strength in the other two areas. Can an employee remain Engaged when Capabilities are low and customers are dissatisfied? Can employees stay Engaged when they work hard, but don't see the connection to business or personal success? Working smart means focusing on the shortest, most effective path to achieving objectives, assuming those objectives are aligned with business strategy.

The remaining four profiles in Table 2.2 likewise are characterized by one or more key deficiencies that must be addressed for an organization to operate at the top of its game.

Conclusion

We discovered in this chapter why People Equity is so valuable to organizations. And we have seen that the three components of People Equity—Alignment, Capabilities, and Engagement—are each important in unique ways. Each tends to influence different, but important outcomes for the organization: financial performance, customer loyalty, operational excellence and productivity and employee retention.

We also have addressed two of the key questions listed in Figure 2.1 that guide our journey through this book:

1. What are these three People Equity factors? What role do they play?
2. Do these three factors truly have a decisive impact on business and personal success? If so, in what ways?

The next chapter addresses the third question raised earlier in this chapter, which deals with the issue of managing People Equity:

3. Are the three factors of People Equity predictable and controllable? What are the drivers or levers or control?

Summary of Key Learning Points

- A review of research and practice identified a concept that we have labeled People Equity because of its parallel role to Customer and Financial Equity in capturing the value of a key stakeholder group: people—whether they are employees, contractors, part-timers, or other sources of labor.
- People Equity appears to be critical in financial performance, quality, customer loyalty, and the retention of talent; it is also applicable to all sizes of organizations, and public or private, profit or nonprofit.
- People Equity is composed of three separate but important factors:
  1. Alignment of employees with the business strategy, goals, values, and synchronized processes and behaviors across work groups
  2. Capabilities—talent, information, and resources to increase customer value
  3. Engagement—willingness of employees to put in extra effort and to advocate on behalf of the organization
- Each of these factors influences important business outcomes:
  1. Alignment affects operational and financial outcomes most directly.
  2. Capabilities affect customer outcomes most directly.
  3. Engagement affects performance and retention of employees most directly.
- There are eight major profiles of People Equity. Each of these profiles requires different solutions to close the gaps and optimize performance.

3

How to Manage People Equity

"If you want your people to get an A, help them understand the why.

—Garry Ridge, CEO, WD-40 Company

A package delivery firm completed its first employee engagement survey and spent considerable time assessing the implications. As a result, it decided to focus on supervision. The company decided to design a variety of educational and communications tools for supervisors, and demanded that every supervisor sit down with each employee twice a year for a face-to-face discussion of the employees' concerns, questions, and developmental aspirations. Surprisingly, the next survey revealed that not only did supervisor ratings improve, but scores were much higher on Engagement, Alignment, and a number of other ratings, even though they were not targeted specifically for action. These were simply collateral benefits of getting supervisors to sit down and talk with their people.

In fact, one manager complained to me that another manager initiated both informal beer and pizza nights with his people and straight-talk sessions, obviously trying to buy their engagement. He cried foul, arguing that he had worked on safety and on-time performance—more important issues for the company. His survey results were flat while the communicative supervisor had not only higher supervisory and engagement ratings, but also better turnover, accident, and other productivity numbers. I explained to him that perhaps the manager received higher performance scores because he was just communicating more effectively, and suggested that he try the same.

What happened here? Behind the supervisory actions were some underlying dynamics that have major benefits for the overall management of talent. First, it may not be necessary to attack everything. Perhaps some factors, like supervision, might drive improvements in multiple areas. Second, while there may be multiple ways to get higher Engagement (or Alignment and Capabilities) scores, some approaches might provide higher return on limited investment money. Third, there may be a way to *predict* which factors will have the greatest impact on People Equity, and therefore performance and retention.

Beyond "What Happened?" is the question, "Why?" This question is key to raising performance levels in an organization, as Garry Ridge, the CEO of the WD-40 Company (WD-40), points out in the opening quotation. It is the same with People Equity. To optimize it, you have to understand what drives it—and why. And here is another caution: Be aware that there are no universals in human behavior. Some drivers will be more important in one organization, work group, or culture than others. "Nothing ever works all the time."

This chapter addresses the question of predictability and controllability—important issues in managing talent. We established in the last chapter the criticality of People Equity for business performance. We will now investigate *whether the three factors of People Equity are predictable and controllable. If so, what are the drivers or levers of control?*

In the course of our research in this area, we were looking not only for the major factors that capture the value of human capital investments, but also a model or framework for how those factors operate, so that we would understand which levers could be pulled or changed to create positive—or negative—results. Tapping these levers or drivers of Alignment, Capabilities, and Engagement puts great power in the hands of executives in an organization to anticipate and influence those business outcomes.

We found five compelling drivers and four enablers that underlie People Equity. These are depicted in Figure 3.1. When these drivers and enablers are effectively managed, Alignment, Capabilities, and Engagement inevitably increase. As a result, human and organizational performance improves substantially and measurably.

A *Driver* is typically the most direct element influencing the three ACE factors, whereas an *Enabler* has broader influence, often through the Drivers. For example, in the opening example, the supervisor attacked some communications, recognition, and performance management drivers, and thereby improved employee Engagement (and Alignment). We will talk about the more general role of the Enablers after we discuss the Drivers.

Figure 3.1 illustrates the relationships among the five Drivers and four Enablers of People Equity.

FIGURE 3.1   People Equity: Drivers and Enablers

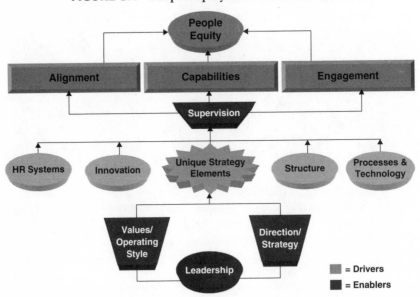

The Five Drivers of People Equity

The drivers of Alignment, Capabilities, and Engagement fall into five categories.

1. *Human Resource Systems*, which include talent acquisition, talent development, and talent retention. Supporting these broad systems are subsystems such as rewards and recognition, training, staffing and selection, and performance management. Each of these major Human Resources systems can be important in managing and developing the workforce:

   - The *Talent Acquisition* systems focus on identifying, recruiting, and selecting qualified talent. Another key aspect of talent acquisition, especially in areas of talent scarcity, is employer branding—developing an image that enables an organization to become the employer of choice of qualified candidates.

   - The *Talent Development* system supports employees through their life cycle with the organization. Included are subsystems such as onboarding, which focuses on the initial orientation and acculturation of new employees. Training focuses on both new and future skills and knowledge. Performance Management deals with Alignment, ensuring that each employee has clear goals and performance feedback that is designed to optimize value for both the organization and the employee. Finally, the reward systems support both Talent Acquisition and Development, providing an attractive incentive for potential employees as well as helping to motivate and focus current employees.

   - *Talent Retention* is supported by effective recognition and rewards, strong positive communication systems, learning and growth systems, and effective supervisory behaviors.

      I address the connection of People Equity to talent acquisition, development, and retention in more detail later in the book.

2. *Processes and Technology*, which includes information and knowledge systems, tools, and work processes of all sorts. These can influence all of the ACE elements, but typically play the most important role in supporting Capabilities.

   - Do employees have access to the necessary information to reach peak performance?

   - Do the IT systems provide timely and relevant information at the moment of truth for customers?

   - Are processes smooth and efficient, reducing employee frustration, and increasing employee success rates with their customers?

- Do employees have the tools they need to accomplish their goals and create high value?
- Do employees have ways to obtain the necessary knowledge about customers, products, and other relevant information?

3. *Innovation*, including the ability to develop and implement new ideas, creativity leading to better products and services, and the agility to adapt to changing environments or competitive landscapes. Innovation is one of the most complex elements within organizations because it is not contained within a single department. It can happen at the organizational, unit, process, or individual level and is misunderstood in part because of a lack of agreed-upon definitions, varying from creativity to "creating new things" to organizational agility at the broadest level.

Regardless of the specific definition, most of these approaches (outside of very narrow technical ones) can have a profound impact on ACE. Consider the following:

- In GlobalCompute, the high technology company described in Chapter 1, executives struggled with sparking creativity and innovation after a merger. It seemed the merger had a chilling effect on innovation, especially in one of the two firms that was most noted for leading edge products. As the market began demanding newer, more innovative products, customer-facing employees began to shudder because they no longer had much to offer. This began to affect their Capabilities dimension, especially since they didn't have the right solution at the customer moment of truth. The firm was now ill-equipped to deliver on a core value that was perceived by both customers and employees as a source of competitive strength. And as the merger evolved, the lack of innovation took a toll on Engagement. Old-timers had placed a great deal of "their souls," as they described it, in an innovation-based brand image.

4. *Structure* encompasses the way the company, function, and unit are organized and the concomitant impact on teamwork, seamless processes, and delivering high value to customers. For example, some organizations are hierarchical by design, while others have become flattened, having removed many layers of management. Some organizations have well-integrated functions that add value to products or services, while others are managed in more isolated silos. Each of these structural trade-offs can have an impact on ACE.

In flat organizations, there is, or at least should be, more effective communications flow, which will likely have an impact on Engagement. People are in the loop more quickly without having to wait for bureaucratic information to come down from on high. Also, if the structures are hierarchical in the customer value chain, this can mean that the Information component of Capabilities may be more stressed.

When a major lending organization restructured and reduced layers of management and decision making, it found that the Capabilities dimension of ACE improved dramatically. Why? The change meant that Information—a key component of Capabilities—was now more readily available to customer-facing account managers. The result: quicker loan decisions, and faster access to customer information when needed—a positive outcome for customers.

5. *Unique Strategic Elements* are those aspects of an organization or function that are important in differentiating it from its competitors, including competitive advantage, brand identity, strategic project portfolio management, business processes, and the like.

This is a critical element that can make or break the effectiveness of a given strategy. This driver is the unique DNA that separates this business from others.

Listed below are three different strategies that are related to concepts introduced by Treacy and Wiersema,[1] who argued that there is room in most industries for competitors that have different expertise domains and who serve different customer niches. They identify three[2] primary differentiators:

• The Customer-Intimate leader
• The Innovation leader
• The Operationally Excellent (typically, the low-cost) leader

Take a moment and think about an exemplary firm that matches each of these profiles in retail. Where do they fit?[3]

When I ask audiences a similar question, the responses tend to include a familiar list of companies:

Operational Excellence: Wal-Mart, Costco, McDonalds
Innovation: Apple, Amazon, boutique importers
Customer Intimacy: Nordstrom's, Lexus, local merchants

How does this relate to People Equity? Every firm has limited resources and must differentiate those resources in ways that provide them a competitive distinction in the marketplace. You cannot be excellent at everything; those who try to do so run out of capital or market runway—they have confused their buyers. Human capital must be lined up in a way that facilitates the unique positioning of the firm: talent that is aligned, capable, and engaged with a particular strategy.

Table 3.1 (shown below) contains three market-differentiating strategies. Notice that different strategies lead to different financial, customer, operational, and employee priorities within each cell of the matrix. For example, Customer-Intimate organizations like the Ritz-Carlton or Lexus place a great deal of emphasis on long-term client relationships and service, whereas Operationally Excellent counterparts may focus on productivity and cost.

With regard to talent, customer-intimate firms like the Ritz-Carlton emphasize different priorities to their people from hotel chains that are primarily price-driven.

When these profiles are connected to People Equity, we begin to see dramatic differences in how ACE may look in different organizations. On page 49, Table 3.2 takes the *People* row from Table 3.1 and breaks it into the three ACE factors. It is then possible to think about the implications of the

Table 3.1
Different Strategies—Different Emphasis Points

Areas of Focus	Operational Excellence	Innovation	Customer Intimacy
Financial/ Operational	• Margin • Productivity	• % revenue from new products • Return on Innovation	• Account share • Revenue dollars/ customer
Customer	• Market share • Price orientation	• Customer value • Acceptance of new products	• Customer versus competitor value • Customer loyalty/ retention
Product/Service Quality	Attributes like: • Maintenance costs • Warranty costs	Attributes like: • Innovative • Serviceability	Attributes like: • Reliability • Responsiveness
People	• Efficiency • Revenue per employee	• Idea Generation • Autonomy	• Empowerment • Service Skills

Table 3.2

Different Strategies—Unique ACE Differentiators

Areas of Focus	Common Across Strategies	Operational Excellence	Innovation	Customer Intimacy
People:				
Alignment	• Goal alignment • Values alignment • Customer alignment	• Cost driven • Values: – Efficiency – Spartan	• Innovation driven • Values: – Creative applications – Autonomy	• Customer intimacy driven • Values: – Customer focus – Empowerment
Capabilities	• Talent match • Information match • Resource match	• Efficiency • Cost awareness	• Idea generation • Creativity	• Service skills • Customer knowledge
Engagement	• Satisfiers • Commitment • Advocacy	• Task fulfillment	• Diversity	• Team fulfillment

three different business strategies on Alignment, Capabilities, and Engagement. For each People Equity factor, such as Alignment, you can see how these three business models might emphasize different features.

Repairs Unlimited, described earlier in the book, is an example of customer intimacy. Dave looks for employees who are willing to relate to the customer. He realizes that he does not have unique products or services—you can get the same products and services from auto dealerships. And, he is not the low-cost provider, like the quick lube shops competing for some of his services. What he has built is a model of long-term trust and relationship. Dave goes to great lengths to satisfy his customers, and he counts on his people being aligned with his model. They understand that building solid customer relationships and providing competitive products and services are what set their repair shop apart from others. There are no backroom people who must be leashed to their lift lest they scare customers away.

You might ask, however, doesn't every firm have goals that employees should understand and support? Or, aren't there generic Capabilities that play across all three strategic models in Table 3.2?

The answer is yes, but it is important to understand what is generic and what is unique. As you can see in the first column in Table 3.2, there are some elements of Alignment, for example, that every firm must have: clear, aligned goals; processes aligned with the customer; and agreed-upon values. It is the content of the focus that is different, however. In the case of the Customer-Intimate business, the goals have a distinct customer service flavor—with distinct measures of those service goals—compared to the quick lube business. With regard to Capabilities, service skills and customer knowledge will be at a premium in the Customer-Intimate model compared to, perhaps, task efficiency in the Operationally Excellent firm.

The Four Enablers of People Equity

Is a football team, regardless of the raw talent, competitive salaries, and great training, likely to win without a good team captain and coaching staff? Hardly. Nor is it likely that they will win a championship without a superior strategy and winning set of values against the competition. Winning teams always point to similar factors: their captains and coaches, management support, their winning culture, and a sound strategy for defeating the competition.

The same is true for business organizations. There are four key Enablers of People Equity, which in turn, drive business results.

1. Effective supervisory or managerial actions
2. Strong, senior leadership behaviors

3. Clearly understood business strategy
4. Compelling organizational values

The supervisor is the daily captain, often drawing on the five Drivers to achieve people and business results (which is why Supervisor is drawn between the Drivers and ACE in Figure 3.1). Senior leadership, the business strategy and the values set the overall context and typically influence the architecture of the Drivers, such as the organizational structure, reward philosophy, or innovation (which is why those three are placed before the Drivers in Figure 3.1). These four Enablers combine with the Drivers, as depicted in Figure 3.1, to increase or decrease People Equity.

The Supervisor

The immediate supervisor, manager, or coach of an employee or work team has a dramatic impact on performance.[4]

Supervisors, when skilled, can either create superior performance or drain the People Equity of a business. Why? Because they have a profound impact on all three factors of People Equity. They motivate, focus, and both develop and match capabilities with customer requirements.

Recalling our package delivery supervisor that we opened the chapter with, note that he had a profound impact on team morale through the use of both sanctioned and unsanctioned tools and motivators. He used some sanctioned motivators such as formal recognition awards and programs, financial rewards and incentives, flexible hours, and access to training programs. Unsanctioned, and arguably more potent, are the informal bonds that were built between himself and his employees through shared pizza and conversation. Positive, casual interactions between managers and employees can lead to high trust, loyalty, and commitment.

On the Capabilities front, supervisors have an important role in assuring that the unit has the critical Capabilities required to meet internal and external customer requirements. In this role, the supervisor must ensure that the unit is acquiring, developing, and retaining the talent necessary to achieve this. Conversely, the supervisor or coach has a role in helping to prune or redirect talent that is not effective in meeting standards or customer requirements.

On the Alignment front, supervisors have a major role in ensuring that the individual goals that are set are highly aligned with the business strategy, that people are focusing energy on high value activities and that they are delivering on the brand promise of the organization. The package delivery supervisor, for example, received numerous questions about company direction, rewards, and the reasons for certain performance measures at those informal sessions. By answering those questions, he was creating a line of sight from the strategy to what these employees were doing daily.

The supervisor is a powerful player—really the Drivers' captain—in the performance equation. Direct managers or coaches[5] help deploy the Drivers in the right doses. If it were legal, you might go to the pharmacist and get a prescription for an antibiotic because you think you have an infection. However, without guidance, you might also kill yourself, treat the wrong disease, have an interaction effect with other drugs or allergies, or take it in the wrong doses for your ailment. By analogy, consider a doctor who adopts a coach-like role. She doesn't set the standards (the pharmaceutical companies and FDA do), she doesn't set the values (national health care policy does), and she doesn't negotiate the financial arrangements (the health care plans do). She helps navigate the complex medical world for you by guiding you through a series of steps to determine cause and providing you with expert advice.

The supervisor (or coach) does essentially the same thing. The supervisor cannot dictate reward policy, develop his own recruiting policies, choose independent goals, or make the final determination on distribution of resources or the type of information system that will be available. Instead, he is dealt a set of Drivers—rewards, structure, technology—within which he must work to maximize People Equity. By using the Drivers in the optimal way, a skilled supervisor can create the highest level of Alignment, Capabilities, and Engagement. For example, in using rewards, the supervisor may apportion rewards differentially across employees by addressing developmental needs for certain employees, financial needs for others, and work-life balance for still others, while staying within the boundaries of the overall rewards architecture.

The Supervisor versus the Leadership Team: Different Ways to Drive Alignment, Capabilities, and Engagement

In the past decade, there has been a resurgence of focus on the central role that the supervisor plays in the performance equation. While this is appropriate, an unfortunate by-product has been a lack of attention to the crucial role of the leadership team in driving workforce performance. After all, without the right support and focus from the leadership team, the supervisor or manager lacks a context from which to drive performance.

We recently found a sales and marketing unit in an energy company that was led by a charismatic manager, who had created high motivation and workforce commitment to him, but he, himself, was misaligned with the leadership of the organization. The people of this unit were consequently serving the manager, not the organization. In the end, the misalignment with the leadership team compromised the manager's personal effectiveness, and consequently, that of his unit, which was subsequently reorganized.

The Leadership Team

One of the primary roles of the leadership team is to ensure that managers and supervisors—the on-the-ground point people of business strategy—are themselves highly aligned with the business strategy, capable of aligning and motivating others, and motivated to do so. Typically, leadership accomplishes this through several activities.

- The What—Setting Clear Goals
- The Why—Communicating Purpose
- The Three Hows:
  1. Ensuring that the long-term values are being lived
  2. Allocating resources such as information, technology, and staffing, determining structure, and funding Capabilities
  3. Shaping the drivers of People Equity, such as the philosophy and architecture of reward systems, performance management accountability, and information access

For example, organizations like the Ritz-Carlton and the Lexus division of Toyota, which embody a high customer intimacy strategy and strong service values, require senior leadership teams whose behaviors and decisions exemplify that philosophy and who create a reward architecture that drives employee behaviors to create high customer loyalty. A few years ago, I had an unexpected problem with my automobile trunk and drove over to a Lexus dealership for a look. The service associate was quick to diagnose a latch problem that prevented the trunk from remaining shut. Correcting the problem required leaving my car at the dealer's repair shop. Unfortunately, there were no loaner cars available. As I discussed my dilemma with the service associate, the service manager at the dealership overheard the conversation and immediately offered to drive me to my office and have someone pick me up once the repair had been made. This was not only a powerful service message for me, but also for the relatively new associate that watched the boss do something impressive at the moment of truth.

While we frequently hear about leadership communication and access, the key to leaders' impact is in what and how they communicate, their behavior as role models for the values and areas of strategic focus, and their decisions regarding the resources and policies associated with the *Hows* described earlier. This, in effect, sets the context for all other performance-related activities to follow.

In hundreds of surveys that we have conducted over the past 20 years, we find that leadership teams vary substantially across these dimensions, and that the variance is highly related to business performance. Figure 3.1 shows the respective locations in the impact chain that the leadership team and supervisors have in building People Equity.

Strategy and Direction

Senior leaders typically formulate the overall direction or strategy, which then gets cascaded to different business units and functions, where it gets integrated into operating plans and day-to-day decision making. Strategy defines a firm's future competitive advantage. It identifies which customer segments the organization will focus on. Strategy also informs the overall organizational goals that serve as a guide for current and future effort. The strategy also begins to define the high-level competencies that will be required to win in the marketplace.

The talent strategy focuses on the role of people in executing the overall strategy. It establishes the framework for how the workforce will increase the equity of the organization. The connection of the talent and organizational strategy is critical. Without a clear differentiated business strategy, any people strategy will suffice—but to what end? It is hard to identify whether employees are devoting their efforts to high or low value activities without the clarity provided by a good strategy. It tells as much about what we won't do as about what we will, what competencies will be less important, and what promise we are *not* making to the market.

Values and Operating Style

Each organization has a culture that has been developed over time—a unique set of shared beliefs and behaviors about "the way business gets done around here." Also, each leadership team adds its signature to the prior culture, modifying it with unique biases, preferences, and ways of doing business. This largely determines *how* we are going to operate to achieve the business strategy.

Some organizations will place a significant emphasis on teamwork, while others will value individual achievement. Certain organizations will place a premium on rewards for performance while others do not. Some focus on internal development while others place more emphasis on buying from the outside. Each of these approaches is valid *if* it is matched to the strategy and guided carefully by leadership to ensure that the organization is not schizophrenic in its internal and external behaviors. It is through this lens that the supervisor must orchestrate performance.

Table 3.3 provides a summary of ACE and its Drivers and Enablers, with examples in the right column of key content in each area.

Table 3.3
Examples of Content in People Equity Factors, Drivers, and Enablers

Factors of People Equity

Alignment	• Clarity of strategy, understanding of and alignment with goals • Alignment of Values • Sychronization of processes, functions to deliver value to customers
Capabilities	• Skills and knowledge to meet customer requirements • Resources to meet customer requirements • Sufficient information to meet customer requirements
Engagement	• Employee commitment and satisfaction • Willingness to advocate on behalf of the organization • Willingness to give extra effort

Drivers of People Equity

HR Systems	• Recognition and rewards • Talent acquisition and development • Performance management
Processes & Technology	• Operations and process drivers • Process effectiveness • Adequacy of performance tools • Effectiveness of knowledge management and information usage
Innovation	• Idea production and usage • Creativity • Adaptability
Structure	• Staffing adequacy • Cross functional information flow • Functional silos
Unique Strategy Elements	• Customized to the organization's strategic priorities

(Continued)

Enablers of People Equity

Direct Supervisor or Manager	• People skills • Technical skills • Performance Management skills • Communication
Leadership	• Direction setting • Confidence in leadership capability • Walk the talk
Direction/Strategy	• Clarity of strategy • Strategic measures
Values	• Core values • Custom values

Predictability

While we have identified the key Drivers and Enablers of high People Equity, and therefore, high business performance, how do we know which Drivers or Enablers are most important at any given time? Which buttons should we push? There are several keys to that answer. The first is to obtain good measures of each of these Drivers and Enablers as well as the three components of People Equity. This will allow you to statistically identify Drivers and Enablers that are most important to your organization or to particular operating units at a given time.

The second is to build in methods to peel back the layers of People Equity—methods like those instinctively deployed by our package delivery supervisor—that help to identify the Drivers and Enablers that may be the biggest blockages to high performance, retention, customer satisfaction, and financial performance. In survey feedback sessions, for example, with the right facilitator, structure, and environment, it is usually easy to open up dialog that informs the root causes of low Alignment, Capabilities, and Engagement.

I address the former issue in the measurement chapter, and the latter issue is addressed further in the talent chapters.

Summary

This chapter addressed one of the key questions posed in Figure 2.1 from Chapter 2. Are the three factors of People Equity—Alignment, Capabilities, and Engagement—predictable and controllable? If so, what are the drivers or levers of control?

Going below the surface of People Equity, we discovered a rich layering of important Drivers and Enablers that help answer the "How to Control" question. With this accomplished, I next address the fourth question in Figure 2.1 from Chapter 2: Are these factors—Alignment, Capabilities, and Engagement—measurable and predictive of important personal and business outcomes? And how do you measure the Drivers and Enablers of ACE?

Summary of Key Learning Points

People Equity and its three key components—Alignment, Capabilities, and Engagement—can be controlled through five Drivers and four Enablers.

- The Drivers include:
  1. Human Resources Systems
  2. Processes and Technology
  3. Innovation
  4. Structure
  5. Unique Strategy Elements
- The Enablers include:
  1. Supervision
  2. Leadership
  3. Direction and Strategy
  4. Organizational Values
- There are standard People Equity elements in all organizations, but it is more effective to customize the ACE dimensions to the organization's unique strategy.
- While much attention has been paid to the supervisor's influence on employee Engagement and productivity, the leadership team should not be overlooked for their important role in shaping the various Drivers of People Equity.
- Values and the business strategy provide important context for the effectiveness of various Drivers.
- The ACE factors are predictable and influenced by changes to the Drivers and Enablers.

SECTION II

Measuring the Unmeasurable

"Victors are those who execute strategy the fastest; to do so, we need good measurement."
   —Carlo Cetti, retired senior vice president of human
   resources and strategy, Jack in the Box restaurants

Whis the People Equity framework is compelling in theory and has proven research support, what is its on-the-ground cash value? The next section breaks apart this question to explore how People Equity can assist those charged with driving strategic decision making and increasing the impact of talent on how an organization is directed and run: How will we know if our talent is being well used? What measures can we use to track this?

- Are we getting a good return on our talent investments?
- How can the ACE framework help us in making more strategic decisions regarding talent?
- How can the ACE framework help us in pinpointing performance gaps more effectively?
- How can we make better decisions on initiatives or activities to eliminate?
- Which talent investments would have the biggest payoff for us?

These are some of the questions that are addressed in the next section— ones that are core to the value equation.

4

Measuring People Equity

"*Organizations cannot improve—unless they change the measurement system.*"

—Dean Spitzer, IBM Corporation

H ow do you capture the value of a disembodied presence—something you cannot feel, touch, smell, taste, or weigh? Measuring intangibles: it is one of today's biggest challenges, both in organizations and our personal lives. In organizations, much has been written about the critical value of intangibles such as brand, intellectual capital, innovation, agility, and of course, human capital.[1] On a personal level, parents wrestle not only with their children's aptitudes and abilities, but with the motivation and drive that is essential for their future success. Scout leaders address teamwork and achievement—it's not just about selling Girl Scout cookies! Preschool leaders tackle development. Sports leaders talk about energy. Religious leaders discuss ethics. And artists talk about aesthetics. Sure, Aristotle and Plato started those conversations several millennia ago. But measuring them is still a challenge.

You might say, "Hey wait a minute. Art is in the eyes of the beholder." True, but what about market value? Why does a Renoir outsell a Pissarro or a Picasso drawing outsell a Mondrian? Of course, there are different tastes, but among art aficionados, there is a pecking order of value that distinguishes paintings, sculpture, and other art forms in similar classes.

Today, eBay has been a great market maker that helps establish strike price and value within a global virtual community. At least in monetary terms, you can compare your grandma's armoire with a painting or vintage car. The monetization of these items in a broad market helps set the market's perceived value of these items.

In business, Brad Gale defined value with a concept he termed *Market Perceived Value*, which attempted to capture the perceived value by the defined market—an aggregation of the perceived value across customers. Basically, it is a ratio of the perceived value of the brand, products, and services of any organization compared to the perceived cost of doing business with that organization. At the simplest level, you assign a *benefit score*, let's say eight (on a 10-point scale) to the specific product—say, your favorite candy—and you assign a perceived *cost* of four to that same product. That would produce a Perceived Value score of 2.0 ($^8/_4$). The higher the score among similar products, the higher your affinity—and your purchasing patterns—for those products, according to research by Gale.[2]

Reality is slightly more complicated. Scores for a given product (or product group) are made in the context of the buyer's perceptions of other product alternatives.

What was particularly interesting in Gale's work was the research that showed strong relationships between Market Perceived Value (MPV) and market share and financial performance. So while MPV is an intangible concept attempting to capture value, it is very useful for two reasons. First, it helps to explain why people make certain decisions. Second, it is predictive of important business outcomes.

On the personal front, parents face the same issues with their children. Parents learn informally about their offspring's inclinations, often through trial and error. Tests have been designed,[3] however, that are calibrated to provide greater understanding (and numerical measures) of the aptitudes and interests of a child. While they are not a perfect predictor of future tendencies or even careers, they can help parents, guidance counselors, teachers, and others to better understand and support that child by focusing on those areas that hold greater promise for success and happiness.

The Value of Measuring People Equity

The same is true as we approach the measurement of people and, more specifically, People Equity. Without the ability to measure it, the concept is not very helpful, as we posited in Chapter 2. If, on the other hand, we can obtain effective measures of People Equity and its components—Alignment, Capabilities, and Engagement—then they can be used to understand why people make various decisions and why certain behaviors occur. And similar to the point made earlier about Gale and his MPV concept, the ability to measure People Equity can make it an important strategic concept, enabling it to predict important outcomes, such as customer loyalty and retention, quality and productivity, and financial performance.

On the decision and behavioral front, if People Equity can be measured, it would help us explain some of the great management questions, such as: why people decide to come to work or not; why people quit their jobs; why some people put in more effort than others; or why some employees decide to put more energy into certain tasks that produce greater organizational value than other tasks.

On the predictive front, if the measures of People Equity could predict employee retention, performance, quality output, customer loyalty, and other important outcomes, then the organization would have an opportunity to intervene in a timely fashion to improve drivers of People Equity that may be limiting performance in these areas.

How to Measure People Equity

Today's organizations are awash in a wide variety of tools that provide at least some understanding of aspects of People Equity and other human capital concepts: interviews, focus groups, competency profiles, 360-degree feedback tools, formal assessment centers, exit reviews, and surveys. But most of these are one-dimensional and fail to capture the holistic People Equity concept. For example, exit interview scores may detect gaps in Engagement based on supervisory practices, reward systems, or growth opportunities. However, the information is often biased by people who have already decided to leave ("I am leaving for a better job"), and the measure occurs well after corrective action should have been taken.

Based on much trial and error with alternative tools over the past decade, we have found that surveys—despite some shortfalls (see the sidebar)—are one of the most effective tools for obtaining a broad assessment of People Equity in an economical and practical way. Surveys work well for several reasons.

- First, people are the key stakeholders we are trying to understand and measure, so their perceptions are crucial.
- Second, people have a wonderful vantage point from which to observe the organization's processes, practices, successes, and failures.
- Third, the information can be captured in a format that readily enables comparisons not only within an organization, but also across functions and organizations.
- Fourth, surveys enable decision makers to not only assess levels of People Equity, but also the Drivers and Enablers of People Equity.
- Fifth, survey information is usually cost effective to obtain.
- Finally, and maybe most important, survey information differentiates high and low performance. That is, it provides profiles within and across organizations that are correlated with other important business outcomes. Units that are higher or lower in Alignment tend to have different performance, making the Alignment score a leading indicator of important business outcomes.

The author and his colleagues have experimented with various approaches and found that by asking the right questions you can achieve a gauge of the three People Equity components, along with the drivers of People Equity.

Overcoming Survey Gaps

Surveys have not always lived up to their promise. For example, employee surveys have historically placed a strong focus on the leader's or supervisor's role in creating satisfied, committed, and most recently, engaged employees. Such surveys have placed a great deal of emphasis on rewards, benefits,

(Continued)

supervisory fair treatment, and similar "motivators or demotivators." Some survey efforts, such as Gallup's Q12, have included items on clear expectations, coaching, recognition, and feedback, but they do not tell us whether the goals and the feedback are aligned with the business strategy. So while knowing that goals exist is an important step, having the right goals—that is, goals that are aligned with the organization's values and direction—is essential to high performance.

Also, few surveys have tapped the Capabilities factor, or they have done so in a fragmentary way. For example, some surveys have asked employees if they have enough staffing in their unit or sufficient information to do their job, but most survey items are cursory at best in these areas, missing crucial drivers such as having the right resources to meet customer expectations, having sufficient technology to deliver high performance to customers, having processes that are efficient and effective in meeting customer requirements, or leveraging skills to best advantage.

Managers are often befuddled about employee surveys. Surveys are at times viewed as an easy way to pacify entitlement-seeking employees, or simply a good thing to do, although little attention or action is anticipated. Or, they are looked upon as a way to generate a to-do list for management. This latter goal rarely leads to productive action for two reasons:

- Weaknesses identified by the surveys are not viewed as important, controllable, or strategic, or the action items simply pile onto an already overloaded agenda. Many managers we have talked with have become somewhat cynical about the actions or outcomes of their employee survey efforts—almost a "We tried, but it just doesn't seem to get much better" attitude. Very few have questioned why. They go through the motions because they are expected to by top management or HR prodders.
- The to-do list is passed down to lower levels. Senior managers recognize that not every issue is under their control, but instead some result from supervisory practices or flaws in the design or execution of human resources and other systems. The problem with this approach is that the supervisors or systems designers have little impetus to change. After all, it is not on the agenda of senior leadership. As a result, many managers pay just enough attention to the list to check off items on paper, without changing things in the workplace.

One solution is to make the surveys more strategic. Our experience suggests that well over 60 percent of organizations do very little of strategic relevance with their surveys. But those that use them strategically have five-year ROIs of 136 percent compared to 71 percent for those that do not. Why do the organizations that use surveys strategically do so much better? For one, the information is focused on the linkage of employees (or other sources of labor) to customer and financial issues. That is, senior leaders can see how Alignment, Capabilities, and Engagement connect to strategy execution. A second reason is the "Alignment" factor, which helps make the connection to strategic goals explicit. With the performance laggards, the survey content is frequently designed to capture employee satisfaction with various organizational issues—often the look and feel of entitlement. They often miss the opportunity to capture, through employees' eyes, the many issues that reflect strategy execution and whether the labor investment is at peak performance. Is the employee engine not only tuned to purr at high speeds, but also headed down the right road?

A few years ago we created a short diagnostic survey that captures the three crucial components of People Equity. In practice, we typically include additional survey questions that assess the Drivers and Enablers of People Equity. While a top-line assessment of People Equity can be attained by asking as few as 18 questions, we generally prefer to use versions that include the Drivers and Enablers in Table 3.3 in Chapter 3. This often results in very powerful surveys of both ACE and the causes of high or low ACE. Only 35 to 45 items[4] are required for this more complete assessment. Frequently, this information is combined with interviews of leaders and managers for further insight.

Assessing Your People Equity

To give you a stronger flavor of People Equity, Table 4.1 is an abbreviated People Equity questionnaire. Take the survey. Try completing the questions for an organization with which you are familiar. Rate each question from Strongly Agree to Strongly Disagree.

Scoring

You can determine your Alignment, Capabilities, and Engagement scores by adding up your scores for each area. Questions 1 to 3 address Alignment; questions 4 to 6, Capabilities; and questions 7 to 9, Engagement. The maximum score for each factor—A, C, and E—is 15 (a score of 5 on each of the three questions) and the minimum is 3 (a score of 1 on each). If you scored 13 or more, you are High in that area; 9 to 12, Medium; and below 12, Low. As you can see, there are different profiles that might occur as a result of the combination of your scores.

Table 4.1
People Equity Questionnaire

	Strongly Disagree	Disagree	Neutral	Agree	Strongly Agree
Alignment					
Most employees understand the overall goals of the organization and how it plans to reach them.	1	2	3	4	5
My unit has clear performance objectives that are tied to our customers' expectations.	1	2	3	4	5
My individual performance goals are clearly linked to our department performance goals.	1	2	3	4	5
Total Alignment Score (add up your score for the three questions)					
Capabilities					
My unit has the people skills it needs to meet our customers' expectations.	1	2	3	4	5
My unit has the technical resources and tools it needs to meet our customers' expectations.	1	2	3	4	5
My unit has the information it needs to meet our customers' expectations.	1	2	3	4	5
Total Capabilities Score (add up your score for the three questions)					
Engagement					
I would recommend this organization to a close friend or colleague as a place to work.	1	2	3	4	5
This is one of the best organizations to work for.	1	2	3	4	5
I am proud to be working for this organization.	1	2	3	4	5
Total Engagement Score (add up your score for the three questions)					

If you found that your organization or unit is High in all three elements of PE, then consider yourself very lucky. A typical organization—even a very effective one—often has units and individuals that vary from over 90 percent favorable (giving 4s and 5s to the questions) to less than 40 percent favorable. That variance provides an important opportunity for both understanding and improvement.

Organizational or Unit Profiles

In Chapter 2, we described the eight key profiles of People Equity. Figure 4.1 illustrates how leaders can use this quick snapshot to determine how effectively they are executing their strategy and how well their workforce is being used at the corporate, business unit, or department level. This profile was obtained by creating ACE scores from this organization's employee survey. Each dimension of People Equity, A, C, or E, could have a top score of 100 or a bottom score of zero.[5] The shading provides a quick indicator of areas of strength, weakest and intermediate for each of the three factors of People Equity—Alignment (A), Capabilities (C), and Engagement (E).

The picture reveals a number of *Aha*'s. Take a moment to see if you can discover what they are. Assume all the divisions of the company are selling the same products to similar customers and that employees are hired using similar selection tools and run through similar training programs. Everyone is on a common reward system. What do you think is happening?

When properly analyzed, Figure 4.1 provides an understanding of how effectively human capital is being deployed throughout the organization. Furthermore, the profile identifies some key concerns. Here are a few:

• The low A and C scores in the Central division indicate it is struggling, with considerable talent that is misaligned and low in Capabilities. Some are also disengaged. Clearly, this division is scoring much lower than its peer divisions. Why?

• In contrast, the West is effectively using its workforce, and most likely uses many best practices that can be shared. What is the West doing that allows it to use its people more effectively than the others?

• Although hiring and training are relatively uniform across all geographic regions, Central has by far the lowest Capability scores. This is puzzling because most employees, when hired, essentially have the same competencies across each region.

• Overall, of the three human capital ACE areas, the entire organization is lowest in Alignment, including the West.

• One of the units in the Central scores a 76 in Engagement and yet its Alignment and Capabilities are quite low—an odd profile.

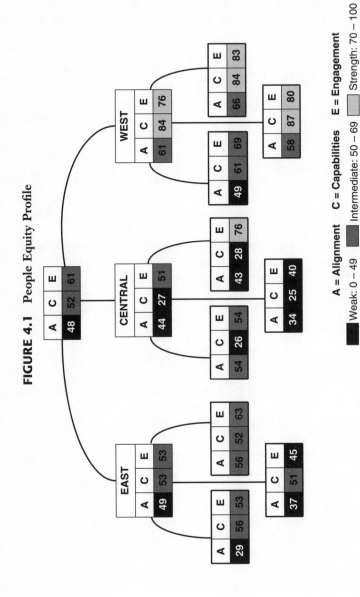

FIGURE 4.1 People Equity Profile

A = Alignment   C = Capabilities   E = Engagement

Weak: 0 – 49   Intermediate: 50 – 69   Strength: 70 – 100

- The variance across units is enormous in most areas:
  - Alignment ranges from 29 to 66.
  - Capabilities range from 25 to 87.
  - Engagement ranges from 40 to 83.

From a decision standpoint, such information enables senior leaders to make a number of important decisions.

Where to direct corrective resources and how broadly to target those resources. In our example, the organization as a whole is deficient in Alignment—the weakest dimension for all regions. Additional questions in the survey revealed gaps in employees' understanding of the overall business direction and therefore key priorities, and gaps in goal setting.

In contrast to the broader Alignment gap, the Capabilities dimension requires more pinpoint solutions. A driver analysis indicated that some units with low Capabilities will need coaching, some more effective staffing, some teamwork enhancements, and still others, better training.

The Human Resources organization was about to launch a company Engagement initiative that included training for all managers. These data helped HR team members refocus and target that effort on only a subset of units for which the initiative would be most valuable. In fact, it allowed them to investigate further what Engagement best practices were being deployed in the West to obtain such strong scores.

Where to focus leadership development efforts. This is a critical area for top management, as recently reaffirmed in a SHRM Foundation study of more than 500 C-Suite executives.[6] The tree diagram highlights the relative strengths and weaknesses of managers regarding their performance in leveraging human capital. When combined with market and financial performance, this information provides valuable feedback on leadership performance and potential.

For example, the Central Division leader, a high flyer from another organization, arrived about a year ago with high expectations on everyone's part. The ACE information in Figure 4.1, which was obtained from a People Equity employee survey, was certainly disconcerting to this business unit leader, as well as to the leadership team. He was struggling to connect with his team but his style was off-putting, given this organization's culture of getting close to people.

The assessment gave both the manager and the leadership advance notice that something was amiss, with time to address it. The president was able to focus more attention on this unit, provide additional coaching and resources, and monitor developments more closely.

Another information-rich example occurred in a Central Division unit—the one scoring a 76 score in Engagement, with low Alignment and

Capabilities scores. Further investigation of this leader, who had struggled with his boss and on occasion with peers, identified a leader who had built an organization that was very loyal to him, but not to the overall organization—an us-versus-them situation had emerged. The leader had carefully protected his subordinates in regard to their competencies (note the low C scores) from scrutiny by others. The market, however, provided independent feedback that reflected this gap—lost customers, complaints, and mounting unhappiness from internal customers.

Where to invest resources to boost employee retention, customer buying behaviors, operational effectiveness, and financial performance. Driver analysis, with its use of advanced statistical methodology, helped identify whether improvements in A, C, or E—or drivers of ACE, such as Rewards, Training, and Leadership communication—would have significant impact on important outcomes, such as employee or customer retention, productivity, and customer loyalty.

For example, in the organization depicted in our illustration, such an analysis identified Respect and Dignity as key drivers of Engagement. Communication and interdepartmental teamwork were two other key drivers of importance relating to Capabilities that were identified through the linkage analysis.

Where to hold, fold, or increase prior investments. The ACE tree diagram provides useful data about the past to make decisions about the future. If initiatives have already been deployed to improve some of the weak areas, they should be reexamined for their efficacy. Perhaps they need to be redesigned or implemented with greater effectiveness.

It is frustrating for everyone involved to watch a key area remain weak because of inattention, or because the resources being deployed have had little impact. An often-quoted definition of insanity comes to mind: continuing to do the same thing while hoping for a different result.

Mining the Organizational Profiles

People Equity profiles enable organizations to invest the right resources to bring their human assets to highly competitive levels. Our experience suggests that it is important to focus on the weakest link in the People Equity chain. For example, if the entire organization is low on Alignment, then generally this should be the primary area of leverage, and the other areas—Capabilities and Engagement—can be spot-treated.

Low Alignment across the organization, as was the case in our example, points to a disconnect in the line of sight from strategy to unit goals to individual accountabilities or performance targets. Perhaps it is a lack of a clear strategy, or the lack of adequate measures—a strategic scorecard, for example—to define the strategy sufficiently to set clear goals. Or the strategy and scorecard might be excellent, but the process to communicate and connect it to units throughout the organization could be faulty, or the performance management and goal-setting process could be weak. In such cases, the survey data will point managers toward the root causes and solutions, and across the organization investments can then be made with increased confidence that the money will be well spent.

Continuing the example, Figure 4.2 (shown on the following page) shows the advantage of having additional items that measure Drivers and Enablers in the survey. As depicted in Figure 4.2, two of the Drivers (HR systems and Innovation) are weak. By drilling down one more level within HR systems, it is further evident that the Performance Management and Rewards HR systems (not selection or development) need attention.

When the top-level findings were first shown to the leadership team, they were quick to jump on performance coaching and possible recent hiring of weaker talent. But the supporting data proved otherwise. By clicking down one more level under Performance Management in Figure 4.3 (Pg. 77), to driver items that support Performance Management, it became clear that the biggest gaps were clear goal setting and accountability. (Remember, some units might be stronger and some weaker.) In the area of Reward systems, lack of recognition is a major culprit.

Instead of channeling knee-jerk resources to coaching or selection, or spending countless hours troubleshooting likely causes, management was quickly able to target resources to key gaps. We also recommend deeper discussion or the use of focus groups to further pinpoint the issues and to identify examples of particularly good and weak performance, so that fixes are specific, relevant, and aimed at removing root causes.

In this case, the corporation redoubled its effort at communicating the strategy and goals to create better Alignment at the local level. One tool they adopted to improve the communications flow was a cascaded balanced scorecard. It focused the top team on the critical drivers and enablers of value for the business; the cascading allowed each business unit and department to connect its goals and measures to the overall strategy and goals. This was a major help to managers in carving out smarter and more understandable goals with their people.

The issue of Accountability was a tougher one, and it began at the top. It was clear that the leadership team had not really held many of its direct reports accountable for performance on all fronts—especially those related to people and customer issues. The president, who had come under increasing pressure, had to work with his team to bring a disciplined performance review process forward. Here, top management used the

FIGURE 4.2 Drivers and Enablers Survey Results

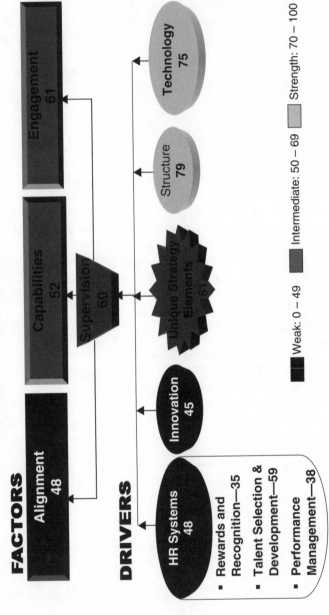

FIGURE 4.3 Human Resource Systems Survey Results

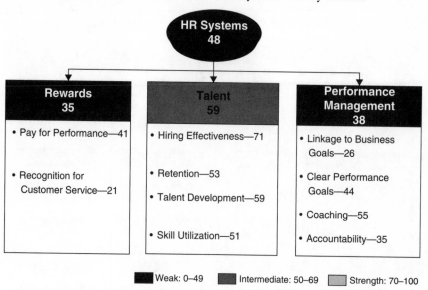

balanced scorecard for double duty. On one hand, it communicated and reinforced what the key priorities were. Second, it was now linked to rewards—reaching targets for each of the scorecard elements was now linked to rewards at multiple management levels. The information from the People Equity survey was a great catalyst to important discussions, decisions, and actions.

Variance Matters

While it would be nice to assume that organizations have a single consistent People Equity profile, reality proves otherwise. We have found a great deal of A, C, and E variance not only across companies within the same industry, but within companies. For example, Figure 4.4 shows a professional services firm with operations across the globe. While there is moderate variance at the business unit level, when you drill down across their various operations in different countries, the variance is enormous. It initially appears that their Asia scores are a disaster, but further peeling of the layers suggests that the biggest concern is Korea, where the scores are low for all three ACE areas. Japan, in contrast, is particularly high on all three areas. It also is interesting to note that there are 10 different unique profiles (combinations of high, medium, and low scores on the three ACE

FIGURE 4.4 People Equity Scores for Global Professional Services Firm

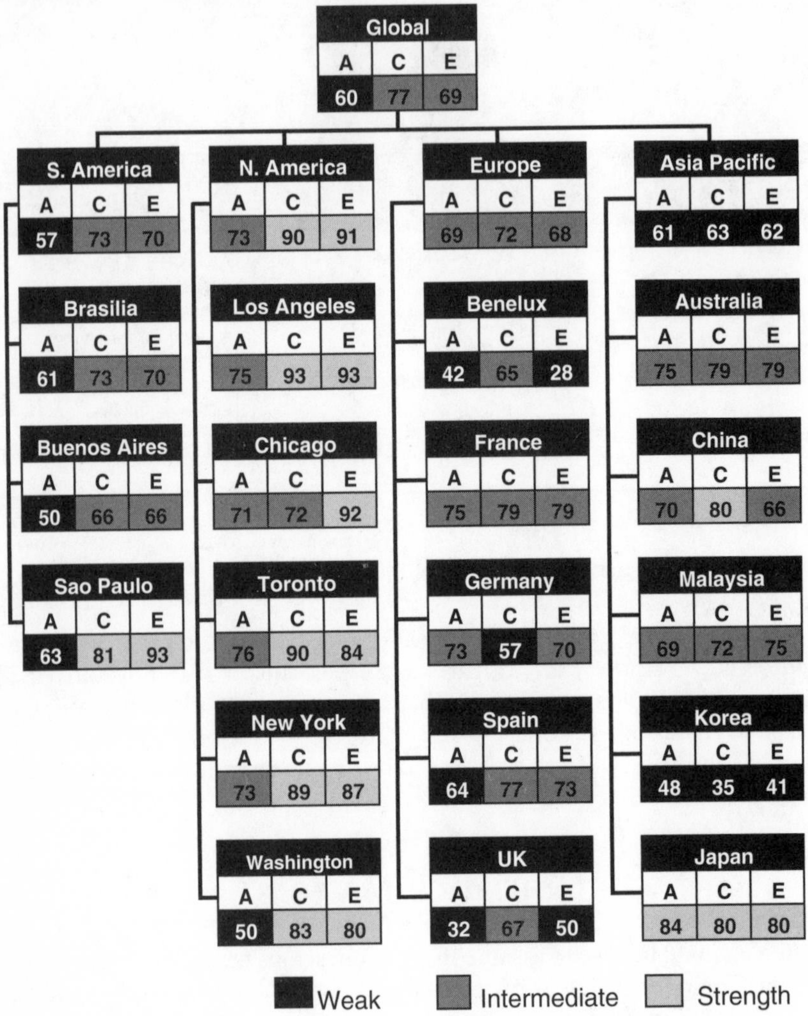

Global		
A	C	E
60	77	69

S. America
A	C	E
57	73	70

N. America
A	C	E
73	90	91

Europe
A	C	E
69	72	68

Asia Pacific
A	C	E
61	63	62

Brasilia
A	C	E
61	73	70

Los Angeles
A	C	E
75	93	93

Benelux
A	C	E
42	65	28

Australia
A	C	E
75	79	79

Buenos Aires
A	C	E
50	66	66

Chicago
A	C	E
71	72	92

France
A	C	E
75	79	79

China
A	C	E
70	80	66

Sao Paulo
A	C	E
63	81	93

Toronto
A	C	E
76	90	84

Germany
A	C	E
73	57	70

Malaysia
A	C	E
69	72	75

New York
A	C	E
73	89	87

Spain
A	C	E
64	77	73

Korea
A	C	E
48	35	41

Washington
A	C	E
50	83	80

UK
A	C	E
32	67	50

Japan
A	C	E
84	80	80

■ Weak   ■ Intermediate   ☐ Strength

dimensions) represented across the 18 country units that report in to the major global regions.

This variance, however, has enabled us to examine how these three factors of People Equity affected business performance. For example, in a recent study of over 70 hospitals, we found some hospitals with Engagement scores below 25 (on a scale of 100) and while others were above 90. At which hospital would you prefer to have your next operation? When we examined the People Equity scores across the 70 hospitals, we found that scores were highly correlated to a hospital's financial performance. Hospitals with low Engagement and Alignment, for example, had union troubles, lower patient and physician satisfaction, and poorer financial performance than their high People Equity counterparts.

Within a large restaurant group, we discovered some restaurants with People Equity scores below 20 and others that scored above 90. (This also included widely varying A, C, and E scores.) As a customer, if you were to walk into two of the restaurants in the organization—one with high People Equity and one with low—you might think you were in two different companies. We found high People Equity restaurants with a sense of excitement—a vibe. Employees were highly attentive to customers and seemed to self-manage their behaviors in a positive way. Their speed, focus, and quality were much higher than their lower People Equity counterparts, where there appeared to be low morale, lack of focus, and inattentiveness to the customer. Restaurants with higher People Equity scores had higher customer satisfaction scores, lower turnover, and they were financially more successful.

Internal variability is a critical factor to consider, not only because it is difficult to manage swings in human capital, but because it dramatically affects customers—internal and external. Customers value product and service consistency. They tend to dislike playing Russian roulette with their wallets.

Wal-Mart and Nordstrom's vary dramatically in their service offering, which is no surprise given the different market segments that each serves. Where an organization is likely to run into trouble is having a mixed portfolio of outlets in which some are aligned with the intended corporate strategy and others appear to be more aligned with the strategy of a competitor.

Even in the best organizations, top-to-bottom Alignment is rare. There will be pockets that for a variety of reasons are low scoring. Maybe the managers need additional skills or coaching, or perhaps the translation of strategic and operational goals has broken down for a particular business unit or function. This same inconsistent pattern is true not only for Alignment, but for Capabilities and Engagement as well.

Five Actions to Boost People Equity

While there are many actions that you can take to boost the overall People Equity of the organization, we have found the following five to be particularly effective:

1. First, have a good talent strategy—in what ways does your human capital differentiate you in the marketplace? Those differentiators should be emphasized and exploited. Without such focus, your measures will simply be the same as everyone else.

2. Next, have good metrics that capture those differentiating human capital factors. The metrics should include both leading and lagging success factors.

3. Have a way to capture Alignment, Capabilities, and Engagement—the three big drivers of human capital value. While we have standard surveys of People Equity, the ones that are customized to the unique features, such as organizational strategy and culture, are most powerful. When a unit head sees Alignment questions that reflect the specific values of his organization, or key service Capabilities that reflect the organization's brand, then the ACE dimensions are even more valuable.

4. Drill down below ACE to ensure that there are measures of the drivers of ACE—these could be training, core values, leadership skills, supervisory practices, and so forth. Typically, these can be included in the ACE employee survey. Questions relating to these factors were at the root of the analysis we did earlier on the drivers of low Alignment for the organization in Figure 4.1.

5. Put in place a strong tracking system that ensures the ongoing review of these measures, along with customer and financial performance.

With these steps, you are on the road to powerful human capital measurement that will give you both insight and foresight, and distinguish your firm in a world of increasing competition and scarce resources.

Connecting the Dots

People Equity and the dimensions captured on the survey example just discussed are part of a network of interrelated business constructs that fit together in a cause-and-effect manner for driving overall business performance and shareholder equity, as illustrated in Figure 2.5. Once information is available for the People Equity elements, it can be connected to operating metrics (such as speed of response to customers, cycle time, quality metrics), supplier metrics (partnering, quality), regulatory metrics, customer drivers (reputation, service quality, price) and outcomes (loyalty, client retention), and financial outcomes (productivity, overhead costs, revenue growth, and margins).

Such analyses will provide an organization with its unique profile of drivers and results, thereby enabling it to pinpoint its value chain gaps. We have conducted scores of such analyses, and they vary considerably from organization to organization. There are a number of consistent predictors of ACE and employee, customer, and financial outcomes such as leadership, supervision, respect, and customer focus. But the exact level of prediction and unique profile varies across organizations, based on their current gaps, areas of strategic emphasis, and unique cultural history.

Conclusion

As we have seen in this chapter, measurement of People Equity is crucial to good decisions. When done correctly, it provides a window into the workings of the organization as we saw in Figure 4.1. Leadership teams can readily use this information to assess how well executives are managing and leveraging their human capital.

We next examine how these measures of People Equity can be used to answer the fifth question from Figure 2.1: How can People Equity and its three components help in making strategic talent investment decisions? Can it inform alternative investment choices in talent programs and practices?

Summary of Key Learning Points

- Intangibles of various types—brand, customer loyalty, human capital, and job satisfaction—are increasingly important in managing and measuring organizational and personal value. For many businesses, human capital intangibles represent far more than 50 percent of their total value.
- The ability to measure People Equity means not only that it can be understood and managed, but it can be used to predict important outcomes such as, performance, quality, customer loyalty, top performer retention, and internal service value.
- The best available way to measure People Equity is through the eyes of the key stakeholder of People Equity—people.
- Surveys can be designed to measure Alignment, Capabilities, and Engagement in such as a way that these concepts can be compared and prioritized for action. Surveys that include the Drivers and Enablers of People Equity add more value because they allow

(Continued)

managers to determine which factors will have the biggest influence on ACE—and therefore, where to invest resources for improvement.

- One-size-fits-all People Equity solutions rarely work because ACE scores typically vary considerably across managerial units within an organization. Different People Equity profiles will call for different solutions. Some managers may need to focus on Alignment while others focus on Engagement. Even managers who share low scores on an area such as Alignment may be low for different reasons, calling for different solutions.
- Because of rapid organizational change, ACE should be monitored on a regular basis to:
  - Identify the current gaps that are inhibiting greater success
  - Provide feedback to managers that enables them to improve their talent management capabilities
  - Test whether different Drivers or Enablers of ACE are becoming more or less important in optimizing ACE and therefore business results

Action Tips: What Can I Do Tomorrow?

As you begin the journey toward managing and increasing People Equity, it is imperative to have a clear, accurate understanding of your current organizational profile. Here are a few questions to ask and steps to take to get that clear reading.

- If you are using an employee survey, does it capture the three key elements of People Equity—Alignment, Capabilities, and Engagement? If not, your survey instrument is most likely missing the power to holistically understand and manage your people issues.
- Are your senior executives eager to see their next survey results? If not, why not? This is typically a result of survey content that is not viewed as strategically significant. Or, it may be a result of misuse. When the information adds significant value, people will surmount challenges to secure it.
- Next, assuming you want to capture the People Equity concept, compare your survey with the content in Table 3.3 from Chapter 3 to determine the level of overlap or uniqueness.
- Once you have assessed the purpose and value of the various surveys already in place, you are positioned to make a choice: either enhance an

existing survey to include missing content in People Equity, or introduce a separate People Equity survey to provide the leadership team and all management levels with a tool that is more strategic.

- Consider coupling the survey with interviews and focus groups to provide more depth of understanding of why and how the drivers and enablers are enhancing or diminishing People Equity.

5

ACE and Resource Allocation

"One of the golden rules is to make sure that we as an Executive team allocate the right resources to the right priorities."
—Doug Michels, CEO, Orasure Technologies, Inc.

W e are often asked to help an organization evaluate (or justify) the return on investment in specific programs such as management training, security enhancements, accident prevention, recognition programs, and many others. The ACE framework helps address this question.

Let's take a specific example. A human resources group is currently deciding how to allocate a budget across the many potential initiatives that are expected to improve key strategic scorecard measures relating to talent management. Table 5.1 illustrates some of the initiatives they are considering for the upcoming year.

The problem is how to choose among many potentially sound initiatives. After all, these were all being advocated by various entities within the organization, including members of the Human Resources leadership team. Some represent continuations of existing programs and others are new. Do you have some favorites among the alternatives?

To answer the question, we need more information. Enter the *strategic value map* in Figure 5.1. This figure is an abbreviated version of the overall strategic value map, which drives the company's balanced scorecard, showing the key factors needed to achieve the organization's goals (shown on the right). The financial or other end goals (for example, increase membership of an association, or cancer reduction for a cancer foundation) are listed at the right. Connected to these longer-term outcomes is what leadership believes are the most important factors that must be managed to achieve those outcomes. For example, customer retention and market share are important intermediate outcomes leading to increased sales and profit. To reach the customer and

Table 5.1
Sample HR Initiatives

Initiatives

HRIS Implementation: improve efficiency of managing HR data.
Talent Selection Initiative: improve the selection of top talent.
Ethics Training: improve understanding of and adherence to corporate ethical standards.
Business Acumen Training: increase financial understanding and decision making for all employees.
Performance Coaching Enhancement: improve ability of supervisors to provide feedback and coaching to their employees.
Benefit Outsourcing: cost savings in overall benefits program.
Customer Service Training: deliver enhanced customer experience.

FIGURE 5.1   Strategic Value Map

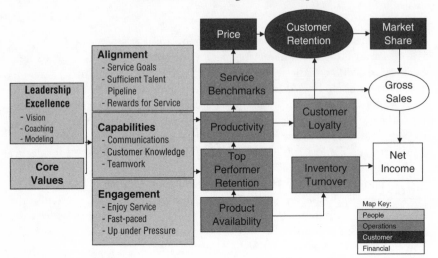

financial goals, there are a number of operational and people outcomes that must be achieved. These are listed to the left of the customer outcomes. Note: There are a few additional drivers relating to Suppliers and Community that are not included in this map for the purposes of clarity and quick understanding.

While there could be many more drivers of success, leadership has agreed that the 14 factors leading to Gross Sales and Net Income are the most strategic areas that need to be managed, while other important tactical drivers can be identified (typically at the functional level—operations, human resources, information technology) that will support this broad scorecard.

As you can see, People Equity and other drivers of People Equity are captured in this scorecard. Many are quite specific to the strategy of the organization. For example, the organization is trying to use customer intimacy as an important differentiator in the marketplace, and as such has a number of Capabilities and Alignment factors that are focused on these issues. Under Alignment, there is a particular focus on strong service goals and rewards for outstanding service; under Capabilities, customer knowledge and stellar communications (customer and internal team) are viewed as critical to differentiate them from competitors. Even Engagement focuses on employees who enjoy serving others in a fast-paced, often pressure-filled work environment.

For our purposes, there is no need to go into the detail relating to the Leadership and Values Enablers. Suffice it to say that the values emphasize service excellence, accountability, and the creation of a high trust environment while placing a strong emphasis on leader role modeling and coaching.

FIGURE 5.2   Talent Value Map

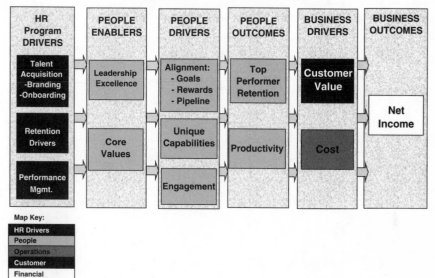

For every element in the strategy map, there is a measure of success, with a clear operational definition, a measurement owner, and both short- and long-term targets that have been agreed upon by the leadership team to ensure success.

Figure 5.2 shows a *talent value map* that is strongly linked to the earlier *strategic value map* of the organization. This map focuses on the talent elements of the overall strategy and therefore makes it easier to focus attention on processes, activities, and initiatives that are directed at human capital. For example, in this case, the map adds some of the important drivers that are often designed and administered by the Human Resources function, such as talent acquisition, performance management, and top performer–retention programs. Note: there are typically some additional HR drivers, but for clarity here, they have been abbreviated. It should also be noted that there is a measure (some the same) for every box on the chart.

We can now apply this information to our key question of choosing the right initiatives. The matrix in Figure 5.3 provides a way to integrate the two, with the initiatives listed down the left side of each row and the key scorecard measures across the top of each column. The shading of each column header indicates whether the organization is currently meeting its target for each scorecard measure, falling somewhat behind but within reach of the target for the year, or far behind the target. Those far behind the target are under-standably of greatest concern, as all of these measures were deemed to be critical to success.

FIGURE 5.3 Resource Allocation Map

Strategic Performance Measures

Initiatives	People Equity Enablers		People Equity Drivers			People Equity		Business Outcomes		
	Values	Leadership	Performance Management	Talent Acquisition	Alignment	Capabilities	Engagement	Top Performer Retention	Customer Impact	Productivity/Cost
HRIS Implementation						S				(P)
Talent Selection	S	S		P	S	P		S	P	P
Ethics Training	P	P			S		S		S	
Business Acumen Training		S	P		S	S			S	S
Performance Coaching		P	P		P	P	S	P	S	P
Benefits Outsourcing							(S)			P
Customer Service Training	S					P			S	

■ far behind target ■ within reach of target ■ meeting target

P = primary S=secondary ( ) indicates negative impact

Each box shows the expected impact of a particular initiative on each scorecard measure. A *P* indicates that we would expect a particular initiative to have a primary impact on this scorecard measure. An *S* shows that this initiative should have a secondary impact. While this classification of impact may appear imprecise, we have found it to be in fact quite powerful for making major decisions relative to the strategy and scorecard. This approach will get most people to the 80–20 solution or better.

Armed with this information, how would you allocate your resources?

- What would be your three most important initiatives? Why?
- What initiatives provide the biggest bang for your buck?
- If you were asked to cut your budget by 15 percent, requiring you to cut two initiatives from the list, which initiatives would they be?
- If the *Talent Selection* initiative has been an ongoing effort for more than a year, what would you conclude?

This resource matrix should help you answer these questions:

What are your most important initiatives? The first challenge is to improve the areas that are substantially below the strategic targets. Remember, leadership has determined that for the organization to grow and reach its strategic goals, each of the columns should be at or near targets. So, a first order of business is to examine whether there are sufficient resources being allocated in those areas to close the performance gap. As indicated in Figure 5.3, the Engagement goal is substantially below target and does not seem to have sufficient initiatives directed to improve that gap; in fact, the benefits outsourcing is expected to have a negative impact (noted by the brackets) on Engagement in the next year. The productivity-cost gap, in contrast, has multiple initiatives that should help address this gap.

Biggest Bang for Your Buck, Yuan, or Euro? Another criterion that may be of importance is looking for initiatives that serve multiple purposes. For example, you can see in Figure 5.3 that the *Performance Coaching* and *Talent Selection* initiatives are expected to positively influence five or six strategic goals, including two that are key gaps today. If it takes similar funding for either of these two initiatives versus other initiatives that perhaps influence only one scorecard area, these initiatives may provide more strategic impact.

By this time, you are probably getting the impression that we are using the scorecard as the criteria for Return On Investment (ROI). Because the leadership team has determined that the scorecard factors are the most important for success, it seems a relatively useless exercise to go about calculating the ROI on secondary factors. In fact, it may be counter-productive to do so. We frequently find organizations suboptimizing functional outcomes at the expense of overall enterprise success measures.

ROI Reality Check

Our investigations of ROI across companies came up with an interesting finding. While many companies have increased the rigor of their evaluation of proposed initiatives during the budget planning cycle, most do not evaluate how well those funded initiatives actually did. While I am sure there must be one out there, I have yet to find a CFO who says that he evaluated the actual ROI on previously budgeted initiatives. When I asked a CFO at a health care company about this, his response echoed what I have heard from most financial leaders: "We don't have the kind of staffing to really do that." This process essentially favors those who can create great models that show enormous benefits (regardless of their implementation) versus those who are actually modest proposers and great implementers. This is an area in dire need of change in organizations because it assumes that all of the best assumptions that were used in building the ROI models and implementation were perfect, but in reality, they almost never are.

If you had to eliminate two initiatives, which would you select? Because of budget cutbacks, or perhaps a need to fund more important strategic initiatives identified earlier, assume you have been forced to reduce the budget and undertake fewer initiatives. If you said *Customer Service Training* and *HRIS Implementation*, those would be reasonable choices. Each of these initiatives has little or no impact on the key gap areas in the strategic scorecard, and the IT initiative, in fact, will have a very large negative impact on the cost goals for this period as indicated by the (*P*) in the *Productivity/Cost* column. This, of course, must be weighed by whether the IT investment would have a larger positive productivity impact over a longer strategic horizon—say, three years.

Program Evaluation. If the *Talent Selection* initiative has been an ongoing effort for more than a year, what would you conclude? What if I additionally told you that the Talent Acquisition measure has gone from "within reach of target" to "far behind target" this past year? Given that this was the only initiative that was targeted to improve the Talent Acquisition measure, clearly something has gone wrong. Perhaps it has not been implemented well. Or, perhaps it was not funded as fully as originally proposed and the impact was choked off. Or, perhaps it was simply the wrong initiative. Before continuing to fund this initiative, it will be important to answer these questions.

How Much Is Enough?

Another important issue relates to initiatives that are meeting targets. For example, we have reached or surpassed our targets in the Values and Capabilities areas (see Figure 5.3), so it may be possible to reduce or eliminate initiatives in these areas and redeploy the focus on the bigger gaps. This is obviously a judgment call about the level of continuing support needed to keep those areas on target.

While hitting the targets is a good thing, surpassing the targets by too much may be problematic. Take the cost target, for example. There is a desire to have Selling, General, and Administrative (SGA) expenses at 30 percent of revenue. Introducing additional initiatives to drive SGA lower may be detrimental to the organization. One of the keys to the balanced scorecard is the word *balance*. The organization is trying to balance or optimize often-competing factors such as revenue generation, cost, and customer impact. By slashing advertising budgets or sales costs below a given target, the organization may well be sacrificing its revenue target.

The same can be true of Human Capital trade-offs. Certain skill levels may be required to satisfy customers. Additional training may not have any measurable advantage to one of the key indicators. Higher employee benefits may not improve your ability to further retain or attract the best, as we have seen in high talent-competition locations such as Hawaii. In a desire to become a "best place to work," employers often escalate employee benefits of all types in an attempt to lure employees to their organization. This is a one-way street, in which employers did not really get a more loyal workforce; they just paid more to raise the level of entitlement expected by employees without gaining any more loyalty—a losing proposition.

We next examine how these measures of People Equity can be used to answer the sixth question from Figure 2.1: How can leaders and employees use People Equity to optimize performance?

Summary of Key Learning Points

- People Equity combined with strategic scorecarding can provide a powerful tool to help allocate limited resources across a whole host of potential initiatives.

(Continued)

- Powerful strategic scorecards provide a way to link organizational results with People Equity, the drivers and enablers of People Equity, and human capital initiatives.
- An initiative matrix that combines strategic scorecards and potential initiatives can help answer the following questions:
  - What are the most important initiatives?
  - If a budget must be adjusted, which initiatives should be added or subtracted from the plan?
  - Which initiatives provide multiple benefits, and therefore might be more value than those that influence only one area?
  - Which initiatives should perhaps be redesigned or retired?
- Another important consideration is how much of an initiative is needed to maintain a particular scorecard area in the green or target range?

Action Tips: What Can I Do Tomorrow?

Here are some thoughts on actions you can take right away in your organization.

- Do you have a talent strategy map and a talent scorecard? If not, begin building one because it can help you do the following:
  - Have important conversations with senior leaders about talent priorities and how they support the business strategy.
  - Examine your own unit's initiatives, actions, and communications to ensure that you can justify the existing practices.
- If you are building a strategy map and scorecard, best practices suggest that it is wise to:
  - Involve the key stakeholders who will be implementing it. For example, if you are building a talent map and a supporting Human Resources map and scorecard, it will have far more power and likelihood of being executed if you involve the various leaders of stakeholder groups such as Training, Organizational Development, Compensation, and Benefits.
  - Get a strong facilitator—internal or external—who is not a member of that organization. Self-facilitation is likely to have you wander the scorecard desert until the initiative dies of thirst.

- If you don't have initiative matrixes, build them. Obviously, they require a scorecard of some sort for prioritization. Several tips:
  - Start with a broad brainstorm of initiatives generated by the various functional stakeholders (for example, head of training, benefits), but create a framework for thinking out of their functional silo. It is far more dangerous to start with each subfunction bringing in a *must* list, which is too often a dusted-off version of last year's list. Most often, they will defend that list leaving you more initiatives than can be funded.
  - Stick strictly to the scorecard criteria or you will create too many exceptions.
  - Have what-if discussions to test how important various initiatives are. What if we lost 10 percent of our budget? Can we justify a 5 percent greater budget based on sound logic and connection to the business strategy?

SECTION III

Optimizing Talent

"We believe our fundamental strength lies in our people."
—Sam Johnson, S.C. Johnson

F ew would argue with Sam Johnson's observation that people are, or at least can be, the cornerstone strength of any organization. They can also be a strategic vulnerability. Talent that is squandered creates a competitive disadvantage as fast as shoddy products or service quality. Manage talent to yield optimal value and you are on your way to becoming a fiercely competitive enterprise.

From an organizational viewpoint, talent optimization means higher performance, better quality, more satisfied customers or clients, fewer accidents, and greater profitability. If your talent optimization is better than that of your competitors, it means that you are investing less in labor costs to achieve high performance, a key factor in a tightening world of competition and cost management.

From an individual's perspective, maximizing potential means becoming the best you can be—better skills and experiences, achieving new levels of accomplishment, building strong relationships, and increasing personal value. And that means increasing your value to your current or potential future employers. Individual talent optimization is not just about money or prestige; it is about accelerating progress toward your life goals.

As David Ulrich[1] has pointed out, "No matter how interesting or valuable an activity may seem to those doing it, if those who receive the output of that activity don't find it of value to them, continuing the activity cannot be justified. Value is the great equalizer, and as the planet becomes more crowded and organizations compete for increasingly scarce resources, value will be the factor that differentiates those who gain or lose in the quest toward their goals—personal or organizational."

People Equity and Talent Optimization

People Equity is a helpful framework to use in thinking about optimizing both organizational and individual value. In this section, we will look at the role of People Equity in helping to guide decisions that will optimize workforce performance and worker fulfillment.

People Equity plays a central role in assessing and guiding talent optimization in several key ways.

1. Immediately following the hire of a new person, People Equity provides a way to track talent development in the fragile, formative employment period that is decisive in determining future performance.

2. People Equity and its nine Drivers and Enablers provide a framework for understanding the major drivers of workforce optimization and when coupled with an appropriate measurement of these factors, they provide an ongoing way to track how well talent is being used.

3. By understanding the drivers and enablers of Alignment, Capabilities, and Engagement, leaders can effectively target limited resources to the right root causes that will most improve People Equity and by extension key business results.

Let us focus for a moment on the alternative ACE futures that we have discussed earlier. Remember, in our examination of hundreds of organizations and thousands of work units, we find ACE scores that vary from winning cultures with scores over 90 to ones that score below 20.

Figure III.1 shows two talent optimization futures that we encounter every day in our organizational assessments. The profile on the bottom continues the growth of ACE from the onboarding period while the one on the top shows a pattern of an organization that squanders its human capital.

The low People Equity profile on the top is typically fraught with conflict, low productivity, and employees who either physically leave or mentally leave their employer. Our experience suggests that it is unfortunately more often the top performers who leave while the performance indigent remain with the organization.

In low People Equity firms, Alignment never reaches high levels; in fact, it generally reaches middle levels and then recedes slowly. This often happens because the organization stops realigning. It fails to communicate changes in the strategy and new priorities, to modify or change measures and targets required of new market conditions, or to rethink rewards that reinforce old behaviors. In some organizations, longer-tenured employees are more out of touch than new hires.

The future Capabilities curve can veer in different directions, as you can see from Figure III.1. For high People Equity firms, Capabilities continue to grow. They are adjusted to remain relevant to new or changing customer expectations. Employees are encouraged to develop their potential. Individuals are often trained across knowledge or skills areas. In these learning organizations, the Capabilities dimension grows and grows, often with scores into the 90s.[2]

For low People Equity organizations, the initial rapid growth in Capabilities scores often resembles a roller coaster ride. Veteran workers often think that they have already been trained; training is for the new people. Employees may tout skills that are no longer relevant. The skills of computer programmers, for example, can become obsolete in as short as one or two years when deep expertise in one technology has been supplanted with the next technology generation. Research suggests that many don't make the

FIGURE III.1 High and Low People Equity Profiles

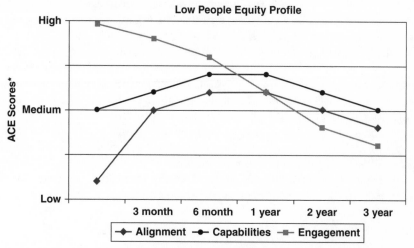

*Favorable responses of new hires to survey questions on each ACE factor.

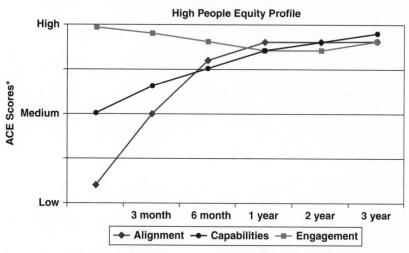

*Favorable responses of new hires to survey questions on each ACE factor

change and ultimately look for other work. Another study found that some managerial skills become 50 percent obsolete within five years.[3]

Still another profile that we frequently find in these low Capabilities units is talent that lacks tools or resources to meet customer expectations. The talent is being choked off. It may seem absurd that an organization would do this, but the resourcing decisions, behaviors, and subsequent consequences are often indirect, occurring over many years of making small choices that suboptimize the Capabilities needed to meet changing customer requirements. While at times this is a conscious decision for budgetary or strategic reasons—for example, a cash cow unit that the organization is milking until disposal—more often the change is incremental, often going unnoticed because of insufficient measurement tools to track the impact.

And finally, in high Engagement organizations, employees are exuberant about the organization, its mission, and their roles. They are willing to advocate to others to come join or invest in their organization. They exhibit high loyalty to and identification with the organization and their unit. The low Engagement profile is often fraught with employees who do the minimum, would not encourage others to follow their plight, and are only as loyal as their pensions and compensation require.

Let's now take a look at how each of the three ACE factors helps to optimize workforce performance and personal fulfillment.

6

Aligning Strategy, Culture, and Talent[1]

"If the CEO is going in one direction, and employees are going in another, that's a serious problem."
—Connie Rank-Smith, Jewelers Mutual Insurance
Company and HR Certification Institute

In the 1970s, Alignment was a major concern for me and thousands of other drivers escaping for a weekend to Tijuana, Mexico. The road to Tijuana was pocked by hundreds of potholes that could swallow whole tires, leaving only two strategies: drive excruciatingly slowly while maneuvering circuitously around this moonscape, or step on the gas and hope to hydroplane over the impediments. Neither really worked, as evidenced by the smiley faces on mechanics in the vast number of auto alignment and body shops that dotted the entrance to Tijuana.

Alignment is a flock of birds or a squadron of planes flying in a perfect V formation, or a team of rowers moving surely and swiftly along a lake's surface. Within an organizational context, "alignment is focus," as one of our CEO interviewees put it. It implies that from top to bottom everything is connected in the most effective and efficient way possible so that there is maximal output using the least amount of input. In this chapter, we focus more on the role of Alignment in optimizing employee performance and allowing employees to become more successful.

In our strategy work, we advise clients to follow a golden rule: Once you have chosen your strategic goals and customers[2]—those to whom your products and services will add value—the organization must have its work processes, structures, systems, capabilities, and culture aligned with that objective (see Figure 6.1). From a talent standpoint that means having behaviors that are riveted on those high value-added tasks and processes needed to serve those customers and achieve the organizational goals.

While it is a generally accepted truism that alignment is crucial to business success, there are many forces at work that cause organizations to limp along, seriously misaligned. Some misalignments are brought on by a merger. When Hewlett-Packard (HP) merged with Compaq, for example, there were clear misalignments between the cultures—HP had a long history of research and innovation primacy and Compaq was better noted for excellence in marketing. These differences in values and priorities led to the many reported conflicts of the two cultures: battles over product selection, product features, and benefits. Misaligned roles, priorities, and behaviors within the organization, coupled with serious misalignments of investment goals and strategic priorities within the HP Board,[3] led to stalemates that delayed the organization in achieving its objectives.

Misalignment is often an insidious phenomenon. It typically comes about after years of poor organizational posture—creeping role scope, processes that have not adapted to new customer requirements, fuzzy strategies and priorities, or gradual service slippage. Misalignments can grow unchecked

FIGURE 6.1 Creating Alignment

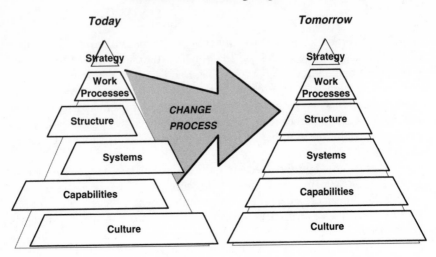

for months or years, until some traumatic event occurs—a major recession, a merger or restructuring, loss of major customers, or an internal stakeholder group that outsources services.

Misaligned values are especially subversive and have a way of going undetected at the top of the organization, though those at ground level often know or at least suspect what's really happening. Enter Enron, Tyco and, more recently, just about any of the Wall Street financial firms.

McDonald's, by contrast, provides an example of a tightly aligned organization. In the late 1990s, McDonald's tried to shake off unprofitable growth using a number of strategies that ultimately did not succeed. When James R. Cantalupo returned from retirement after McDonald's same-store sales hit rock bottom in 2002, he immediately focused on Alignment. He helped McDonald's launch its "Plan to Win," a playbook that aligns people, products, place, price, and promotion. Within a short time, employees at all levels had clear guidance for prioritizing their actions and resources. By studying the customer more effectively, and aligning company practices with the marketplace, everyone in the company was able "to focus on quality service and restaurant experience rather than simply providing the cheapest, most convenient option to customers."[4] Looking back on McDonald's 55 consecutive months of same-store sales growth as of November 2008, CEO Jim Skinner said, "Alignment of the organization has been a pivotal factor in its success." It shows; McDonald's was one of only two firms in the Dow in recessionary 2008 for which the stock went up.[5]

Big or Small

Alignment is not just an issue for large corporations. At the WD-40 Company (WD-40), a truly global brand with fewer than 400 employees, CEO Garry Ridge says, "Having people aligned with your vision and strategy is imperative." Henry S. Givray, chairman and CEO of SmithBucklin Corporation, the world's largest association management and professional services firm, with 750 employees, stated that the most important Alignment involves cultural values: "If people share the same values, their organization can pursue any strategy successfully."

What Does the Evidence Say?

While more research is needed, the research and case examples that do exist strongly support the connection of Alignment to important organizational outcomes.

For example, Jack in the Box, the 30,000-plus employee quick-serve restaurant company, found that Alignment was significantly correlated (.38) with people's intention to leave (a good predictor of actual turnover), and that, in turn, was significantly correlated (.33 and .38, respectively) with sales and profit.

In a study the Metrus Group conducted among 56 hospitals, they found that Alignment was significantly correlated (.23) with EBITDA (earnings before interest, taxes, depreciation, and amortization). In another study conducted by the Metrus Institute by Kostman and Schiemann[6] with the American Society for Quality (ASQ), which included approximately 2,000 organizations, the authors found that two-thirds of the firms that were in the top quartile on Alignment were also in the top third in financial performance. In contrast, for those in the bottom quartile on Alignment, only two in five were strong financial performers.

Another way to look at Alignment is in terms of the negative consequences of being misaligned. Table 6.1 summarizes a range of consequences of low Alignment from theory, practice, research, and interviews with senior leaders.

One of the most negative outcomes of low Alignment is wasted time and energy. When individuals (or teams or units) are not well aligned with the vision, organizational goals, or what customers need and want, extra energy is required to reach the goals because time is often diverted to low or no value-added activities. This misalignment not only reduces the team's impact on results, but also frustrates team members. The sense of low accomplishment engendered by misalignment is a morale buster that, in turn, leads to stress

Table 6.1
The Business Impact of Low Alignment

Low Alignment
• Confusing brand promise • Many urgent, but not important activities • Non-competitive costs due to misdirected energy, talent • Burnout or talent loss—working hard, but not smart • Overstaffing to compensate for time lost on low-value activities • Low teamwork–high conflict across interdependent units

(related to work-life balance; perceptions of time waste) and other dysfunctional outcomes, ranging from poor performance to turnover.

Strong evidence exists supporting the connection between Alignment and performance. To listen to most of the leaders interviewed, it is a key factor for success, which raises the question: What is Alignment?

Three Key Alignment Elements

To ensure that everyone is rowing in the same direction, see Figure 6.2, which illustrates three critical elements that compose Alignment.

- *Strategy and Goal Alignment.* The line of sight from organizational strategy and goals and measures to employee behaviors, including the intermediate alignment of appropriate unit structures, processes, goals, and measures—vertical alignment.
- *Values Alignment.* Consistency of behaviors in support of agreed-upon organizational values—the *How* we do things that define a culture.
- *Customer Alignment.* The synchronization of organizational processes, resources, and employee behaviors across interdependent individuals and teams to meet customer requirements—horizontal alignment.

Before we examine some of the drivers of Alignment, take the survey in Table 6.2 to assess your unit's or team's Alignment proficiency.

As you answer the survey questions in Table 6.2, focus on your current organization or another in which you have worked at some point in your career.

Add up your score: A score of 24 or above indicates that your organization is doing a reasonably good job in the Alignment arena. Scores below 17

FIGURE 6.2 Key Elements That Support Alignment

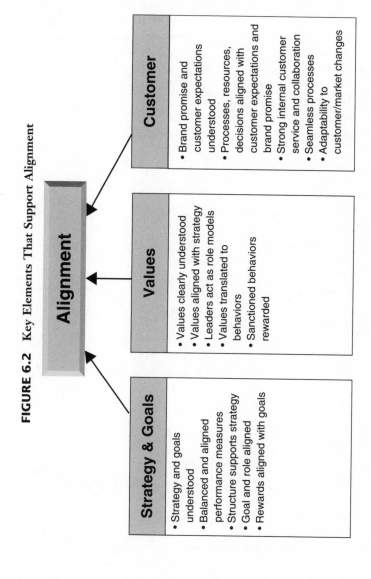

Alignment

Strategy & Goals
- Strategy and goals understood
- Balanced and aligned performance measures
- Structure supports strategy
- Goal and role aligned
- Rewards aligned with goals

Values
- Values clearly understood
- Values aligned with strategy
- Leaders act as role models
- Values translated to behaviors
- Sanctioned behaviors rewarded

Customer
- Brand promise and customer expectations understood
- Processes, resources, decisions aligned with customer expectations and brand promise
- Strong internal customer service and collaboration
- Seamless processes
- Adaptability to customer/market changes

Table 6.2
Quick Alignment Check

	Strongly Disagree	Disagree	Neutral	Agree	Strongly Agree
Most employees understand the overall goals of the organization and how it plans to reach them.	1	2	3	4	5
My unit has clear performance objectives that are tied to our customers' expectations [Answer for your direct customers, whether internal or external].	1	2	3	4	5
My individual performance goals are clearly linked to unit and department performance goals.	1	2	3	4	5
The goals of my department are tightly linked with the overall goals of the company.	1	2	3	4	5
Employee rewards are linked to achieving performance goals.	1	2	3	4	5
There is good teamwork and cooperation between my department and other departments.	1	2	3	4	5
Total Alignment Score (add up your score for the six questions)					

indicate serious concerns in this area. Scores below 30 indicate that you are leaving money on the table in the form of Alignment drag, which almost always costs you something in the form of missing customer connections or missed productivity opportunities. For more information, go to **reinventing talentmanagement.com**.

FIGURE 6.3 Order Fulfillment Department—Alignment Results

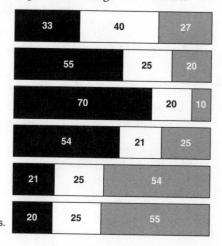

Most employees understand the overall goals of the organization and how it plans to reach them. — 33 | 40 | 27

My unit has clear performance objectives that are tied to our customers' expectations — 55 | 25 | 20

My individual performance goals are clearly linked to unit/department performance goals — 70 | 20 | 10

The goals of my department are tightly linked with the overall goals of the company. — 54 | 21 | 25

Employee rewards are linked to achieving performance goals. — 21 | 25 | 54

There is good teamwork and cooperation between my department and other departments. — 20 | 25 | 55

■ Favorable □ Neutral ▦ Unfavorable

This short evaluation[7] should help to underscore the types of issues that can be measured in the Alignment area. While our assessment includes only your ratings, in practice we would want to have the aggregate ratings of all team members (for example, delivery team, shift, department). While the overall score is important, it is the individual items that represent an opportunity for improvement.

For example, in the organization profiled in Figure 6.3, a majority of employees report having individual performance goals that are linked to their department goals, but only one-third of employees understand the overall organizational goals. Also, rewards are not seen as linked to goal achievement, and horizontal alignment represented by cooperation across work units is low.

What Drives Alignment?

Organizations such as Volvo, American Express, Federal Express, WD-40, UPS, CIT, Caterpillar, and others have devoted considerable energy to ensuring that there is Alignment between their organizational visions on one hand and employee behaviors on the other, leading to important organizational outcomes such as employee productivity, quality, employee and customer retention, and customer loyalty. And to ensure this, the leaders

Table 6.3
The Nine Drivers of High Alignment

1. A clear, agreed-upon vision and strategy
2. Translation of the vision and strategy into clear organizational and unit measures
3. Cascading and communicating the strategy and goals
4. Meaningful individual goals and roles
5. Rational acceptance of the strategy and goals among implementers
6. Clear, timely feedback on goal attainment and the drivers of those goals
7. Strong internal customer service and collaboration
8. Meaningful rewards that reinforce strategically aligned behaviors
9. Culture alignment

focus on a host of Alignment drivers to give them an edge in strategy execution.

Some of the most important drivers of Alignment are listed in Table 6.3.

Before examining each of these factors, it is important to note that strength in one factor does not compensate for weakness on another. For example, from a logical standpoint, it is hard to imagine that excelling on feedback, while not understanding the strategy, will help drive performance (except perhaps in the wrong direction). Experience suggests that you need to start at the top—agreeing on strategy—and then work through other elements to be the most successful. So let's begin at the top.

A Clear, Agreed-Upon Vision and Strategy

Despite its discussed importance, there is often much confusion about what strategy is and how it should be formulated. Strategy, vision, mission, goals, values, and organizational philosophy are often confused or combined.[8] At the simplest level, strategy is securing agreement from the key stakeholders about "What products we are delivering to what markets so as to achieve certain long-term goals, and what capabilities are required to do that." If the leadership team is together on the strategy, then it is off to a good start. Strategy should also tell us about what we will *not* do. The not-do part is key to Alignment because it helps reduce the amount of energy that may be wasted by key stakeholders—employees, suppliers, partners—on low-value activities.

In a study we did with attendees at Conference Board strategy conferences, nearly one-third of vice presidents and directors reported that the top leadership team did not have a clearly agreed-upon strategy. This may explain why Jerry Seibert, the global director of diagnostic services for the Metrus

Group, quoting data from a current cross-industry database of more than 100 organizations, reports that only about two-thirds of employees report having clarity about the overall business strategy.

While many organizations do have an articulated strategy at the top, it often means different things, depending on which seat you occupy at the executive table. In our strategic advisory work, for example, we have seen many leadership groups endorsing statements such as "We will be the most admired brand," or "We will be the most customer intimate," but then fail to push to the next level of specificity where resource trade-offs and tactical priorities occur. Does customer intimacy mean that the company will forego some less customer-intimate, but more cost-effective processes? Does "most admired" mean by customers, employees, communities, Wall Street, or all of these? And how will that be translated to processes and behaviors? The failure to effectively play through these themes often results in functional silos defining their own strategies that are aligned only at the 50,000-foot level.

Translation of the Vision and Strategy into Clear Organizational and Unit Measures

"Linking strategy to measurable goals is not only a good idea," says Scott Shull, assistant director of strategic planning at Intel, "from a strategic planning perspective, it's required." If you don't have overarching goals linked to measures, then you have no control, and no way to direct people towards short- and long-term goals. Shull adds, "Doing this is always harder than anyone gives it credit for."

Most winning organizations are good at translating their vision and strategies into quantitative measures.[9] One popular approach called *balanced scorecard*, introduced by Kaplan and Norton in the 1990s and adapted by Schiemann and Lingle to cover a broader set of strategic issues, offers a powerful way for executives and employees alike to make their strategies more tangible.

Well-balanced strategic measures, coupled with strategic value maps (discussed later) that provide a picture of the cause-and-effect relationships among goals and the critical success factors necessary to achieve those goals,[10] help to create strong Alignment in organizations by:

- Making explicit the vision and long-term goals by translating them into clear outcomes in areas such as financial performance, environmental impact, market share, or reputation (most admired brand).
- Making explicit the value proposition of the business—what are the drivers of the vision and long-term goals and how will they be measured? This allows people in every unit to then ask how they help the organization reach its measurement targets.

- Creating a tool for cascading or connecting goals (or drivers) throughout the organization.
- Creating accountability once measurement owners have been identified.
- Providing focus by highlighting the areas in which the organization is doing well or poorly, thereby enabling leaders and employees to focus resources and energy on a limited set of areas.

Cascading and Communicating the Strategy and Goals

A great vision or strategy that is locked in the head of the CEO is not likely to have much impact on the performance of an organization. That is exactly what we found when we interviewed leaders for a global materials company. Members of the leadership team described a clandestine meeting in the Pocono Mountains at which the strategy was revealed by the CEO. Despite having little input to the strategy, team members were expected to go out and execute it. There was one minor problem. They needed exceptional memories, because after the getaway meeting, the strategy document was actually locked in a secured file drawer, with access limited to the CEO.

When we confronted the CEO about this, he pulled out the key, opened the file drawer, and held up the strategy document, proudly refuting our challenge that his company might not have a written one. He bellowed, "We have a great strategy, but we cannot let anyone see it." We asked why, and he spouted, "If employees know, the unions will know it, and then our competitors will know it." When we asked him how it would be effectively executed if people—especially his top team—did not understand it, he replied "I have divided elements of it on a need-to-know basis." This approach hardly ensures that the entire team is rowing in the same direction.

The employees of this company are not alone. According to Ventana Research,[11] only about 50 percent of the companies surveyed do a good job of aligning departmental plans with overarching corporate goals. An additional challenge is that while many employees may report having clear goals, these goals may not be aligned with organizational objectives. Elaine Pulakos reports in a recent review of the research in this area, "The most effective practice is to establish a hierarchy of goals where each level supports goals directly relevant to the next level, ultimately working toward the organization's strategic direction and critical priorities."[12] This is far better than setting goals based on incremental adjustments to past performance or on a best-try basis, which may not be what is currently needed.

Cascading goals works only when combined with effective strategic communications. For example, Volvo with its 92,000 global employees, has grown from a baseline level of 67 percent to 84 percent of employees who report they understand the company's overall strategy and direction.[13] Much of this success was attributed to a concerted effort to strengthen the capabilities of their middle managers by providing more effective communications tools.

Meaningful Individual Goals and Roles

This is an area that has been well researched, with some outstanding early work done by Ed Locke and Gary Latham[14] that demonstrated a number of critical components that drive organizational performance. One of these factors was goal clarity. Early experiments concluded that those with clearer and more difficult (but attainable) goals had better performance results. From their global database, the Metrus Institute tells us that, on average, 76 percent of employees report that their performance goals are clear. There are a number of organizations, however, in which less than 50 percent of employees say they have goals or that their goals are linked to the department or company goals.

Given the speed of change today, it is also important to periodically (for example, quarterly) reexamine and update goals when changing circumstances demand. Flexibility is a key ingredient of successful goal setting. Some, in fact, argue that too much emphasis is placed on rigid goal setting early in performance planning. In reality, business (and life planning) is often too complex for those goals to remain fixed.[15]

This view is consistent with a growing global movement in accounting, led by Jeremy Hope and Robin Fraser, which originated in Great Britain in the late 1990s. The approach called "Beyond Budgeting" strongly contests the value of traditional budgeting and goal setting.[16] Their approach is grounded in a philosophy that does away with command-and-control systems and cultures in favor of moving accountability closer to the customer in accordance with a set of guiding principles. The authors argue that the Beyond Budgeting approach—now embedded in organizations such as the World Bank, Toyota, the German retailer Aldi, and Southwest Airlines—adjusts goals (and budgets) throughout the year as the external (for example, competitor moves, customer demands) or internal (for example, new products, research discoveries, restructurings) conditions warrant. (See Table 6.4.)

But clear, aligned goals alone are not enough. Employees must accept the goals as their own.

Rational Acceptance of the Strategy and Goals among Implementers

People must understand and accept the business strategy. When we were engaged on a consulting assignment for Wal-Mart a few years ago, an employee approached me seeking a private meeting. She described how she had worked at Nordstrom's in the past and how "they really understand service." She went on to describe how she was building a covert operation of

Table 6.4
Beyond Budgeting Processes and Principles

Adaptive Management Processes

- Goals are based on maximizing performance potential.
- Base evaluation and rewards on relative improvement contracts with hindsight.
- Make action planning a continuous and inclusive process.
- Make resources available as required.
- Coordinate cross-company actions according to prevailing customer demand.
- Base controls on effective governance and on a range of relative performance indicators.

Six Devolution-Based Principles

- Provide a governance framework based on clear principles and boundaries.
- Create a high-performance climate based on relative success.
- Give people freedom to make local decisions that are consistent with governance principles and the organization's goals.
- Place the responsibility for value creation decisions at the front line teams.
- Make people accountable for customer outcomes.
- Support open and ethical information systems that provide "one truth" throughout the organization.

"service trekkies" who would help employees of Wal-Mart eventually get it. While she was obviously passionate about her mission, it was not the strategy of Wal-Mart. Their strategy is built on operational excellence leading to low prices; in contrast, Nordstrom's has been built on outstanding service, leading to customer intimacy. She might be labeled as "right person—wrong fit."

Clear, Timely Feedback on Goal Attainment and the Drivers of the Goals

Ed Liddy, the former chairman, president, and CEO of the Allstate Corporation and Allstate Insurance Company, said at a recent presentation, "If you have people who don't want feedback, you might not have the right human resources."[17] As discussed in our comments on goal setting, clear goals are not enough to achieve the best performance. Research has shown that those who receive more frequent and specific performance feedback and coaching are better performers than those who do not.[18] Researchers have shown that feedback that is closer to the performance itself is most effective. Perhaps this is why Intel has weekly one-on-one meetings between employees and their managers, ensuring that communication and feedback are continuous.

Some organizations that are quite good at setting goals are weak on performance feedback or coaching. In 104 organizations that we studied recently, 76 percent of employees agreed that their performance goals were clear. The favorable responses for receiving feedback regarding the goals, however, were approximately 10 percentage points lower, on average. In some organizations, less than 40 percent of employees rated feedback favorably.

Nearly all of the research and customary wisdom suggests that reviews should be conducted in a supportive manner, and that continuous discussion, rather than an infrequent formal review, is most effective.

Strong Internal Customer Service and Collaboration

We have thus far been discussing multiple aspects of vertical alignment—each part of the organization focused in the same direction on key strategic goals. If you have ever watched an elite crew team, it is immediately apparent that all the rowers are pulling in the same direction, much like our aligned organization. Something more stands out, however. The rowers are perfectly synchronized, with each team member dipping his oars at the same moment, pulling back together. Should even one rower lose the rhythm, the craft immediately starts to slow.

So it is with highly aligned organizations. Not only is everyone pulling in the same direction, divisions, departments, and individuals work in a synchronized manner, each supporting the work of the other.

Siebert and Lingle[19] recently published a study conducted with ASQ in which they examined the ratings of more than 1,200 respondents of the degree to which departments other than their own provided them with superior *internal* service. In short, how well do other departments support the work of your department? The results were clear. Companies in which employees rated supporting services of other departments positively were significantly more likely to be in the group of top companies in financial performance, productivity, and external customer satisfaction.

In summary, vertical alignment is not enough. It must be supported by a horizontal synchronization of departments if an organization is to reach its maximum potential.

Meaningful Rewards that Reinforce Strategically Aligned Behaviors

A few years ago, while working with a global medical diagnostics firm, we observed a phenomenon of sales plummeting in December, repeatedly causing the firm to miss its forecasts. When we conducted focus groups with sales reps, the phenomenon was easy to understand. The reward system paid handsomely only for target results; there were minimal incentives for overachievements. This resulted in sales reps holding back on closing sales until the beginning of the next year so they could provide themselves with a head start on the next payout cycle. The company got what it rewarded, not what it wanted at the broader financial level.

There has been considerable research conducted on reward and incentive systems, from basic piece-rate payouts to more holistic reward systems, such as Scanlon plans, which reward the collective accomplishments of groups of employees. A compensation system based on enterprise success allows everyone to share the organizational success and helps focus individuals' attention on how their performance contributes to the whole.[20]

Rewards in various forms—bonus plans, recognition, the job itself, and incentive systems—have been shown to be effective in different circumstances. Much of their effectiveness appears contingent on the ability to link individual or team performance to meaningful rewards and to provide those rewards in close proximity to the performance.

Culture Alignment

Organizational culture has been identified by many of the highly successful companies we studied as a foundational driver of effective Alignment. Givray of SmithBucklin was perhaps the most vocal about the criticality of the right culture for Alignment. When he thinks about Alignment, he thinks first about the Alignment of people's values. "While the mission and goals may be the brains, or rational side of Alignment, a company's cultural values are the heart of its long-term success and endurance." Givray is quick to point out that people who are not aligned on values will have difficulty working together on any mission. He says, "Even executives who have different operating styles can overcome those differences if they share the same vision and values."

Garry Ridge, the Australian CEO of WD-40, is also passionate about culture. He speaks and lives by the values he espouses. He answers his own phone, returns e-mails in 24 hours (usually much faster from my experience), offers a daily e-mail thought to all employees (always upbeat and inspirational), provides an update on the business weekly, and is ready to quickly address any violations of cultural norms. According to others in the organization, he sets the standard and does not expect employees to do anything that he would not hold himself accountable for. The company's performance management system is solidly based on values of shared accountability for results, teamwork, open communication, and action. WD-40's incentive systems and high revenue to employee ratio (low overhead) require that each employee pull his own weight.

Table 6.5
WD-40 Company Corporate Values

WD-40 Company Corporate Values
• We value doing the right thing.
• We value creating positive lasting memories in all of our relationships.
• We value making it better than it is today.
• We value succeeding as a team while excelling as individuals.
• We value owning it and passionately acting on it.
• We value sustaining the WD-40 economy.

WD-40's corporate values (see Table 6.5) were generated through a process that engaged many employees. The senior team also generated a set of overarching principles that govern how employees should behave, reducing the need for many detailed and narrow rules and policies. When difficult situations occur, or tough decisions need to be made, the leadership team uses the principles as a template to ensure that their actions are consistent with company values.

Culture—the living values of the organization—helps to provide clear guideposts for the acceptable ways to do things. Cultural alignment reduces an enormous amount of organizational rub that can derail even the most brilliant strategy.

While these concepts are compelling drivers of Alignment, I am frequently asked how they come together practically in successful organizations. Let us now take a look at an example of aligning the organization, including strategy, goals, feedback, rewards, and culture.

Outreach Airlines: From Vision to Results

I have selected a combination of two U.S. airlines, Southwest and Continental, to illustrate how these Alignment drivers come together to create an Aligned and effective organization.

Clear, agreed-upon strategy. When Southwest decided to challenge the historical airline business model, it identified several strategic assumptions, or pillars, that if executed well would allow the company to outmaneuver long-established rivals and achieve greater profitability: leveraging of aircraft (all 737s) and maximizing their "in-air" time; lean, productive, and flexible workforce with winning attitudes; and low-cost ticketing.

These pillars represent the unique value proposition of the business. The test, of course, is in the execution. The pillars needed to be understood and supported by employees (and suppliers) at all levels.

Translating strategy to measurable goals. Whether it is the strategy of Southwest, Continental, or Singapore Airlines, successful organizations translate their strategies into a critical few areas that must be managed well. Schiemann and Lingle[21] and Kaplan and Norton[22] have demonstrated the importance of using balanced, or strategic, scorecards that capture the critical strategic results and drivers (for example, market share, on-time performance, high productivity) that reflect the value proposition—the strategic pillars—of the business, as well as the measures of those concepts. Measures provide a quantitative way to determine how much of a particular concept (for example, on-time arrivals) is occurring; targets provide a desired level of achievement (for example, 85 percent on time). While measures in general can be motivating in the short term, targets provide more focus and sustainable energy, especially if they represent stretch targets that need to be achieved over more than a single budget cycle.[23]

In the airline example, pillars such as those previously described can be more fully developed into strategy maps (see Figure 6.4) that describe the value proposition of the business. Maps typically contain the critical financial, customer, operational, employee, supplier, and environmental (for example, "green" impact, community, safety, regulatory, social responsibility) dimensions that are essential to support or implement the pillars.[24] The benefit of such maps is that they display the cause-and-effect relationships of the strategic concepts, including both strategic results and the drivers of these results. For example, "high return on capital invested" (ROCI) in Figure 6.4 represents a desired result, while faster turnaround of aircraft, on-time

FIGURE 6.4   Strategic Value Map

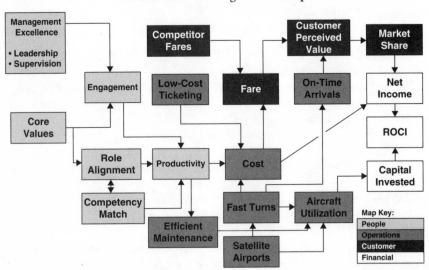

performance, and maintenance that allows the planes to stay in the air more, are drivers of ROCI. You can see the cause-and-effect links in Figure 6.4, with downstream results displayed on the right and upstream drivers displayed to the left with key cause-and-effect connections shown by the connecting arrows.

Each of the elements in the model has a corresponding measure. For example, on-time performance could be measured by the time the plane leaves the gate against the published departure time, or by the wheels-down time or the gate arrival time against the published arrival time, or other possibilities. The important thing is that everyone understands what *on time* means. The major advantage of clear measures is that they leave no doubt as to how an objective is defined.

The advantage of identifying and articulating these scorecard elements is that the visual model provides a blueprint and rallying point for performance. One reason Continental Airlines went from worst to first[25] was the strong commitment to a minimum number of key performance indicators, such as on-time performance. The CEO and his leadership team believed that almost all employees could rally around the on-time goal because so many different roles had an impact on it: logistics, pilots, flight attendants, gate agents, maintenance, and baggage handlers among others. Even more important, on-time departures affect financial performance on many different levels. Thus, this single measure served to align the different functional groups that were essential to superior performance. Not only did it help create vertical Alignment from strategy to roles, but it also helped create horizontal Alignment across functional groups.

Cascading the goals. The next step toward total Alignment is making these goals relevant (understandable and meaningful) to all of the key functional roles, such as gate agents. This helps middle managers and functional people quickly understand what the scorecard means to the organization and to them.

Figure 6.5 shows the current (baseline) and target performance for on-time performance that represented success for the airline. It also shows some of the roles that influence that performance (four are shown in Figure 6.5). Gate agents, for example, influence on-time performance through such activities as check-in timeliness and boarding efficiency.

Figure 6.5 also shows the impact of potential improvements in boarding speed (in this case, from 37 to 25 minutes) on important outcomes such as customer satisfaction, customer retention, and operational costs. To achieve improvements, the gate agents might need to negotiate more effectively with customers with connection problems or manage an overbooking situation with dispatch. Such an analysis enables gate agents to focus on the factors that, if improved, will have the most impact on a highly desired outcome, on-time performance.

FIGURE 6.5 Linking Strategic Scorecard to Accountabilities

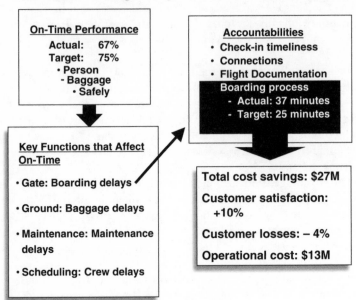

Rewards are critical. While the example and figures just presented show the linkage of the overall goals with key roles (for example, gate agent), they do not show the behind-the-scenes challenges of securing understanding and motivation needed to support those goals. During the turnaround at Continental, Gorden Bethune met with union leaders, employees and managers, and banks—among others—to convince them of the importance of changes being made in areas such as on-time performance.[26] He had to convince his audiences that it made sense economically to peg rewards to achieving results, such as on-time performance. He then offered incentive compensation to all employees each month that the airline finished in the top three[27] in on-time performance against their competitors. The result: Pilots, flight attendants, gate agents, logistics, and maintenance employees saw themselves as being in the game together.

The success of Continental serves as an impressive example supporting Locke and other behavioral researchers in their arguments that clear goals (on-time performance), and frequent (monthly), specific (on-time performance records) feedback connected with rewards (monthly payouts) drive change. Continental Airlines went from bottom of the pack to a top five performer in only a few months and a top-three performer for much of the next year.[28] It was such a good idea that U.S. Airways has borrowed the idea to propel its on-time performance from a dismal back-of-the-pack carrier for many years to number one in mid-2008.[29]

Alignment: The Unfinished Agenda

In preparing this chapter, we found very few organizations that truly demonstrated wholesale success in linking strategy to individual performance management. Organizations such as GE, WD-40, and SmithBucklin are exceptions that demonstrate what is possible, not illustrations of common practices. Several major gaps stand out across most of the less-than-stellar organizations. First, lack of disciplined execution and accountability are two common interrelated gaps. While organizations increasingly talk about their much-improved performance management systems, many still lack the organizational discipline to hold themselves accountable for designing and executing such systems well. While no system is perfect, it is clear that organizations need effective processes to ensure that employee performance is in Alignment with the company's vision, goals, and customer expectations.

Second, while there are a set of best principles, many of which are long known, each organization is also unique—its culture, leadership style, and strategy, for example. This means that those principles must be tailored to a particular context. Copying one's performance management neighbor does not seem to work well. Instead, the leading firms interviewed appear to uniquely tailor the performance management system to their strategy, culture, and management style.

Summary of Key Learning Points

- Organizational mis-Alignment is sometimes obvious, but often remains hidden until it becomes severe.
- Even small organizations can have serious Alignment problems.
- Alignment has a strong, direct impact on customer satisfaction, stress, inefficiencies, waste, conflict across groups, customer service effectiveness, intentions to leave, as well as actual turnover, performance, productivity, sales and profitability, among others.
- Alignment is needed on three fronts—with the organizational goals, values, and customer expectations.
- Alignment is driven by a number of important factors:
  1. A clear, agreed-upon vision and strategy
  2. Translation of the vision and strategy into clear organizational and unit measures

3. Cascading and communicating the strategy and goals
4. Meaningful individual goals and roles
5. Rational acceptance of the strategy and goals
6. Clear, timely feedback on goal attainment
7. Strong internal customer service and collaboration
8. Meaningful rewards
9. Culture alignment

Action Tips: What Can I Do Tomorrow?

Is your organization Aligned? Here are a few ideas to answer this question.

- Answer the survey questions in Table 6.2, or better yet, conduct a customized survey that is specific about your organization's unique strategy, goals, and culture. What percentage of your employees say:
  - They understand the organization's strategy?
  - They understand their unit's goals?
  - There are clear performance measures?
  - They have clear goals and roles?
  - They received performance feedback that helps to improve their performance?
  - Rewards are connected to performance?
- Make sure that your organization has a strategy map that shows the cause-and-effect relationships between the goals you desire and the drivers of those goals.
- If you don't have one, create a balanced scorecard that captures the critical few financial, operational, customer, people, environmental, and supplier success factors.
- Ensure there is a defined process for cascading the strategy and score-card targets throughout the organization. How well is it working? Do functional groups have connected dashboards?
- If you pulled any group together and asked them to write the top three organizational priorities on a piece of paper and then share it with the group, how many would select the same priorities? How well would that match their customers (or internal stakeholders) list?
- If you do not currently conduct an Internal Customer Service assessment, consider doing so. This is an outstanding way to better align with your internal stakeholders better.

- What are the most important deliverables and service features to them?
- Do they see your current deliverables aligned with those expectations?
- If the organization Alignment is low, there are some immediate things you can do.
  - Improve the clarity of the strategy.
  - Conduct an audit of work activities. What percentage of time is spent on low-value activities? What percentage of time is spent on urgent-versus-important activities? What actions are required to change those numbers to increase value?
  - Look for ways to reduce intergroup conflict, which has been shown to be a major time and energy waster. You may need to bring in a facilitation resource who is outside of any political issues for this one.
  - Improve the frequency of your communication about the strategy and how well it is being executed throughout the organization.
- If the diagnostic shows low values Alignment, consider:
  - Bringing the top team together for a discussion of the role that values play and the importance of their Alignment. Get your employees' input because they are incredibly astute on this issue.
  - If you don't have an updated value statement, create one and:
    - Communicate and test for understanding.
    - Identify desirable versus undesirable behaviors.
    - Be clear about the consequences of violating the values.
- Keep employees informed on the progress toward reaching the goals—monthly postings, quarterly town hall meetings, memos from leaders.
- Ensure that compensation is linked to performance against goals, and where appropriate, to corporate performance.

7

Capabilities: Fuel for Growing Customer Value

"To have a competitive advantage, it is not enough to assemble a group of great individuals; the individuals must function together in ways that deliver outstanding organizational performance."
—Ed Lawler, director of the Center for Effective Organizations, University of Southern California[1]

N ot long ago, I conducted a program in a hotel where the corridors were plastered with large posters displaying management's "Customer Commitments," which included service excellence and outstanding communication. I registered at the front desk, confident that with such a strong commitment to service excellence there would be no problem getting my program materials, which were due to arrive early the next morning, in time for an 11:30 A.M. start.

What followed was a comedy of service errors: miscues between the hotel's front desk and its business center, clerks missing in action, and promises made and broken. Bottom line: The next day, 11:30 A.M. came and went, but there were no materials. I was forced to begin the program with a song and prayer and the old soft shoe.

Eventually, my package materialized. It was sitting in a cubicle at the front desk, where it had been since 9:30 that morning. "Were you in a hurry for this?" asked the clerk on duty (whom I had approached during the first break!). History need not record my response. Clearly, this was a case of a hotel staff that lacked the talent, information, and resources to meet a customer's expectations—expectations that management had made a point of proclaiming were a clear priority.

Why Capabilities Are Critical

Employee Capabilities are one of the most important factors in predicting customer loyalty, retention, and lifetime customer value.[2] Of the three factors in People Equity, this one correlates most directly to customer outcomes (while the other factors influence profitability, efficiency, and employee outcomes such as turnover, to a greater extent). Even when organizations are high in Alignment and Engagement—that is, their people are focused on business goals and are energized—if they are low in Capabilities, they will have a difficult time satisfying customers or gaining customer referrals. They are constantly recruiting new customers, only to lose them after a short time. And, since the cost of finding a new customer can be up to 10 times the cost of retaining an existing one, the losses fall to the bottom line. Think of Alignment as the focus, Engagement as the energy, and Capabilities as the skills, technology, and processes needed to deliver successful products and services to customers.

Beyond customers, Capabilities gaps can also hurt the organization in other ways (see Table 7.1), such as creating turnover because employees might not have the skills to succeed. Or, low Capabilities require the organization to incur additional costs to make up for those Capabilities

Table 7.1
Examples of Business Impact of Low Capabilities

- Unable to meet customer requirements
- High rework
- High warranty or guarantee claims because of product deficiencies
- Overstaffing to meet standards or customers requirements
- Low customer-relationship scores; lower customer retention
- Employee and Supervisory burnout; turnover because of performance shortfalls with customers

gaps. While writing this chapter in Colorado, my Internet access went down. The Internet provider had a help desk person who wasted two hours of my time debugging my computer, only to have a more competent employee subsequently discover that the server to the building had gone down—something he figured out in minutes! This was followed by corrective calls, manager reports, and finally a call from the vice president of operations responding to my complaints to the building management. The lack of Capabilities cost the firm perhaps 10 times what it should have cost in rework and very likely overstaffing.

Assess Your Capabilities

Take the survey in Table 7.2 to assess your unit's or team's Capabilities proficiency.

Add up your score: A score 24 or above indicates that your organization is doing a reasonably good job in the Capabilities arena. Scores below 17 indicate serious concerns in this area.

Table 7.2
Quick Capabilities Check

	Strongly Disagree	Disagree	Neutral	Agree	Strongly Agree
Capabilities					
My unit has the people skills it needs to meet our customers' expectations.	1	2	3	4	5

My unit has the technical resources and tools it needs to meet our customers' expectations.	1	2	3	4	5
My unit has the information it needs to meet our customers' expectations.	1	2	3	4	5
We regularly evaluate our customers' satisfaction with our products and services.	1	2	3	4	5
People in my unit have the training necessary to perform their job well.	1	2	3	4	5
There is good teamwork and cooperation within my work unit.	1	2	3	4	5
Total Capabilities Score (add up your score for the six questions)					

Our mini-survey[3] should help to underscore the type of issues that we measure in the Capabilities arena. To learn more, go to **reinventing talentmanagement.com**. While this example includes only your ratings, in practice we would want to have the aggregate ratings of each team member. Figure 7.1 shows the profile for a large order fulfillment department, counting *Agree* or *Strongly Agree* as Favorable and *Disagree* or *Strongly Disagree* as Unfavorable. For example, while almost four-fifths of employees believe that they understand their customers' expectations (data not shown), the organization does not regularly evaluate its customers (first item in Figure 7.1). Perhaps that is why they received a mediocre value rating for "understanding their customer" in their customer survey. It suggests that their assumptions about their customers and their service delivery are not highly aligned with the customer. Ratings of people skills are mediocre at best, perhaps as a result of training gaps or weak teamwork and cooperation (see the last three items in Figure 7.1).

Getting a Grip on Your C—Combing for Causes

Table 7.3 shows the major factors that drive low Capabilities scores from our experience.

FIGURE 7.1   Order Fulfillment Department—Capabilities Results

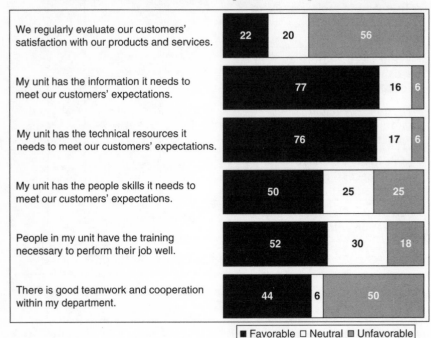

We regularly evaluate our customers' satisfaction with our products and services.	22	20	56
My unit has the information it needs to meet our customers' expectations.	77	16	6
My unit has the technical resources it needs to meet our customers' expectations.	76	17	6
My unit has the people skills it needs to meet our customers' expectations.	50	25	25
People in my unit have the training necessary to perform their job well.	52	30	18
There is good teamwork and cooperation within my department.	44	6	50

■ Favorable □ Neutral ▨ Unfavorable

Table 7.3
Typical Root Causes of Low Capabilities

- Inadequately defined customer value
  - Don't understand the customers' value proposition (and how your product or service supports it)
  - Weak customer measurement
  - Poor customer contracting
- Poor talent match with role requirements
  - Insufficiently defined role requirements
  - Inadequate competency profiles
- Insufficient talent (quantity or quality) to meet customer or stakeholder requirements typically arising from
  - Recruiting issues
  - Selection issues
  - Development and training issues
  - Insufficient diversity

- Inadequate innovation
- Insufficient information to meet customer expectations
- Inadequate or poorly allocated resources
- Weak teamwork
- Silo suboptimization
- Weak supervision or coaching related to Capabilities

When we conduct organizational surveys or internal audits of Capabilities issues, the issues in Table 7.3 are the most frequent causes of low Capabilities. The key is to have a measurement instrument that enables you to quickly identify which of these are gap areas so that you can focus your time on the ones that are in greatest need of improvement or that will provide the most impact on the customer.

An examination of the root causes of low Capabilities reveals, against the backdrop of our research and interviews, a number of important insights about effectively managing Capabilities. Let's explore.

Corralling the Nine Capability Killers
Inadequately Defined Customer Value

The large retailer Circuit City announced in 2007 that it was replacing more senior sales associates with lower-paid and less-skilled workers in its network of 1,300 stores in the United States and Canada, demonstrating to Wall Street and others its idea of cost control to help improve margins. In less than two years, Circuit City announced that it was shutting its doors. The new strategy did not meet the needs of customers, who migrated to other stores in search of a company with more knowledgeable employees.

Many Capabilities' gaps begin with a weak understanding of a company's customers, both internal and external. Our research has found that less than half of *internal* customers believe that the departments they rely on every day understand their business needs. If this is true inside a company, imagine the lack of understanding of *external* customer needs! Said William Crouse, the former president of Ortho Diagnostics and managing director of HealthCare Ventures, "It all begins and ends with the customer. Without them, you don't have a business," as Circuit City quickly found out. Our customer studies indicate that while most people tell us that they generally understand their customers (Who would admit otherwise?), in reality few have a strong understanding of their customers' value proposition—that is, how their customers create value (or if they are a consumer business, what the consumer values).

Recent techniques, such as customer value mapping[4] offer promise in helping suppliers create value maps that describe how their customers create value for *their* customers. This means getting into your customers' heads to understand their world and how they win, which then becomes the basis for building your value proposition to them. Table 7.4 shows two examples: one for external customers and one for internal stakeholders.

Once the customer's value proposition is understood, it becomes possible to extract how you might add value to that customer. Customer value is a function of three elements: requirements, expectations, and needs.

1. *Requirement*—what customers specify they need from you as a supplier—"I require your deliverable on time and on budget."

2. *Expectations*—include requirements that are specified, but also often include other elements that are desired or assumed, and which customers judge you on—"I know you delivered on time and met my price requirements, but your people were less knowledgeable than I expected." When someone has exceeded expectations, they have gone beyond requirements and even the hidden belief about what would most likely be delivered.

3. *Needs*—elements that create customer fulfillment—may be known or unknown to the customer, such as the need for instant messaging that we saw our children addicted to almost before it became available. If you understand more about your customers' overall value proposition— what creates value for them—then it is easier to both meet their stated requirements and expectations and to make some assumptions about other features or benefits (for example, speed, or durability) that they might value given their underlying needs. We address the hidden needs further under Innovation later in this section.

Bottom line: We must truly understand our customers if we are to create and execute plans that add value for them and address the Capabilities needed by the workforce.

Talent Match

A second big gap leading to low Capabilities scores is a poor match between competencies and role requirements. This is particularly important in pivotal jobs[5] that are most strategic for the organization. One dilemma, especially in a world of changing customer demands and role requirements, is discovering a gap between what employees were trained for and what they are now being asked to do.

Table 7.4
Customer Value Map

Customer Value Map (External)
Customer Organization: RetailCo
Key Customer Relationship: Elizabeth Brown, Regional Director of Sales
Primary Objective: Increase customer loyalty, thus growing same-store sales.

Constituencies		Objectives	Metrics	Strategies		Challenges	
Internal	External			Internal	External	Internal	External
Buyers	Product suppliers	Provide product selection that meets cost and quality objectives of our target market	% inventory returned unsold	Work with buyers to clarify brand strategy	Develop partnership with selected product vendors	Poor forecasting	Suppliers driven by overall market: limited ability to drive timing of delivery
		Update merchandise more frequently than competitors	Frequency of new seasonal line introduction				
Customer Satisfaction Team	Customer	Provide a superior customer experience	$ volume per customer/ profit per customer	Increase level of direct contact between customer satisfaction team and customers in stores	Enhance overall customer experience, with product at center	Ensuring focus on profitable customer growth	Cost restrictions on providing enhancement to customer experience
			Frequency of customer visit				

(Continued)

Table 7.4
Continued

Customer Value Map (External)
Customer Organization: RetailCo
Key Customer Relationship: Elizabeth Brown, Regional Director of Sales
Primary Objective: Increase customer loyalty, thus growing same-store sales.

Constituencies		Objectives	Metrics	Strategies		Challenges	
Internal	External			Internal	External	Internal	External
Sales Force		Every interaction with the sales force enhances the shopping experience	# of customers who nominate "Top Service" salesperson # service complaints Avg $ volume/ sales person	Provide adequate training in sales skills and our customer philosophy		Frequent turn-over of sales staff	

Prepared by Frank Davis, regional representative of ProductCo to RetailCo.
(RetailCo. is one of the primary channels for ProductCo sales.)

Table 7.4
Continued

Customer Value Map (Internal)
Customer Organization: NewTech Business Unit, New World, Inc.
Key Customer Relationship: David Dennison, SVP, NewTech BU
Primary Objective: Grow market share through introduction of new products that leverage our technology developments.

Constituencies		Objectives	Metrics	Strategies		Challenges	
Internal	External			Internal	External	Internal	External
Sales	Customers	Continue to increase sales, with primary focus on increasing share of wallet with current customers	Customer loyalty Customer spend	Continuous training for sales force	Provide multiple access channels for products	Not over-promising to the customer	Projecting desires of customer in next generation products
R&D	University Relationships	Deliver leading edge results in our identified areas of focus	Commercialization of research results	Ensure that longer-term projects have multiyear funding approval	Increase R&D team involvement with University partners	Competition for people with the right skills mix	Identifying long-term partners

(Continued)

Table 7.4
Continued

Customer Value Map (Internal)
Customer Organization: NewTech Business Unit, New World, Inc.
Key Customer Relationship: David Dennison, SVP, NewTech BU
Primary Objective: Grow market share through introduction of new products that leverage our technology developments.

Constituencies		Objectives	Metrics	Strategies		Challenges	
Internal	External			Internal	External	Internal	External
BU employees	Outsource partners	Maintain an innovative, highly skilled workforce that is committed to the objectives of NewTech BU, and the company	Products delivered on projected schedule, cost, quality	Ongoing training and communication	Develop win-win partnerships with limited number of key suppliers	Making sure that employees understand our business strategy	Maintaining quality control across multiple partners
			Key employee/partner retention Employee alignment and engagement	Rewards aligned with performance			

Prepared by Jean Thompson, VP Human Resources for New World, Inc.

For example, in earlier years, many line managers thought that human resources management was something you could practice if you had good people skills. Not so today! The HR Certification Institute, a division of SHRM, has defined a set of strategic, regulatory, statistical, selection, and other specialties that are required to truly excel in Human Resources. In manufacturing, mechanical skills were once preeminent, but with increasing automation, plant workers must also become fluent with IT tools.

To identify if talent match is the culprit, take a look at the following.

- *Clarity of role requirements.* What do we really expect from this role? Who are the key stakeholders? What are the deliverables? What constitutes good, great, or inadequate performance?
- *Defined competencies.* What competencies—knowledge, skills, experiences— do we need from the job incumbent so that we can be successful?

It is possible to have clear role requirements and updated competency profiles, yet still have a talent gap. This occurs most often when incumbents are insufficiently trained and developed, which we will discuss momentarily.

Before leaving this area, keep in mind that a number of employee development advocates suggest placing individuals in stretch assignments that will enable them to gain skills outside their traditional comfort zone. Organizations such as Deutsche Bank, AMD, GlaxoSmithKline, and GE regularly do exactly that, especially in their leadership development practices. Such practices can help stretch Capabilities—perhaps increasing comfort with customers in new regions or industries or mastering new functional specialties or product and service areas. The art here is akin to changing the wheels of a moving automobile—getting the job done without stopping, and without rolling over your customers in the process!

Insufficient Talent

This is the third deadly Capabilities killer, and typically has two major root causes.

1. Insufficient number of people—a numbers gap
2. Insufficient competencies—a quality gap

While the former is clear and often tied to headcount, the latter is often the result of four different issues: recruiting, selection, training, and diversity. Many of these are addressed in other parts of the book. Recruiting can help by creating a robust talent pool. Selection is important in screening for skills, experiences, or attitudes that will satisfy customers. And, depending on the talent model of the organization—grow skills or buy skills—training may be crucial in getting a new player up to full productivity.

The diversity issue is a complex and difficult one to categorize, but it is worth raising here. As organizations are operating in more diverse areas of the globe with more differentiated customers, it is also important to extract the rich Capabilities of a diversified workforce to enhance an organization's ability to identify with different customers, and challenge the status quo and old ways of doing things. Diversity is rooted not only in global variety, but also in race, religion, age—or generation, family structure, sexual preference—and the myriad other ways that human beings differentiate themselves from one another. The wealth of perspectives that emanate from such diversity have many advantages, not the least of which is that they can produce a wide idea pool for innovation.[6]

Inadequate Innovation

This is often a hidden culprit of low Capabilities scores. This is particularly acute in certain industries (for example, technology) and job types (for example, scientists, product managers, creative public relations roles). If innovation is not sparked in these groups, a limit is being set on performance and results.

I had this very experience a number of years ago with a long-term client that re-bid its ongoing project every three years. My team had great scores on customer intimacy and other important quality dimensions, but we were surprised to receive feedback that our competitor had introduced a new technology that we had not yet deployed, and was thus chosen to continue the project. The evaluation committee (a group that did not have the deep relationship experience with us) saw this innovative capability in our competitor's arsenal, and recommended the change. A hard, but important, lesson for us!

The other key thing to remember—and this relates back to my earlier note about needs, requirements, and expectations—is that oftentimes the market, and your customer in particular, do not express a need (remember, some of those needs are latent), but when someone creates a new solution to a latent need, they quickly migrate to it, *a la* iPods, Lotus Notes, and Blackberries.

Insufficient Information

In an earlier chapter, I described a bank that had built an excellent strategy for cross-selling financial services. Yet, in spite of a good model, training, and promotion, the sales effort was a failure. Loan officers were unable to access information about those customers' accounts—mortgages, personal loans, IRAs—that had not been opened at the local branch. Loan officers did not have the requisite Capabilities, not because they lacked skills or training, but because they did not have the information they needed to meet customer expectations. Customers do not care about how your information systems are structured; at the moment of usage, they expect them to be effective in helping the delivery resource to achieve the right level of performance.

Ed Lawler offers some eye-opening statistics in his book, *Talent: Making People Your Competitive Advantage*, in which he shares some research from 100 large corporations on the effectiveness of information measurement and analysis systems relating to human capital.[7] HR executives, some of the people closest to the human capital systems, rate all of the areas in Table 7.5 less than 30 percent in effectiveness, and some areas, such as "Connecting human capital practices to organizational performance" receive a less-than-10-percent effectiveness rating.

Apparently, CFOs agree. Most were not satisfied with how human resource systems allow them to assess their human capital and make decisions with human capital in mind.[8] In fact, less than 16 percent were satisfied with information relating to measuring employee skill levels, return on human capital investment, and systematic workforce planning.

Another key information issue is the extent to which employees receive other information about the business that will enable them to be more effective. Again, based on Fortune 1000 companies, Lawler concludes that the typical employee gets limited information about competitive performance, business plans, and new technologies, and more than a quarter of employees do not receive information on unit operating results.[9] Says Lawler, "Without this information, it is impossible for employees to participate in many of the workplace decisions that are part of influencing an organization's strategy and operations."[10]

Table 7.5
Human Capital Information System Effectiveness

How effective are the information, measurement, and analysis systems of your organization when it comes to:	Effective or Very Effective (%)
Connecting human capital practices to organizational performance	9.1
Assessing and improving the human capital strategy of the company	27.6
Contributing to decisions about business strategy and human capital management	27.2
Identifying where talent has the greatest potential for strategic impact	24.2

Adapted from Edward E. Lawler III, *Talent: Making People Your Competitive Advantage*, Jossey-Bass 2008.

As important as skills and training are, they are only part of the Capabilities picture. Organizations need to measure employee Capabilities holistically, making sure that all three components—talent, information, and resources—exist.

Inadequate Resources or Poorly Allocated Resources

More often than not, our employee surveys uncover a variety of resources—tools and equipment, space—that are insufficient to meet employee performance needs. Some relate to customers directly and others to desires of the workforce. A bigger issue, and one not readily uncovered in the survey process, is the allocation of resources. The organization may have the right number of PCs, but they may be inappropriately allocated to users, who most certainly have a variety of different needs and usages.

Weak Teamwork

This is a perennial issue of concern in most surveys that we conduct in the Capabilities space. It is rare to find an organization in which teamwork is not a problem in some unit or across units. While the cross-team conflict is often caused by Alignment issues, within-unit conflict is more often a function of divergent processes, cultural values that do not reinforce teamwork, pay systems that incent people to compete rather than cooperate, performance appraisal systems that pit team members against one another, and a variety of other issues. The good news is that identifying teamwork problems is relatively easy; it then requires having targeted discussions with members of those units to uncover the real root causes of low teamwork.

While customer expectations are probably the most important reason for fixing teamwork, another is cost. Poor teamwork leads to poor quality, rework, resource depletion, and overstaffing.

Silo Suboptimization

Even when teamwork is strong within particular units, silos can drive down your Capabilities scores. With structure, come silos. It is the nature of the beast. In a majority of the organizations that we have examined in the past several decades, management of employee talent, information, and resources is frequently siloed into different functional specialties that often fail to come together at the customer moment of truth. Functions such as sales, HR, IT, and customer service divide the responsibilities for product and service delivery into distinct accountabilities. In one organization I worked with, no fewer than five departments each had its own approach, definition, and measures of success for the role of a service representative. Not surprisingly, service was overdesigned, yet still contained many gaps.

Customers don't care about a company's internal structure; they want employees with whom they interact—regardless of department or function—to possess the information and skills to solve their problems. Do you want a customer to boil over? Just say, "That's not my problem!"

And yet, we have discovered organizations that have reduced silos, where cross-functional teamwork is par for the course. Springfield Re-manufacturing (as described in *The Great Game of Business* by Jack Stack and Bo Burlingham[11]),WD-40, and SmithBucklin come to mind as great examples of seamless teamwork over the past 20 years. What these organizations have in common is a focused leadership team, strong measures, and rewards that are focused on overall success, rather than on the success of many different functional silos. We have conducted many customer studies over the years in which customer loyalty has nosedived because silos cannot play together.

Weak Supervision or Coaching Related to Capabilities

As has been described earlier, supervisors and coaches play a key role in creating high People Equity and do so distinctly in A, C, and E. Some of the ways in which they play a key role in the Capabilities area are fairly obvious and are alluded to in the root causes discussed earlier, such as matching talent effectively to customer requirements, or providing sufficient resources to meet objectives. Managers who are adept at coaching are helping in three very important areas:

1. Helping employees to understand where there are skills gaps that are hindering them from success and supporting them to build a developmental plan to improve those gaps.
2. Helping to coach employees in areas of skill development that will assist them in stretch assignments and potential growth positions.
3. Helping employees leverage their strengths. Marcus Buckingham and his former Gallup colleagues have questioned the traditional wisdom of being able to "change employees' weaknesses," and instead, encourage managers to help employees find roles that fit their strengths and build on those competencies. What is unclear is what happens to an employee who is missing several key competencies that are important to most roles and stakeholders. Unless those gaps are corrected, or those employees are terminated, the organization will deliver suboptimal value to its customers.

Capabilities in Closing

Recall the opening example to this chapter in which a hotel had failed dismally to provide a promised service. It may have been Aligned (employees understood and agreed with management's focus on service excellence) and Engaged (they wanted to provide it), but as it turned out, they just didn't have the Capabilities required to turn the vision into reality. In our People Equity typology described in Chapter 2, this is the *Under-Equipped* profile.

While some organizations are woefully under-equipped on many of the drivers of Capabilities, most fall short on a few gating drivers or enablers that are hindering Capability excellence. The key is to identify and correct the root cause.

In our hotel example, a discussion with hotel management after my experience provided some needed facts about the organization's Capabilities.

- An experienced manager had recently left the hotel, and no one had been trained to take his place.
- There was no information system in place to communicate my request across different departments.
- The "outstanding communication" in the values statement was a slogan; there was no systematic training in communication. It was assumed instead that because it was a value, people would practice it.
- The hotel was process-poor. There were no systematic methods for dealing with fairly standard requests such as mine.
- The hotel was measurement-meager. While basic customer satisfaction with room, food, and check-in was measured, there was no rating of business services.

An organization needs to develop its Capabilities to meet or exceed what is valued by its target customers—this is the essence of value creation for any given strategy. An organization does not need to provide world-class service to score high in its Capabilities. For example, Ramada, Wal-Mart, and Ryan Air have all built brands based on low cost rather than service excellence. Their service is not terrible, but it is not of primary importance to their targeted customer base. In contrast, Ritz-Carlton and Singapore Airlines have put a much greater premium on service as a brand differentiator. Either model can work, but whichever you choose, your employee Capabilities must be aligned with your strategic model.

And we should not forget to apply the *pivotal job* criteria[12] (strategic job, considerable performance variance, talent scarcity) discussed earlier. Some roles will be far more important to the organization or will offer higher opportunities for improvement because there is substantial performance variance that could be improved. In the case of scarcity, however, we often find that managers will live with subpar competencies because replacements are hard to find. There is a risk to this because those inferior competencies, unless improved or replaced, can lead to low customer or stakeholder ratings of value.

To obtain a complete, accurate measure of how well your employees are equipped to do their job, we recommend moving from detailed competency measures to more general questionnaires, which ask both customers and employees to tell you how talent, information, and resources come together in the right way at the right time in support of the business strategy. Only then will you be able to determine in which of these three areas you need to concentrate your resources to improve Capabilities.

Summary of Key Learning Points

- Capabilities are a significant contributor to important business outcomes, especially to customer satisfaction, loyalty, and retention, among other valuable outcomes.
- Capabilities include three factors: Sufficient Talent, Information, and Resources to meet customer expectations.
- When Capabilities are low, many dysfunctional outcomes occur:
  - Inability to meet customer requirements
  - High rework
  - High warranty or guarantee claims, because of product deficiencies
  - Overstaffing to meet standards or customer requirements
  - Employee and supervisory stress. Burnout and turnover because of performance shortfall pressure.
- Capabilities can be managed, but it requires understanding of the key drivers. The following is a list of some of the major Capability drivers:
  - Clearly defined customer value
  - Good talent match with role requirements
  - Enough talent to meet customer requirements
  - An innovative climate
  - Sufficient information to meet customer expectations
  - Sufficient resources
  - Good teamwork
  - Cooperation across functional groups
  - Strong supervision or coaching

Action Tips: What Can I Do Tomorrow?

Does your organization have the right Capabilities? Here are a few ideas to answer this question.

Regarding customer or internal stakeholders:

- Have you prioritized your customers by their value to your organization?
- Does your organization measure customers' perceptions of your brand, products and services, and relationships? Customer loyalty? Do you measure your internal stakeholders to understand how they value your services? Do you know which services are rated most important by your stakeholders?

To assess your Capabilities proficiency, consider answering the survey questions in Table 7.2, or better yet, conduct a customized survey that is specific about your organization's unique Capabilities proficiency. What percentage of your employees say:

- Their unit understands and develops the skills needed to meet customer requirements?
- Work processes are well designed to make delivery of products or service to the customer smooth and seamless?
- They are able to meet customer requirements on a regular basis?
- Their job is well matched to their competencies?
- Their unit understands the requirements of internal stakeholders?

If the organizations' Capabilities are low or running short, here are some possible actions you might take to improve:

- Better define the customer value.
  - What does your strategy say about customer value?
  - Consider creating customer value maps, as described in the chapter.
  - Use surveys to ask customers about value.
- Communicate the customer value proposition to all employees. Clearly define how your product or service supports it.
- Consider improving customer or stakeholder contracting. Can you and your customers come up with agreed-upon success criteria? How often will they be assessed?
- Meet with Human Resources to discuss current role requirements. Review the following:

- Do we have meaningful competency profiles for most positions? If not, can we put a plan in place to develop them?
- Are recent hires well-matched with the competency profiles? If a reasonable percentage is not, is it related to the recruiting, selection, or development processes?

- Collaborate with the leadership team to assess the current layout of the office. Think about ways to rearrange the workspace to increase teamwork and innovation.

- Identify ways to make customer-related information more readily available to employees.

- Ask employee service teams to identify the tools that, if available, would facilitate customer service improvement.

8

Getting Engaged

"We could not have achieved the incredible results that we have without securing both the hearts and the minds of our employees."

—Henry Givray, chairman and CEO,
SmithBucklin Corporation

Employee engagement has been a driving force in organizations for as long as organizations have existed. It is folklore that Attila the Hun used to have his organizational psychologists survey his soldiers to find out who was unhappy. Those sporting frowns were quickly put out of their misery. They were summarily executed! Things have evolved a great deal since that time. Or have they?

Let's go to the statistics:

- Yahoo survey reveals that 47 percent of U.S. workers are ready to jump ship at next opportunity or plan to change jobs within 12 months.[1]
- In another study, 52 percent of workers are interested in leaving their jobs; 75 percent of those within 12 months.[2]
  - 34 percent of those workers would not recommend their employer to others.
  - 45 percent cited a lack of potential for career growth.
- The U.S. Job Retention Poll conducted by the Society for Human Resource Management and the *Wall Street Journal* reveals that more than 75 percent of employees are looking for new jobs.[3]
- In a Towers Perrin study, disgruntled employees either quit and leave—or they quit and stay.[4]

Many point to these statistics arguing that something is amiss in employee satisfaction, commitment, or engagement. In reviewing the reported engagement results by various firms and research organizations, the percentage of engaged employees in organizations ranges from about one in ten to about half (see Table 8.1). The difference in numbers is most likely a function of definitional differences and whether the researchers were trying to capture a most stringent level of engagement. Nevertheless, while companies vary dramatically in the percentage of their workforce that is engaged (we have seen values ranging from under 20 percent to over 90 percent), it is fair to say that a sizable percentage of the workforce have low engagement or active disengagement—and this was before the economic downturn!

Perhaps Woody Allen had the employee mindset right when he said, *"Eighty percent of success is showing up."* But it is a mindset that won't get you very far in today's turbulent, competitive world.

Table 8.1

Reported Levels of Employee Engagement Over the Last Five Years

---

Corporate Executive Board – 11 Percent based on 50,000[1]

The Jackson Group – 39.5 Percent of over 50,000[2]

Towers Perrin – 17 Percent of 35,000 in global study (also discovered 32 Percent partly or actively disengaged in Canadian sample)[3]

Development Dimensions International – 19 Percent[4]

Chartered Institute of Personnel and Development – 30 Percent of British employees[5]

Metrus Institute – 50-60 Percent at high or moderate engagement levels

---

[1] "Driving Performance and Retention through Employee Engagement" (Washington, D.C.: Corporate Executive Board, 2004).

[2] Connie Poteat, "Employee Engagement: What Works!" The Jackson Group, Society for Human Resource Management Strategy Conference, September 2008.

[3] Towers Perrin Talent Report, op. cit.

[4] Richard Wellins, Paul Bernatha, and Mark Phelps, *Employee Engagement: The Key to Realizing Competitive Advantage* (Pittsburgh, Penn.: Development Dimensions International, 2005).

[5] C. Truss, E. Soane, and C. Edwards, *Working Life: Employee Attitudes and Engagement,* (London, U.K.: Chartered Institute of Personnel and Development Research Report, 2006).

Is Engagement Important?

Even tough-as-nails retired CEO of General Electric Jack Welch has stated that the three most important measures of an organization's health are first, employee engagement, followed by customer satisfaction and positive cash flow. Welch knew what he was talking about. Engagement has a demonstrable positive effect on a number of desired outcomes—employee retention, performance, quality, customer satisfaction and loyalty, and financial performance.[5] Engagement studies have confirmed the importance and impact of Engagement on important business and personal outcomes. For example:

- A 2007 study across 40 global companies by Towers Perrin[6] found that firms with the highest percentage of engaged employees not only had higher retention of their most valued employees, but also collectively increased operating income 19 percent and earnings per share 28 percent year to year. By contrast, the companies with the lowest percentage of engaged employees showed year-to-year declines of 33 percent in operating income and 11 percent in earnings per share.

- Using Engagement survey items that measure commitment and work effort, Caterpillar, the construction-equipment manufacturer, discovered that performance related to these items in one of its European plants led to nearly $9 million in annual savings from reduced turnover, absenteeism, and overtime. It also found that in an Asia Pacific plant these same items led to a 70 percent increase in output in less than four months. Furthermore, Caterpillar reduced grievances by 80 percent in a unionized plant and reported higher customer satisfaction and operating results at other locations, all related to high scores on Engagement items.[7]

- Intuit, the software powerhouse—using Engagement survey items such as being proud to work for the company and motivated to go above and beyond what is expected—found that highly Engaged employees are 1.3 times more likely to be high performers than less engaged employees, and they are five times less likely to voluntarily leave the organization.[8]

- Molson Brewing Company found interesting correlations between Engagement and safety and accidents, reporting that highly Engaged employees were five times less likely to have a safety incident or lost-time accident. Molson reported saving over $1.7 million in safety-related costs in 2002 because of stepped up Engagement efforts. Molson also reported large differences in sales performance between high and low Engaged sales personnel.[9]

Table 8.2 also shows some of the negative consequences of low Engagement, as was illustrated in Table 2.1.

Defining Engagement

So what is this intangible called *Engagement?* To some, Engagement is another name for employee satisfaction—a state of contentment that might be characterized as the look of a smiling Buddha. Others, such as the Institute for Employment Studies, describe it as a positive attitude toward the organization. Hewitt says it is a state of emotional and intellectual commitment to an organization or group producing behavior that will help fulfill an organization's

Table 8.2
Impact of Low Engagement

- Low external or internal customer satisfaction due to disengaged workers
- Low productivity, due to mediocre energy
- Top talent loss when market conditions permit
- Deadwood: Unmarketable employees retire in place
- Low referrals of new talent from existing workforce
- Cynical or apathetic culture

---

promises to customers. Still others, such as the Corporate Leadership Council, Towers Perrin, and Kenexa, use multiple dimensions, such as commitment to something or someone, discretionary effort beyond the minimum, pride in working for the organization, and motivation to contribute.

Behind all the rhetoric on Engagement looms an old-fashioned word, *motivation*. How motivated are employees to produce some positive outcome? To delight customers? To be innovative? To exceed goals or performance targets? Robert Vance, in a recent SHRM Foundation Effective Practice Guidelines report on Engagement, summed it up succinctly by linking Engagement with a willingness by employees to "go the extra mile." Behaviorally, this means the Engaged employees willingly perform their prescribed tasks, are more likely to perform voluntary actions, and will exhibit fewer proscribed behaviors—those discouraged by the organization, such as absenteeism, lateness, and chronic grousing.

Macy and Schneider[10] and others have reviewed and categorized various descriptions of Engagement, ranging from employee traits (for example, are some people more predisposed to be Engaged?) to positive attitudes or a state of being Engaged (for example, I am committed to this organization) to intentions (for example, I intend to stay with this organization) to behaviors that are indicative of added energy or emotional highs— actions such as working longer hours, doing more than is expected, or other forms of adaptive or innovative behavior in the cause of organizational success. They argue that each of these represent different, albeit related, concepts. Research at Metrus Institute and elsewhere suggest that many of the concepts described as Engagement (satisfaction, commitment, pride, advocacy, discretionary effort) correlate highly, and may in fact, be part of one broader motivational factor.

While the organizational and social psychologists continue to wrestle with and conduct research in this area, there is little disagreement that those with high levels of these Engagement elements are across the board more effective than those with low Engagement. No matter which definition is used, most expect Engaged employees to work harder and remain with their employers longer, please more customers, and have a stronger positive influence on organizational results—not because of their Capabilities or their Alignment—but because they are more excited, more energized, and exert more effort—in short, they are more motivated to do positive things!

At the Metrus Institute, we sought a definition of Engagement that would help us capture this sentiment. We chose a definition of Engagement that would do three things:

1. It would capture both positive feelings about the organization (for example, being committed to its success) as well as a level of energy or excitement that leads employees to exert more effort or go beyond the

basic job requirements. It would not, however, include basic personality traits that may make some people more Engagement-prone than others.

2. It would be predictive of important employee behaviors, such things as discretionary behaviors that go above and beyond the minimum, leading to higher performance, or adaptive behaviors such as creative problem solving and decision making that would affect organizational results such as productivity, customer loyalty, or profitability.

3. It can be influenced by actions that organizations and supervisors, in particular, can take.

For us, the ultimate measure would be observing behaviors that are indicative of individuals who are going the extra mile. Sadly though, we have not seen any standardized way to measure those behaviors. In some units, it might be putting in extra hours. In others, it might be creating great ideas. And in still others, it might be doing a very special activity for a customer.

Short of these behaviors, we believe that one of the highest forms of Engagement would be willingness to advocate on behalf of the organization— willingness to promote the organization as a place to work, purchase from, and even invest in. Asking people to pull their wallets out and invest in a public organization is a very strong indicator of one's full commitment. Advocacy is a distinguishing characteristic of Engagement that goes beyond mere satisfaction or commitment. Another key feature short of witnessing actual discretionary behaviors is employees' intention to volunteer discretionary actions.

While we define Engagement as the level of that special energy or advocacy, we typically operationalize an Engagement index as a combination of Satisfaction,[11] Commitment, and Advocacy (see Figure 8.1), because we view the three elements as part of a continuum.

FIGURE 8.1 Components of Engagement and Examples of Each

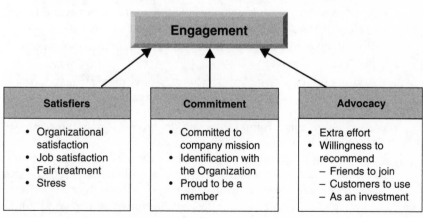

1. Are employees satisfied with the organization? If not, don't count on having many employees with higher-order states of Commitment and Advocacy. A long research literature, sparked by Herzberg with his famous two-factor theory,[12] has identified basic satisfiers and dissatisfiers, such as job security, fair treatment, and benefits that must be at threshold levels to create high organizational satisfaction; otherwise, their absence will remove employees psychologically from the game.

2. At a higher level, are employees committed to the organization and the work? For example, earlier work of Hackman and his colleagues[13] and others provides sound research evidence for creating roles that have task identity, variety, autonomy, feedback, and other features that increase an employee's commitment. Some organizational features, such as mission (for example, save lives or bring food to people) or values (for example, high ethics is an important feature that builds pride for many employees, especially to many recent graduates) may also add to the commitment, identification, or pride that people have with the firm.

   Others have discussed the importance of reciprocity—an employee will reciprocate commitment when the organization or manager commits to the employee. The stronger these features, the more committed employees may be to the organization. Others have also argued that there is also an emotional versus rational commitment. The latter represents an intellectual commitment. For example: You provide me with a salary and I provide you with equivalent labor. This is in contrast to the more passionate feelings described in the next element.

3. At a still higher level, are employees passionate, absorbed, or enthusiastic? Are employees willing to advocate on behalf of their organization?
   - Are they willing to put in extra effort (time, energy, thinking)?
   - Are they willing to go beyond their minimal job description to solve organizational problems and help it achieve higher performance?
   - Are they willing to encourage people they value—friends and family, perhaps—to consider working for this organization?
   - Would they encourage such people to support this organization's products or services?
   - And if a publicly traded organization, would they encourage people who are close to them to invest in this organization?

We settled on these components and definitions for several reasons:

1. We wanted conceptually to separate the states of satisfaction, commitment, and willingness to advocate (these are all states or intents) that characterize Engagement from subsequent actions that result from being Engaged: remaining with the organization, working longer hours,

or exhibiting adaptive behaviors (for example, creative problem solving) as Macey and Schneider[14] have described. By doing so, we can then examine the relationship of these states of Engagement to those important outcomes, rather than muddle the two together. If Engagement is predictive of these important outcomes, then it can be used as a leading indicator, giving managers time to adjust before undesirable outcomes such as turnover occur.

2. We also wanted conceptually to avoid the trap of confusing Engagement with the mélange of many Engagement drivers, such as being treated with respect, or having good pay, which are clear drivers of organizational satisfaction—one component of Engagement. As my wife periodically reminds me, "If we call a tail a leg, how many legs does a dog have? Four—calling a tail a leg doesn't make it one." Engagement is not fair treatment or respect or recognition. Each of those concepts is a frequent driver of Engagement, but they are conceptually distinct. Let's keep them that way.

You can think of Engagement as a pyramid (see Figure 8.2), in which employees increase their overall level of Engagement by first being *satisfied* with their job and organization, then being *committed* to their work, supervisor, and organization, and finally, they reach a level of high Engagement, in which they are energized and *ready to advocate* on behalf of their unit or organization. Below certain levels of job security or respectful treatment, no amount of job enrichment or growth opportunities, or even a cool brand, will create organizational advocates or those willing to put in discretionary effort. When people

FIGURE 8.2 Engagement Pyramid

are satisfied with basics and have developed Commitment, the Advocacy drivers tend to be the ones that create a buzz or energy in an organization that observers can tangibly feel.

When we find employees who are high on all of these, we believe we come close to capturing the motivational energy—the *Force*, as some early psychologists and Star Wars enthusiasts have termed it—that fuels more effective work behaviors. When channeled in a productive way (Alignment) and fueled with the right competencies and resources (Capabilities), we have a powerful set of ingredients to create personal and organizational value.

S.C. Johnson & Son

S.C. Johnson has been noted over the years as one of the best organizations to work for, with frequent awards and recognitions for their outstanding employee culture. When I interviewed Joanne Brandes, the former executive vice president, chief administrative officer, general counsel, and secretary of JohnsonDiversey, Inc., a spinoff of S.C. Johnson & Son, she described some basic elements they continually did well, beginning with a "We really want you to stay and grow here" message from Day One, which was then followed by offering profit sharing, treating employees with respect, offering growth opportunities and a learning organization, and minimizing the separation between leadership and everyone else in regard to accessibility, pay, and status. Furthermore, "We conducted employee surveys on a regular basis," said Brandes, "to ensure that we were living those principles." They built a culture around creating engaged employees.

What's Your Engagement Level?

Take the survey in Table 8.3 to assess your unit's or team's Engagement proficiency. The survey also includes a few Engagement Drivers to illustrate several points.

Add up your score: A score 24 or above indicates that your organization is doing a reasonably good job in the Engagement arena. Scores below 17 indicate serious concerns in this area.

Table 8.3
Quick Engagement Check

Sample Engagement Items	Strongly Disagree	Disagree	Neutral	Agree	Strongly Agree
I am satisfied with this company as a place to work.	1	2	3	4	5
In my work unit, you can feel high energy and excitement.	1	2	3	4	5
I would recommend this organization to a close friend or colleague as a place to work.	1	2	3	4	5
I am treated with respect and dignity.	1	2	3	4	5
My immediate manager inspires the best in people.	1	2	3	4	5
In the past three months, I have had opportunities at work to learn and grow.	1	2	3	4	5
Total Engagement Score (add up your score for all six questions)					

This mini-survey[15] should provide insight into the type of issues that we measure and assess in the Engagement area. While this example includes only your ratings, in practice we would want to have the aggregate ratings of all team members. To see more, go to **reinventingtalentmanagement.com**.

We show in Figure 8.3 Engagement results for a sample of questionnaire items from the People Equity survey of the Order Fulfillment group we described in the Alignment and Capabilities chapters. It includes both Engagement-related items (items 1, 2, and 3) and items that measure drivers of Engagement (items 4, 5 and 6), counting *Agree* or *Strongly Agree* as Favorable and *Disagree* or *Strongly Disagree* as

FIGURE 8.3 Order Fulfillment Department—Engagement Results

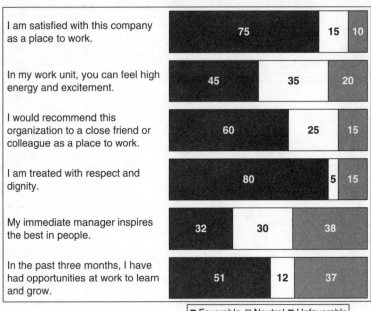

Unfavorable. For example, in the profile in Figure 8.3, we notice that only 60 percent of employees would recommend this organization as a place to work. What is holding some of them back? Three-quarters rate satisfaction high, reflecting this organization's respectful treatment (item 4), as well as strong scores in other satisfiers not shown in this example: good job security and strong benefits.

It is also rated highly as a company to work for because it is located in an area with limited alternatives. On the other hand, the item on willingness to recommend (item 3) and being an exciting place to work (item 2) suggests that this might not be the most exhilarating experience, perhaps holding back employees from recommending it to others. The most important clue, however, may be the lack of inspiring leadership from managers. Recall from earlier chapters that this group of managers had been rapidly expanded, with the original, tightly focused leadership team now in charge of a significant operation. It may be time for a broad-based leadership development intervention. Current employees may remain with the company for security reasons and the strong benefits package, rather than because they are truly energized, or because they are committed to the company.

Examining your *E*—Excavating for Root Causes

Table 8.4 shows the major factors that, in our experience, drive Engagement, or *E*, scores.

When we conduct organizational surveys or internal audits of Engagement issues, the issues in Table 8.2 are the most frequent causes of low Engagement. The key is to have a measurement instrument that includes questions in these areas, thereby enabling you to quickly identify which of these are gap areas.

Many of the preceding issues are likely familiar to you, and you may wish to skip the discussion of those that are; there are some interesting insights to

Table 8.4
Major Drivers of Engagement

- Satisfiers

  - Job security
  - Fairness issues
  - Compensation (wages, benefits, perks)
  - Treatment with respect and dignity
  - Stress (e.g. work and family conflict; workload or performance targets)

- Commitment
  - Reciprocity issues
    - o Employer brand/culture matches promise
    - o Sufficient resources/training to deliver performance
    - o Role matches talent
  - Interesting Work
  - Identification with organizational mission or values; supervisor; peers for example
  - Commitments to peers
  - Inspiring leadership

- Advocacy and Extra Effort

  - Personal growth and development
  - Recognition
  - Involvement and visible identification roles
  - Supervisor takes a personal interest
  - Winning experiences

---

be gleaned from our research and the interviews of practicing managers, however. Let's explore.

Encircling the Major Engagement Killers

Under the umbrella of basic *Satisfiers*, we often find:

- *Security fears*, such as job security or having a financial security net in the form of benefits or compensation.
- *Fair treatment*, based on a literature of organizational and procedural justice, including pay or promotional equity issues.
- *Sufficient compensation*, in the form of pay, benefits, or other perks that enable an employee to meet an expected standard of living.
- *Being treated with respect and dignity* is one of the most powerful elements in satisfaction with the supervisor and the organization, and typically a strong predictor of other outcomes, such as turnover.
- *Stress-related factors*, such as problems balancing work and family demands, task overload, unrealistic standards, and work conflicts have been shown to create low satisfaction. On the other hand, stress can be too low. *U-stress*, or the good stress that creates pleasant excitement, for example, cannot occur when the task demands are too low.

This suite of Satisfaction factors are often ones that are at play in unionization situations. They can be both good predictors of an organization's ripeness for unionizing activities and of the likelihood of contract ratification during contract renewals. Over the years, researchers at the Metrus Institute have been involved in validating these items to predict important organizing outcomes.

Commitment issues that frequently drive Engagement include:

- *Reciprocity Issues.* There are many areas in which there is an expectation that in return for certain behaviors (for example, good performance, satisfying customers) by the employee, the organization (or a supervisor or peer) will provide positive consequences in exchange. These might include basics such as attractive pay or benefits, but it also includes things like skills development, an innovative culture, or certain resources that allow the employee to flourish.
- *Interesting Work.* There has been a great deal of work connecting job design and organizational commitment. Jobs that have task richness— elements such as job variety, autonomy to make decisions or effective feedback mechanisms tend to increase commitment. But some individuals

do not want a highly enriched or challenging job, according to a number of studies, so job-person matching may be more important in gaining their commitment.

* *Identification with the Mission and Values.* People tend to be more motivated when they are committed to the overarching mission and goals. It is often why nonprofits, church groups, or special interest groups can obtain highly engaged people for relatively low compensation. They are energized by the mission itself. Individuals may also identify with their supervisor or with peers.

* *Commitment to Peers.* The Gallup organization and others have described the importance of having a friend at work. A close relative of mine remained with an organization nearly 10 extra years before retiring because of a deep commitment to friends at work, despite being dissatisfied with many other aspects of the organization, including the immediate supervisor. Establishing close relationships in the workplace can exercise a strong influence on decisions related to prescribed or proscribed behaviors. For example, we found that vibrant high-buzz organizations seem to energize themselves. Garry Ridge at WD-40 said that peers who are highly energized demand the same from new recruits, and our focus groups and interviews with employees over the years in such units support the validity of Ridge's observation.

* *Inspiring Leadership.* While supervisors often play a more relevant role to the employee on a daily basis, people look to their leaders for inspiration and commitment to a greater goal. Setting noble goals, communicating consistently, and role modeling of desired behaviors can have a strong influence on employees' willingness to be committed to their organizations. Most employees want to be committed to something noble and honorable, and would like to believe that their leaders can take them there. David Sirota, a long-time scholar of commitment, says that the main question for management is not, "How can employees be motivated?" but rather, "How can management be deterred from diminishing—even destroying—employee motivation?"[16]

There are several issues that drive Advocacy—the highest end of the Engagement triangle.

* *Growth and Development.* This is probably the number one issue today in creating high Advocacy scores. Many firms have the basics, but younger employees in particular want to see much clearer growth and development plans than their predecessors. Providing growth and development opportunities to employees can make a huge difference in retaining top talent. Different forms of development are important to different individuals.

Tamar Elkeles at Qualcomm reminded me that some people may prefer to get their development from formal education, while others may be looking for a strong professional network.

- *Recognition.* While at times related to fairness, recognition can also energize employees. Some are more motivated by team recognition while others seek and thrive on individual recognition. Many sales organization recognize that and besides offering incentive pay, they go out of their way to create prizes, awards, and special event recognition to honor those who are achieving important goals—high sales, more satisfied customers, or even volunteer community involvement.

   In looking at employee survey results from both the Metrus Institute and publicly available databases over the past 30 years, we found that recognition is often rated as important to employees, but is a motivational lever that is underused in most organizations. The average organization in the Metrus Institute database, for example, receives only 46 percent endorsement of the question "I am regularly thanked or recognized when I do a good job." This form of reward scores lower than financial rewards (for example, pay satisfaction is typically 50 to 60 percent favorable) and the job itself (typically 70 to 80 percent favorable).

- *Involvement.* Considerable research points to the fact that people are more committed to things in which they are involved. Recall the old joke: Who is more committed to your breakfast—the pig or the hen? While the hen can provide an egg and return for another day's battle, when bacon shows up on the table, the pig is pretty committed! In our scorecard work, we have found, for example, that when executives actually "grind their own sausage," as one energy executive described it, as opposed to delegating that activity, they create more effective scorecards, and they execute their strategies far better.

   Another form of involvement comes from the roles people play. Individuals who take on leadership roles (for example, team leaders, supervisors, coaches) are apt to proselytize far more for those organizations. Even employees who are in communications videos or other visible symbols of organizational identification tend to be more involved and outspoken about the organization. The flip side of this is that if jilted by the organization, these same individuals might be its biggest critics.

- *The Supervisor.* "The level of engagement is only as good as the leader of the group," says Alison James, senior vice president of human resources for Encore Capital Group, "and leaders have the ability to drive engagement . . . or kill it." Common wisdom says, "People quit their supervisor, not their organization." To many, this implies that supervisors are ogres. But research by David Sirota suggests that many employees like their supervisors.[17] The Metrus Institute has found that typically about 60 to 80 percent of people rate their supervisor favorably.

Supervisors can be a strong inspiration leading to employee Advocacy. They play a major role in many of the Engagement areas we have discussed. Many of us have had one or more managers or coaches whom we remember fondly, perhaps even inspirationally, throughout our lives. When we have asked people about this managerial paragon, most talk about how they were treated individually. That is, the manager was able to connect with them personally—understanding their needs, desires, hopes, fears—and able to help them navigate a successful path. These kinds of supervisors can bring about the Advocacy level of Engagement that we have found to be so beneficial for not only the organization, but for the individuals as well.

- *Winning Experiences.* While more research is needed, it appears that circumstances also play a role in one's Engagement. While some individuals are stronger than others in what is known as locus of control—their confidence in controlling their own future—most employees' views of the organization or a particular unit are shaped by experiences of success or failure. We see athletes who joined winning sports teams rise to greater heights than similar draft picks who ended up on losing teams. Having winning experiences with customers, peers, internal stakeholders, or against team milestones can go a long way to create stronger Advocates—the peak of the Engagement pyramid.

What Is the Role of Communications?

Communications is complex, typically defying classification into one unique category, largely because it covers diverse content and depends so strongly on who the communicator is. For example, supervisory communications can be incredibly dissatisfying when supervisors demonstrate disrespect or they can be powerful motivators when focused on employee development opportunities and delivered in a positive manner. And inconsistent communication can be a cause of low trust and is often intertwined with fair treatment and respect.

The impact of communications on Engagement can also be strongly influenced by cultural differences and expectations. While empowering decisions may get a supervisor strong ratings in United States or Canada, they may offend in Latin America, where the supervisor is expected to make (not shirk) those decisions. French organizations, for example, tend to be characterized by authoritarian leadership behaviors, where collaboration rules in Japan. Bottom line: Understand your local culture and its expected communication norms.

There also are generational communications issues of style and medium, where mismatches can cause low Engagement. Gen X-ers and Millennials are far more comfortable multitasking across different communications platforms (for example, texting, Twittering, phone, and even e-mail). Letters—forget about it! But these are no substitute for face-to-face communications in a situation such as a performance review. While ineffective communications is often blamed on the supervisor, it can also be a function of the broader organizational culture. For example, a closed communications culture is often a turn-off to Gen X-ers and Millennials, who are accustomed to being highly connected.

Is Engagement Enough?

At the Metrus Institute, we have been both delighted and disappointed with the recent flurry of energy directed at Engagement. While Gallup, the Corporate Leadership Council, and others should be commended for promoting this concept to the boardroom and the HR community, there is also an element of silver-bullet mentality that seems to have taken over in practice. One executive confided, "We are Engagement crazy; it drives everything we do." Another said, "Engagement has taken over the silver bullet space for Empowerment." When that happens to the exclusion of Alignment and Capabilities, bad things can happen.

If you remember back to the eight profiles of People Equity that we described in Table 2.2, four of those profiles shown again in Table 8.5 are all high in Engagement, and yet only one of those profiles—high scores across the board—is the desirable one. Our research and experience suggest two outcomes of these high Engagement, low Alignment, or low Capabilities profiles. The first is suboptimal performance as we described in earlier

Table 8.5
High Engagement Profiles

Alignment	Capabilities	Engagement	Profile
⬆	⬆	⬆	Superior Performance
⬇	⬇	⬆	Cheerleader
⬆	⬇	⬆	Under-Equipped
⬇	⬆	⬆	Strategic Disconnect

chapters—energy without focus or perhaps without the capabilities to satisfy customers.

The second outcome is the negative impact of low Alignment or Capabilities scores on long-term Engagement. In recent years, for example, we have had a spate of organizations that have come to us because they have overemphasized Engagement, but somehow their Engagement scores did not improve. When we have had the opportunity to examine these organizations in more depth, we typically have found key gaps in Alignment and Capabilities that are now inhibiting further evolution of Engagement. Is it possible to remain engaged when you have insufficient resources? Is it possible to stay engaged when customers constantly complain? Is it possible to stay engaged when your performance bonus isn't aligned with your performance? Is it possible to be engaged when you don't understand or agree with the company's direction? When the Alignment or Capabilities scores are much lower than Engagement, it is usually a sign that Engagement improvement will be limited at best.

Let's take a look at a few examples of such imbalances with high Engagement scores.

- One example from the measurement chapter included a unit with high Engagement and low Alignment and Capabilities. You may recall that this unit had a manager who had created loyalty to himself and not to the organization (low Alignment) and was shielding mediocre-to-poor performers and performance (low Capabilities) as long as he could. When he was discovered, he left and the unit imploded within a few months, creating havoc for customers and the organization alike.
- An HR team for a bank was about as close to cheerleaders as one could get short of a high school football game. But discussions with the leadership team indicated that the group was not perceived to be Capable in many ways—low business acumen, low stakeholder service ratings, and not viewed to be state-of-the-art on people issues. The bank president began to put increased pressure on the head of HR, demanding greater understanding of the industry and competitor issues, and proof of best practices. At first, this group responded by cheering harder, but never seemed to have time for training themselves or upgrading skills. After continuing to give themselves high fives for about a year, a series of low performance ratings, unfunded initiatives, and less involvement in decisions, the cheering employees became frustrated, leading to cynicism and big drops in Engagement.
- A security team for a health care organization was a high Engagement team for a while. Team members were bright and dazzled many of their stakeholders with their technical prowess at national sales events or in their ability to deter computer theft. One of our diagnostics, however,

indicated that they had low Alignment. In investigating the team of investigators, we discovered that its program priorities were out of sync with a number of key strategic priorities. The assessment indicated that their stakeholders wanted less lock-down building security. And they wanted more help with IT security than they were getting. This mis-Alignment eventually led to funding cutoffs for some of their prized programs and a growing disengagement in the group.

There are many examples of these profiles that limited the potential for Engagement, despite many positive supervisory behaviors and even sufficient rewards.

Engagement in Closing

We began this chapter by pointing to some disturbing statistics about the levels of disengagement. And yet, we continue to discover organizations or units within organizations that are achieving high levels of Engagement. Invariably, when we investigate, we find that they are not only managing each of the 15 satisfaction, commitment, and advocacy drivers well, they have often also built cultures that are consistent with these elements. They expect their senior leaders to role model these behaviors; they expect their supervisors to be coaches and mentors, connecting with their employees in a personal way. And those organizations quickly sanction inappropriate behaviors that may damage those fragile relationships. As with many aspects of organizational life, Engagement begins at the top with leader behaviors, not just a desire to have Engaged people.

Summary of Key Learning Points

- Engagement is a significant contributor to discretionary effort, employee retention, customer satisfaction and retention, and performance, among other valuable outcomes.
- Many studies point to a number of Engagement and morale deficiencies.
- Engagement requires achieving positive ratings in three areas: Employee Satisfaction, Commitment, and Advocacy.
  1. Basic satisfiers can inhibit Engagement when they are below certain thresholds.

2. Commitment is a two-way street between the organization and its people and is often facilitated with strong and meaningful jobs, good leadership role models, recognition, and good values.

3. Advocacy is often driven by strong growth and learning opportunities, an inspirational manager, and high employee involvement.

- Engagement can be managed, but it requires understanding the key drivers of Engagement and addressing those that are inhibiting peak levels of Engagement. We discussed five major drivers of each component of Engagement—Drivers of Satisfaction, Commitment, and Advocacy.

- Engagement alone is not enough. Engagement is oftentimes held back by Alignment and Capabilities factors. But even when Engagement is high and Alignment and Capabilities are low, there are negative consequences for the organization. Recall the eight profiles of People Equity that we described in Table 2.2: four of those profiles are high in Engagement but three of those profiles suboptimize employee and organizational performance (see Table 8.5).

Action Tips: What Can I Do Tomorrow?

- Is your organization engaged? Here are a few ideas to answer this question.
  - Answer the survey questions in Table 8.3, or better yet, conduct a customized Engagement survey that is specific about your organization's unique Engagement drivers. What percentage of your employees say:
    - They are committed to the organization?
    - They talk positively about the company to friends and family?
    - They feel inspired?
    - They are willing to go the extra mile as needed?
  - Do employees advocate on behalf of the organization?
    - Do they recommend good candidates for employment?
    - Do they advocate for your products and services?
    - If you are a public company, are employees significantly invested (while maintaining their investment portfolio balance)? Do they recommend others to do the same?

- If Engagement in your organization is low, here are some immediate steps you can take.
  - Ask a third party to conduct anonymous focus groups with low Engagement units to ascertain root causes.
  - Identify ways to improve the negatives. Come up with action steps to address those issues.
  - Embrace the positives. Communicate what is working and compliment the individuals and the teams responsible.
  - Assess your policies for work-life balance. Work with HR to change the policy to avoid burnout.
- Are the referrals of new talent from existing employees low? Here are some immediate actions to consider.
  - Meet with HR to make sure the referral policy and incentives are clear.
  - Communicate to the employees the value of referrals.
- Is the organizational commitment to employees as high as it should be? Here are some immediate actions to consider.
  - Individualize attention to employees. Do managers go out of their way to make people feel special? Personally compliment those who are putting in the extra time and effort.
  - Customize incentives (as simple as awards or a drawing for a gift certificate) for employees.
  - Employ and communicate an open door policy to serve as a sign of commitment to open communication.
  - Seek out an employee to whom you can serve as a mentor and provide her with coaching.

SECTION IV

Managing the Talent Life Cycle

"It may be a bad economy, but Talent Management is here to stay."
—Leif Meneke, vice president of talent and leadership for the Americas, Deutsche Bank

In this section, we turn to our last question posed in Chapter 2: How can People Equity inform design and delivery of key aspects of the talent management life cycle: acquiring, acculturating, developing, and retaining the right talent for your strategy?

As economic challenges continue to mount, the viability of many organizations, including some of the world's largest corporations, is on the line. Whether we are in prosperous times or lean ones, the future belongs to those organizations that acquire and use increasingly expensive talent more effectively and efficiently. They will enjoy a distinct advantage.

And here is where People Equity can make a significant contribution. When used effectively, the People Equity concept provides help in strategically assuring that your organization realizes the full potential from its human resources.

Making Talent Management Decisions

There are two major factors that will influence your actions in talent management—one external and one internal to your organization.

The internal one is related to the strategic value of particular roles in the organization. Huselid, Becker, and Beatty[1] point out that not all roles are equally strategic, and given limited resources, organizations need to assess how strategic a role is before expending disproportionate resources to acquire, grow, optimize, and retain talent for that role. Dick Beatty, professor of organizational development at Rutgers University has argued that logistics employees occupy one of the most strategic roles for an airline; these folks manage the biggest asset of the business, and have a dramatic impact in balancing on-time performance against cost. Boudreau and Ramstad[2] also talk about strategic roles in the context of managing variability in organizations. They argue that the role of the street sweeper at Disney, for example, potentially has more impact than the role of Mickey Mouse—initially a surprising thought! But they go on to explain that there is almost no variance in the role of good Mickeys and poor Mickeys, but the street sweeper may offer the type of variance in performance that could delight amusement park customers. When a street sweeper overhears customer conversations and offers assistance to find a good restaurant or seek out a particular ride, that exceeds customer expectations by a long shot and that behavior has a much better chance of leaving a favorable impression on customers.

Given limited resources, it is important to think about which roles are most strategic so that your organization can focus its best efforts to recruiting, selecting, training, optimizing performance, and retaining performers who are in these roles.

Second, the external environment will also influence a range of choices your organization must make regarding talent management.

Consider the following three scenarios:

1. Roles for which talent is plentiful in the marketplace
2. Roles for which talent is available but top talent is scarce
3. Roles for which all talent is very difficult to find

In Scenario 1, the primary challenge will be in screening talent for fit with your organization—Alignment, Capabilities, and Engagement readiness. Right-fit individuals will always surpass poor-fit players in performance, retention, and positive cultural impact.

In Scenario 2, the challenge includes getting the mindshare of top talent, and offering an appealing value proposition to that talent. In good economic times, these individuals have many options with which to compete and in poor economic times, they will need serious inducements to leave positive and secure jobs.

In Scenario 3, an even greater challenge is getting through the clutter of many suitors, avoiding the increased risk of sidestepping fit to acquire needed skills, and finding competitive differentiators that appeal to the scarce talent. A further challenge will be retaining this talent in an environment of many suitors.

Managing the Talent Life Cycle

The following talent chapters will help shed light on strategic talent planning and management across these scenarios. Testing for fit, using the ACE criteria, will be a fundamental feature that applies to all three scenarios, but is particularly mission critical for the most strategic roles in the organization. For less strategic roles, applying ACE principles can also have a significant impact on financial performance. The multiplier effect of poor selection, misdirected training, unfocused effort, and high turnover can both escalate cost and negatively affect strong performers.

What's at Stake?

Here are the key questions that we will address in this section:

- How can we *acquire* more *A* performers?
- How do we effectively *acculturate* new employees into the organization to maximize their chances of success?

- What is required to grow the talent reservoir to increase potential future performance and to achieve key organizational goals?
  - What leadership talent will be needed to meet our strategic objectives?
  - What is the role of leaders in maximizing ACE?
- How can we *retain* our best—our top quartile—performers?

These are fundamental talent questions. The answers to them will likely determine the survival and success of many organizations.

9

Finding Fit

"The wrong hire is too costly in this economy."
—Lance Miyamoto, chief human resources officer,
Comverse Technology

Assuming that roles have been clearly defined, effectively communicated, and tightly aligned with the organizational strategy, People Equity provides a framework for thinking about the best way for an organization to source and select candidates likely with the best fit. Will they:

- Buy into the strategy?
- Relate to external customers or internal stakeholders with whom they will be dealing?
- Embrace the brand promise?
- Be compatible with the culture?
- Accept the accountabilities and performance targets?
- Work in concert with other team members or other teams?
- Connect with the manager for whom they will be working?
- Have the necessary knowledge, skills, abilities, and experiences to achieve the role accountabilities?

Look at the talent pool in your organization. Too many negative answers to these questions indicate you are selecting candidates likely to be low People Equity players. Don't be surprised by higher costs; frustrated customers, peers, and supervisors; lower productivity, and most likely—early turnover.

If you disqualify a reasonable minority of candidates for the reasons listed, then consider this to be a positive talent acquisition strategy. This is akin to organizations prioritizing and selecting (and deselecting) certain types of customers. Some customers won't add value, or contribute so minimally that they are not worth the acquisition costs. So too for employees.

If on the other hand, you are eliminating large numbers of potential candidates, then it may be time to reexamine your values, policies, and operating style. For example, in a recent engagement, we worked with one firm that has begun to engage talent in high schools or earlier by creating a desirable brand, projecting the organization as an attractive place to work, and creating a buzz about the wide range of direct and indirect employment opportunities and benefits. Executives in the organization, however, also began to realize that some of their operating policies and styles were not consistent with the favorable brand image. This led the senior leadership team to explore alternative policies and move to create a work environment that would not only bring talent in, but also keep it.

The organization's older communications style (secrecy), rewards (hierarchical and tenure-based), dress codes (strict), and work-life inflexibility (no telecommuting and limited time off) simply eliminated too many of the potentially talented people. Those policies and styles almost guaranteed a lack of Alignment and lower Engagement among early career talent.

Strategic Talent Sourcing

"We see ourselves as 'talent collectors'—everything else will work if you get the right talent," says Ed Guttenplan, the co-founder of Wilkin and Guttenplan, a mid-sized accounting firm headquartered in East Brunswick, New Jersey. He goes on to say "It is very hard to find people mid-career that fit the Wilkin and Guttenplan culture. We have been very successful in hiring accountants out of school and training them in our culture." One of the best sources of talent is promoting internal candidates. From a fit standpoint, they are a known quantity. From an ACE perspective, the organization should know their potential for becoming Engaged, their Alignment with the goals and values of the organization, and their competencies.

A second great source is referrals from current employees or other stakeholders (suppliers) who know the organization well. Current employees—especially your top talent—often associate with other A-list players, and they know who is most likely to fit—or not. Says Jean Holley, executive vice president and chief information officer at Tellabs, "Employee referral programs are often used to help find and recruit talent. Great people know where to find great people, and people who are talented want to work with great people." Others caution, however, that referrals from your poor performers can backfire and should be managed cautiously.

An organization's customer base offers a third great talent source. "Recruiting is easier if they are also customers and have had a great experience with you; and regardless of the outcome of the selection process, you want them to remain great customers," says Dr. Richard Vosburgh, based on his prior experience with MGM Mirage, Taco Bell, and Hyatt Hotels and Resorts. Target and Starbucks are examples of firms that recruit employees heavily from a loyal customer base.

Fourth, recruiters and job search firms historically have been less strategic in their approach to talent acquisition. Said one executive from a Fortune 500 firm, "Recruiting is often a hit-or-miss proposition. Traditionally, our search firms do a good job of matching competencies, but often miss the boat on cultural fit." Another source in the search industry claimed that two out of three candidates recruited from the outside typically fail.

Only recently have we seen an interest in more strategic approaches, ones that:

- Use the full ACE model to identify best-fit candidates who:
  - Have the right competencies for the current position and the skill breadth to adapt to changing future needs and roles

- Have the right Alignment potential—candidates who will be aligned with vision, mission, values, and desired culture
- Are capable of becoming Engaged
- Use strategic talent management or organizational measures that go beyond standard transactional metrics such as fill rates and time to fill positions. These might include impact measures such as:
  - Performance levels achieved after hire. Did they become A-list players?
  - Did they remain with the organization for target periods of time (enough to recoup the investment)? How many hires were subsequently promoted?
  - Did they create satisfied stakeholders?
  - What percentage of the hires are good cultural matches?
  - What was the recruiter's overall success rate in finding best-fit hires?

Finally, internal recruiting and selection managers need to apply People Equity principles when using other resources such as web sites, advertising, job fairs, and campus recruiting.

Improving the Selection Process

According to John Dooney[1] with SHRM Research, their data show that the more profitable firms in a given industry have higher talent acquisition costs, presumably because they invest more money in the recruiting and selection of their talent. While this may be an indication of commitment to talent acquisition, Karl Ahlrichs[2] suggests that most firms could become far more efficient and effective in talent selection. He asserts:

- Current hiring processes waste time and fail to spot high performers who will fit with the company.
- Companies can apply lean principles of continuous improvement to the hiring process to get better.

The reasoning is simple. The selection process does not do a good enough job of screening for straightforward knockout factors early on, thereby incurring many expensive steps (for example, interviewing at multiple levels, job visits) that could have been avoided. Also, it creates dissatisfaction among candidates who may have invested personal and family time, energy, and emotion in the process. If they are screened out later for knowable factors (for example, credentials or experiences), these candidates, like disgruntled customers, will tell other potential candidates.

By applying lean thinking, Ahlrichs recommends using a narrative application followed by a 10-minute phone interview to screen for fit, followed by an online assessment at a minimum before considering a face-to-face. He recommends using a validated online assessment that measures qualities relevant to a company's needs. By the time an applicant comes in for an interview, the HR professional has invested less time, yet gathered more useful information for assessing the candidate's values and attitudes than is traditionally the case.

While this begins to address the issue of improving the talent selection process, what about the criteria for selecting good fit candidates? Richard Reilly, a long-time researcher in this field, suggests thinking about three different categories of attributes for making selection decisions: (1) relevant knowledge, skills, and abilities; (2) personal behavior styles (for example, personality or emotional intelligence); and (3) value alignment. The first two are the best predictors of performance and the last is a good predictor of retention.

Here are some suggestions for how to attack both the process and content, based on both research and successful practices.

- *Be clear about what is a must.* The clearer the organization is about critical values, operating policies, credentials, key skills, or knowledge, the easier it will be to assess talent.
- *Don't miss the inside candidate.* Research has shown that companies continue to be overly enamored of external candidates for top executive positions; most studies show, however, that internal candidates generally outperform external candidates after assuming an executive position.[3]
- *Involve the applicant in the screening process.* By being precise and transparent about the success criteria and the selection decision process, the organization can ask the candidate to contribute helpful information. This will cause some candidates to drop out who are only marginally interested, and it will transfer some of the screening work to the applicant. This can provide information about motivation, attention to detail, fuzzy answers, and verifiable information. Most will not shade the facts when they know they can be checked.
- *Scan for knockout items early.* Today, background checks, drug testing, aptitude tests, and other knockout evaluations can be done quickly up front before more costly steps such as interviewing.[4]
- *Balance the use of application forms and resumes with essay-style applications.* Professor Reilly, based on his selection research, likes this approach saying, "We have asked candidates to provide narrative examples of past behavior prior to arriving at an interview. This served to weed out those who were not serious, provided useful information to make a first cut on viable candidates, and gave interviewers a better starting point."
- *Test for Alignment before more costly competency evaluations.* Eric Greitens, a former Navy Seal, describes[5] two areas that are critical for Alignment:

Alignment with the mission and culture fit. He says that people who are not aligned with your mission or values will never succeed in the long run. This is the best place to avoid self-deception about how this top Capabilities person might be adjusted to fit the culture—it almost never happens. Such assessments may be less costly, and therefore deployed earlier, in jobs in which competency testing is very costly. It also reduces the temptation to allow their *what* to overshadow their *how*.

- *Examine the ability to become deeply Engaged.* Have these candidates been engaged in a mission before? How did they do? Did they act as a leader? Did they engage others? Did they recruit others to the mission? What drives them? Money, relationships, victory, growth—and will your organization provide those things? Will their manager provide those things? The answers to many of these questions will require well-trained interviewers, but basic information can be sought before the interview. A number of organizations that we have examined, for example, ask prospective candidates to write an essay about prior engaging experiences, to describe volunteer activities that they are passionate about, or to describe what turns them on. Much of this background can be started with written information or early recruiter conversations.

- *When assessing Capabilities, don't forget relational or communications skills.* If the role requires interaction with other teams or team members across the organization, even the most impressive technical skills may be squandered because of an inability to communicate or empathize. If candidates are being evaluated for a managerial role, look to decision making, strategic thinking, team development, strong communications skills, good judgment, and motivational experiences before their technical prowess. These capabilities are more likely to sidetrack them than their technical capabilities.

Best Practice

Validate your ACE criteria. While we know that the ACE factors have a strong relationship to performance and to key business outcomes, the specific relationships should be validated in your organization. Furthermore, leading organizations identify the primary predictors of high A, C, and E for key job groups, and then seek to screen and test for any of those factors that they can before making a hiring decision.

Two cautionary notes bear mentioning. First, screening for fit assumes that the culture is healthy; selecting like-minded people into a dysfunctional environment simply exacerbates an existing problem. Second, the organization needs to be on the alert for unintentionally screening out candidates who may be diverse by gender, race, or other important classifications. Fit is not intended to reduce diversity, but instead to screen more effectively so they can remove the major Alignment, Capabilities, and Engagement causes for new hire failure. When defined in a reasonable way, ACE criteria should not screen out different ethnic, gender, age, or other major cohorts. In our surveys of ACE globally, we find high and low ACE scores for every type of diverse population that we have examined.

Measuring The Impact of Your Talent Acquisition Process

Most of what is measured today is the efficiency rather than the effectiveness of the hiring process. We frequently see organizations tracking their time to hire, speed of filling requisitions, cost per hire, and so forth. But efficiency may be a slippery slope, especially if the organization fails to bring talent on board that has high People Equity potential. The last thing an organization needs, especially given the trends outlined earlier, is to hire the wrong talent faster.

There are some more strategic ways to approach the measurement of the talent acquisition process. Much of the focus should be on the impact of the process on key stakeholders, such as prospective hires, and the organizational impact of the process.

One key stakeholder group is prospective talent in the pipeline. Individuals already in the talent acquisition pipeline are easier to assess. For example, Qualcomm surveys applicants about their views of the organization and the talent acquisition process. By surveying separate groups that participated in the selection process, it is possible to evaluate the effectiveness and efficiency of that process and its impact on these stakeholders' views of the organization. For example, we might survey:

- Those who were hired.
- Those who were given offers (qualified) but declined.
- Those who were not qualified. In this group, it is possible to also segment by reason for lack of qualification: technically qualified but had mismatches on other key dimensions (culture fit, engagement); not technically qualified but good cultural fit; and so forth.

All of these individuals were drawn to the company, although they were not all good fits. The most difficult group to assess is those who would be great fits who never enter the pipeline.

Best Practice

Assess the talent market periodically to determine the general beliefs about your organization within the likely candidate pool.

Reasons for pervasive reluctance to consider your organizations could range from brand to perceptions of your hiring process to perceptions about your culture. The real question is whether these perceptions are accurate or not. If they are accurate, then applicants may be deselecting appropriately. If the perceptions are incorrect, however, then the organization will need to increase communication efforts through various channels (for example, ads, employee messaging, web site, social networking). This approach will be particularly important in Talent Scenarios 1 and 2 when the organization is finding shortages in key talent areas.

Don't overlook the perception of important players such as team members, the supervisor, or others who interact with the individual. Their views in the early stages after being hired can be very informative about the efficacy of the talent acquisition process.

Best Practice

To measure talent acquisition effectiveness, include items on your employee survey that address the impact of new hires. For example:

- Are they team players when teamwork is needed?
- Do they have the knowledge and skills needed to meet customer expectations?
- Do they carry their fair share of the load?

When these items are low, we can often garner information about the talent acquisition processes (as well as training and onboarding).

Some organizations use their training system immediately after a hire as a secondary screening tool to weed out candidates who are unable to reach certain training or performance hurdles early on. When I was at AT&T, the service representative job was a difficult to fill, critical customer interface job. The organization had a robust training program that typically could screen out bad fits fairly quickly. Although this was more costly than screening them out before hire, it was less costly than having them fail on the job. Once again, most of these efforts focus heavily on the Capabilities, but the best ones also focus on Alignment and Engagement.

Lastly, but perhaps most important, are the impact issues raised earlier in the chapter.

- What are the performance levels achieved after hire? Did they become A-list players?
- Did they remain with the organization for target periods of time?
- How many hires were subsequently promoted?
- Did they create satisfied stakeholders?
- What percentage of the hires are good cultural matches?

By addressing these questions, an organization is well on its way to becoming a highly effective acquirer of talent.

Effective talent acquisition is a key step in building People Equity, but once selected, talent must go through a fragile step—acculturation—that can make or break success. We address this in the next chapter.

Summary of Key Learning Points

- In good times and bad, finding top talent is a challenge.
- Don't forget internal candidates, who will short-circuit a lot of selection costs, especially for Alignment and Engagement
- Selection processes in most organizations could be far more effective and efficient, requiring attention to several aspects of the process:
  - Examine your talent flow. If you have lots of good talent choices, you can be more selective. If you have few good choices, reexamine your talent value proposition, your employer brand, and your communications.
  - Hiring processes are notoriously inefficient and ineffective. Even the best selection approach is likely to have 15 percent of wrong-fit hires. More typically, it approaches about 45 percent of wrong-fit hires.
  - The order and content of the selection process can be greatly enhanced. Consider:
    - Separating the *musts* from the *nice-to-haves*
    - Having the applicant do more of the screening
    - Moving less costly knock-out steps to the beginning

o Enhancing the validity of the selection tools

o Minimizing the use of traditionally ineffective tools like the interview

o Examining the candidate's capability to become highly Engaged

• Measure the Impact of the talent acquisition process. Most measures of the process are efficiency rather than effectiveness or strategic in nature. For example, consider:

– Measuring the impact of the talent acquisition process on key scorecard indicators

– Identifying and tracking talent life cycle measures

– Measuring stakeholder perceptions of the talent acquisition process (hires, declines, other stakeholders)

– Evaluating what your competitors are doing from a process standpoint, but don't copy their brand attributes unless they fit your strategy and culture.

Action Items: What Can I Do Tomorrow?

• Deploy the People Equity model and its three components to identify high potential candidates. Beyond the typical screening for Capabilities,

– Are you screening for Alignment with your direction and values?

– Are you effectively probing to find individuals who have the Capability to become highly Engaged in your culture?

• Consider involving the applicant more in the early stages of selection.

– Do you have online screening tools? Are they valid? If not, work with a professional to ensure they are.

– Are you asking candidates to provide narrative descriptions? Do you have a standard method for scoring them? Make sure your selection interviewers are well trained. This is one of the biggest areas in which hiring mistakes are made.

• Do you know how key stakeholders perceive the talent acquisition process?

– Have you assessed recent hires, those who turned offers down, and those who you rejected?

- Check blogs or Twitter to find out attitudes of people that have interviewed.
- How do peers of recent hires feel about the process and those hires? Likewise, managers of the hires?
- Do you have good impact measures? Consider:
  - Performance? What level of performance have recent hires achieved?
  - What percent of new hires turn over within one year?
  - What percent of new hires fail training?
  - How do customers (or internal stakeholders) rate the new hires?

10

First Impressions

"Acculturation is critical to get new employees to be believers while inoculating them from catching our old viruses—this is the key to innovation and improvement."
—Sumner Grant, CEO, Ministers and Missionaries
Benefit Board

Y ou just bought a new car and what advice did the dealer offer? Chances are you were told: Be careful how you break in the new car. Early-stage care will determine how well your vehicle will perform, along with its half-life. You might as well pass that advice on to employers regarding their new hires. If you don't seat the new relationship well, it will not yield the value you expected.

Now that your ideal candidate has signed on, what's next? Are there important strategic approaches to managing this fragile, getting acquainted, onboarding period? How can the ACE factors of People Equity help in making this period the most successful for both the organization and the new talent? Is there anything we should be doing before the candidate actually arrives?

While I could devote considerable time to how employees are brought aboard an organization, I prefer to focus on the strategic aspect of onboarding and how it relates to ACE.

There is a good deal of evidence in the psychological literature suggesting that first impressions count.[1] This is especially true during the first days and months of a new hire's employment. People Equity can provide an interesting way to track how well the organization is onboarding, leveraging, and embedding its new talent.

Perhaps you have had a similar experience to mine. Early in my career, I arrived at a new job to find that my boss was traveling for the week, my name was not on the security register, the departmental assistant was not ready for my arrival and said she would get background information for me later in the week, my office still had my predecessor's books and belongings in it, and my company orientation was scheduled for sometime during the next two weeks and later postponed. I was then surprised to be told that I should have fasted for a physical, needed to make benefit choices but without an adviser, and prepare for a weeklong trip starting in four days with nothing more than a nearly indecipherable note: "Bill, prepare to discuss turnover with our clients next week."

Even for as unstructured an individual as I am, this was pretty daunting. Fortunately, a new colleague who knew the ropes took pity on me over lunch and began to do a core dump about my boss, the culture, my peers, and expectations. In the afternoon, my new assistant handed me a to-do list delivered in a "This is the way we do things here; I don't have a lot of time to explain now!" manner.

I lasted nearly three years, but my early disenchantment with that welcome lingered (apparently, since after more than 20 years, I am writing about it!) And I was told that I was considered a really good find. I'm not sure what the welcome would have been for a fair find.

Today, the market is even more competitive for good finds, and the onboarding experience can make or break the return on investment of your hard fought and expensive talent identification and selection process. Some research[2] has indicated that new hires may make up their minds whether to stay or leave within the first four to six weeks of hire. Others have suggested that it might even happen on the first day.

The Role of ACE in Managing Acculturation

Try to answer three questions. What is the level of employee Alignment, Capabilities, and Engagement on the first day of a new position? Is each ACE component high, medium, or low? To help make this more tangible, how would your new hires answer the abbreviated questionnaire in Table 10.1 on Day One? How about 3, 6, or 12 months after their hire?

Table 10.1
Quick People Equity Check

	Strongly Disagree	Disagree	Neutral	Agree	Strongly Agree
Alignment					
I understand the overall goals of the organization and how it plans to reach them.	1	2	3	4	5
My individual performance goals and targets are clearly linked to our departmental performance goals.	1	2	3	4	5
					TOTAL × 10
Capabilities					
I have the knowledge and skills needed to meet our customers' expectations.	1	2	3	4	5

I have access to the technical resources and tools I need to meet our customers' expectations.	1	2	3	4	5
					TOTAL×10
Engagement					
I would recommend this organization to a close friend or colleague as a place to work.	1	2	3	4	5
I am proud to be working for this organization.	1	2	3	4	5
					TOTAL ×10

Best Practice

An organization that has built a clear employer brand and uses the recruitment and selection processes to educate as well as to evaluate will have a head start with higher ACE scores on Day One, which means a shorter road to maximum productivity.

The race to maximize ACE starts well before Day One, during the talent identification and selection process, but that is merely a warmup. The real game begins in earnest on Day One, which may make or break a successful new hire experience.

Figure 10.1 provides a look at ACE starting on Day One for many new hires. Engagement is usually at its highest level. People do not leave other roles and join the organization because they expect to be disengaged. It is often a very exciting day—new friends, new organization, new role, and new opportunities. It should be very high, perhaps 100 (highest score on our Engagement Index) for some employees, unless they are as neurotic as Woody Allen.

However, Engagement soon begins to erode for many. After one year or more, our strategic employee surveys find some organizations with Engagement

FIGURE 10.1   ACE Scores for New Hires

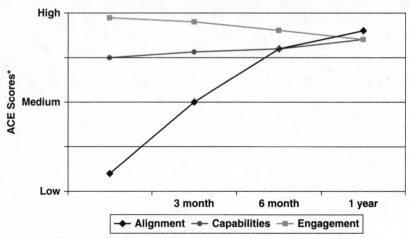

*Favorable responses of new hires to survey questions on each ACE factor.

levels for recent hires in the 90s,[3] compared to others that are struggling to hold scores in the 40s or 50s.

Alignment, on the other hand, is relatively low on Day One for new hires to the organization. For job transferees, this will be less so. They will have much clearer understanding of the overall organization vision, mission, values, and performance management and reward processes; they will not know, however, how these organizational features are interpreted or applied in their new unit. Also, they may not have a good feel yet for how the new role and their goals and measures align with department or business unit goals.

But here is where effective strategic branding and selection pay off. If the organization has done a good job in these two areas, Alignment should not be zero—in fact, we should have some relatively high scores on understanding of values, brand, and overall mission. Most new employees, however, will not as yet understand their unit's goals and metrics, their own specific objectives, how pay relates to performance, the performance feedback and coaching process, the social norms, the horizontal relationships with other units and so forth. This should grow over time, through formal and informal experiences.

While informal sources of information often telegraph a great deal about the way the organization really operates, we have found that strong leaders approach Alignment with a carefully thought-through plan and create processes to accelerate the growth of the Alignment curve. They don't leave Alignment to chance. They schedule formal orientation sessions and training, of course, to help adjust expectations about the individual's role and how it fits with the greater organization. But the best go beyond this with weekly review meetings or sit-downs with the boss to discuss the strategy and values, within some historical context. Some assign a buddy within the department who can help the new hire relate what he or she is learning through orientation to the department's goals and priorities.

For the third component of People Equity—Capabilities—we find two predominant profiles. Some organizations begin with fairly high Capabilities scores because they hire people expected to hit the ground running—true veterans in their profession. The traditional auto industry model has been to hire certified welders or other skilled workers who can become productive quickly. These organizations often look for experienced talent with skills that can be deployed immediately. In this *prêt a porter* skills model, the initial Capabilities score will be relatively high.

Figure 10.2, in contrast, shows an organization that has a philosophy of training from within. They perhaps prefer to hire more for values and ability to become engaged and will provide the skills to those with the right aptitude. This was typical of Nissan when they opened their Smyrna, Tennessee, plant in the United States. The company did not want a unionized workforce, and selected employees who were aligned with their values and willing to become passionate about the company's mission and culture. To that end, Nissan did not hire experienced mechanics, welders, or machinists, but instead, trained for many of those types of skills. The model worked quite well. The Capabilities ratings of new hires on Day One

FIGURE 10.2 ACE Scores for New Hires

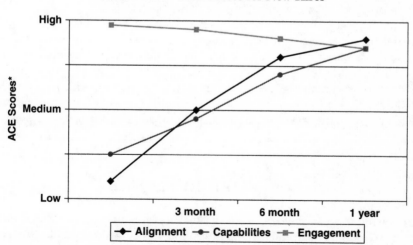

*Favorable responses of new hires to survey questions on each ACE factor.

is typically lower in this model, but increases rapidly in the first months on the job.

In no case, however, are new job incumbents at 100 percent on Capabilities on their first game day. While they may have the skills, abilities, or knowledge, they do not yet have a full grasp of their customers' expectations, have not yet learned local operating procedures, and have not mastered the use of information and resources that are uniquely packaged in this organization (for example, product descriptions, service requirements, intranet information, supporting departments, tools available). This will come with training and on-the-job experience. But these Capabilities can be accelerated by teaming up new hires with experienced peers, or by contracting for skills and knowledge expected by a certain date.

Best Practice

Organizations like JetBlue, Qualcomm, and the Whirlpool Corporation begin tracking new employees through surveys and informal third-party discussions early in their new role—and sometimes, even before they join a company. In the case of the Whirlpool Corporation, for example, interview candidates are surveyed regarding their experience with the company within two weeks of their interview date. The company wants to know how well they are engaging talent before they even extend an offer. Once a candidate joins the company, the Whirlpool Corporation delivers a structured onboarding process and initially surveys its effectiveness once the new hire has been with the company for at least three months. The Whirlpool Corporation realizes that early disconnects are risky in regard to engagement, productivity, and retention.

An effective best practice is to begin surveying new employees early and frequently on a small core set of questions that will help the organization monitor development during the crucial incubation period. We would recommend surveying using the ACE dimensions as well as some key questions regarding expectations gaps—areas that may be disconnects with prior expectations. This is also a good opportunity to get still-memorable feedback on the employee's impression of the talent acquisition and preboarding processes.

Socialization Factors

Following some of the earlier socialization research of Katz and Kahn[4] and others, George Graen and his colleagues[5] introduced a concept called leader-member exchange (or LMX). They discovered that different types of supervisor-subordinate relationships develop over time. Some of these evolve to become strong relationships leading to high productivity, retention and other benefits; others evolve to more arms-length out-group relationships. While the out group may occur for legitimate competency or political reasons, those relationships nevertheless lead to lower productivity, lower engagement, and higher turnover.

This research explains a great deal about why the initial employment period is so important and so fragile. Getting to high productivity and longer retention requires careful attention to and tracking of the early stages in the acculturation process.

Role of the Supervisor or Coach

Given the research just described, how can we intervene with a critical player—the supervisor or coach—to enhance the positive perceptions and behaviors during this fragile period? Our discussion with experienced practitioners suggests that supervisory coaching and onboarding training can be very helpful if done in a culture in which these activities are valued and reinforced from senior leaders. If an employee is not getting an *A*, CEO Garry Ridge of WD-40 asks the coach why not. He expects a great deal from his managers in the form of effective coaching and supportive activities to enable both new and established employees to "be all they can be," which has resulted in a mind-bending $1.25 million per employee in revenue.

A key element of supervisory training is to help supervisors understand the dynamics that are taking place for a new employee: mastering new technical and organizational information, rules and roles, and relationships can be daunting. If done well, this can accelerate your new employees to effective performance more quickly, while reducing the chances that they will opt out because it does not feel right. While most managers still have natural proclivities to create a pecking order of relationships, we have seen good examples of well-trained supervisors who have learned to bring out the best in people, regardless of their current skills and experiences.

A primary role of the new supervisor or coach is to help accelerate Alignment and Capabilities, while keeping Engagement near its peak. Depending on the job, this means helping the new employee become adept (high Capability) and focused (high Alignment) in his or her new role, while trying to remove Engagement blockers that have been described elsewhere in this book.

What about supervisors who are resistant to this type of training and behaviors? When I asked many of our interviewees this question, a majority said, "Get them out of that role!" When I asked senior leaders and retired

Best Practice

Research and best-practice interviews suggest that certain supervisory actions can be quite important during the onboarding stage. See Table 10.2 for examples of such actions. When supervisors become coaches and begin to use these elements, new hires get off to rapid and successful starts.

---

executives to identify the one thing that they would have done differently in their careers, many mentioned spending less time on getting poor managers to do their jobs right—and in most of those cases, the job referred to managing people.

What about Internal Hires—Transfers?

Much of what we have said for new hires is also applicable to new role incumbents. The primary difference is that both parties know a lot about each other, which can be good or bad, depending on what is embedded in that knowledge. As mentioned earlier, Alignment usually begins at a higher level, Capabilities are better known, and Engagement should be high if the individual has sought out this position.

Table 10.2
Positive Coaching Behaviors During Acculturation

- Providing frequent, effective, and transparent communication
- Setting clear expectations about the "What" (for example, goals and accountabilities) and the "How" (for example, what are culturally acceptable ways to reach the "What?")
- Enabling performance (for example, sufficient information and tools)
- Providing effective training (can be formal or informal) to enhance skills needed to be successful
- Connecting new players to teammates and stakeholders (for example, internal customers) in a way that increases relationship building as soon as possible
- Helping to build professional networks
- Providing early recognition for small successes and for behaving in culturally appropriate ways
- Providing the right resources and tools to get the work accomplished
- Treating the new hire with respect and fairness
- Valuing diversity

What can be different is a new incumbent bringing the wrong assumptions about the new unit, based on how his prior unit operated. As we have said many times in these pages, there is wide variation among supervisors in most organizations—a problem in and of itself. If the new internal candidate does not have adequate knowledge of the supervisor and team members, then he may carry inappropriate assumptions about leadership styles, decision-making latitude, appropriate communications, and many other aspects of the work relationship. In this case, the leader and the new member's peers can be helpful in quickly educating him on the rules of the game for the unit.

Intervening at the Right Time

The tracking of ACE during the early stages of the relationship can be very telling. Organizations that are measuring ACE during this formative stage still have the opportunity to intervene in relationships to change behavior before negative patterns take hold. There are many potential causes of low People Equity scores; the following are several typical situations:

- *Supervisory or peer relationships that are not going well.* The first step is to ensure that the new employee was a good hire from an Alignment and Capabilities standpoint. If that is the case, then effort can be focused on the dynamics at play with the supervisor or peer group that may be creating low ACE scores.
- *Training issues.* These situations often include a systemic gap in knowledge or skills that inhibits success in training or early performance. It is not uncommon to run into situations in which the training does not provide enough development for new hires to hit performance targets quickly. We have seen this quite often in sales training. In these cases, it is important to rule out that they were simply poor hires. If quite a few hires are hitting the targets, then it is more likely an individual issue, but when a significant number of new hires are struggling collectively, then look to a training deficiency as a possible cause.
- *Values or culture conflict.* While we discussed the importance of a rigorous hiring process, there are, at times, individuals who accept certain organizational values but are not equipped personally to deal with the implications. Two common examples come to mind:
  1. Many applicants say they insist on being accountable, but often they shirk hitting the numbers once on board.
  2. Some think an entrepreneurial culture is exciting, until they arrive and find that they have to wear six hats.

- *Authority and empowerment can be deal-breakers.* Employees who are used to working in environments that give them a great deal of latitude typically do not do well in ones that make them go through the chain of command for every decision or resource.
- *Weak hires.* Enough said. If this is happening frequently, then it is time to reexamine the talent acquisition processes.

Best Practice: Why Wait for Day One?

While we have addressed the issue of what to do starting on Day One, the clock starts ticking earlier. Interview input suggests that some firms are doing interesting things between the time of signing on and Day One's arrival. Kristen Weirick at Whirlpool, for example, describes a robust pre-onboarding process. New talent is kept engaged with company and product information and early discussions that will help them prepare for their arrival, ranging from work-related issues to personal ones, like where to enroll the kids in school, how to get temporary housing, and daycare.

While many larger organizations, in particular, have had standard packages of information for years, the leaders are doing more to manage perceptions and build a high ACE start on game day. The following are a list of potential actions you might consider to keep Engagement at its peak, and begin to increase Alignment and Capabilities, beginning with the more standard and moving to more engaging actions. Keep in mind that leading firms are already using some of these approaches during the courting and selection stages.

- Information packets on the organization: annual reports, public relations releases, organizational charts, new products, and much more.
- Community information: housing, schools, medical resources, day care, shopping, arts, and the like.
- Human Resource department calls and e-mails before Day One to inform and invite questions.
- Meet the peers. If geographically feasible, in-person meetings are the best, but some organizations have used one-on-one phone calls with peers to begin to establish relationships and a help network.
- Meet the coach. Professor Robert Liden of the University of Illinois at Chicago, has found evidence suggesting that positive early perceptions of the supervisor are significantly related to positive perceptions after

three months on the job.[6] Lunches or breakfasts with the coach just to get comfortable and begin to understand more about the organization in a relaxed setting.

- Direct information to spouses or significant others to bring them into the process and to establish the employer brand with them as well: upcoming picnics, company parties, company-sponsored events in the community, support services. Some firms are quite active in helping a spouse or other family members secure jobs or educational slots to help relieve stress of a potentially traumatic move.

Most of this falls under the category of helping the new hire and her family become embedded in the work and local community; staying at a bad hotel, having a bad meal, or getting ripped off at an auto shop could start a negative spiral. Positive organizational information during this period accelerates Alignment by better understanding context and culture. It also can increase Capabilities by adding to the new hire's knowledge base. And from an Engagement perspective, the relational activities can begin to build trust and mutual respect.

Summary of Key Learning Points

Here are some of the Key Learning Points we covered about acculturation and transitioning into a new situation.

- The early stage of employment with a new organization or unit is the most fragile period and sets the trajectory for long-term performance and retention.
- Because new hires often make early decisions about their long-term prospects with an organization, this period needs to be managed carefully to minimize the risk of early loss or protracted performance ramp-ups. These risks are especially high in difficult-to-recruit roles and with more expensive hires.
- Acculturation begins before Day One on the job and leading firms are guiding this process with a series of actions that ensure they begin the new relationship in a strong fashion.
- Organizations can increase their odds of obtaining high ACE scores by carefully managing and monitoring supervisory relationships during this stage.
- High ACE organizations not only measure their ACE scores on a more frequent basis during this stage, but focus on information, training, supervisory behaviors, peer relationships, and performance assessments to accelerate their ACE scores.

Action Items: What Can I Do Tomorrow?

- Use a diagnostic tool (for example, acculturation survey) to assess the effectiveness of your acculturation process.
  - Does it capture the important Alignment, Capabilities, and Engagement success factors? Does it provide information on:
    - How quickly employees are becoming Aligned (for example, understanding goals, measures)?
    - The adequacy of talent, information, and resources, or the effectiveness of teamwork?
    - The engagement level of the new hire, and factors that influence it (for example, supervisor relationship, communications, employment policies)?
  - Is your diagnostic conducted early and frequently enough to understand if acculturation is not going well, so there is time to intervene?
- If the diagnostic shows weaknesses, consider:
  - Are the goals of the organization, the department, and the role clearly explained to newcomers?
  - Are new employees provided with the right tools and resources the moment they arrive?
  - Are the formal orientation sessions and training available for new employees as well as for employees new to their role but not to the organizations?
- Take these steps to accelerate understanding of your organization:
  - Ensure seamless communication between the talent acquisition team and the onboarding team.
  - Put together a standard package of information about the organization that is sent home with each candidate before arriving on the first day.
- Ensure that direct managers consider acculturation of new employees a priority. Consider taking these steps:
  - Set up a short course or refresher on acculturation with the management team. Lead the discussion around onboarding and how the new hires feel when first joining an organization. Help managers understand the dynamics that are taking place for a new employee: mastering new technical and organizational information, rules and roles, and relationships. It's daunting!
  - Present the important best practices to the managers as described in Table 10.2 in this chapter.

- Establish a new standard: Supervisor calls before Day One to invite questions or solve problems.
- Prune out managers who don't want to spend the time acculturating new employees; they are costing the organization dearly.

• Create a formal process for intervening before an employee becomes unproductive and unfulfilled. Consider legitimate intervention activities with the new hire from someone other than the manager.

- Have human resources, the boss's boss, or another key stakeholder check in with the new employees two weeks after they start their employment to see how they are doing and how the acculturation process is progressing.
- The organization might have an ombudsman, who reaches out to new hires to inform them of his role.
- The boss's boss might schedule a breakfast or other informal activity (for example, just dropping in to chat) to see how things are going.
- Have a third-party organization poll the new employee at one or two key intervals—perhaps end of first few weeks and again at the end of the first quarter.

11

Growing Your Talent Reservoir

"Get the best talent and retain them. It's not just about money, but about development."
—Don Crosby, vice president, HR International, McDonald's Corporation

How Deep Is Your Talent Reservoir?

Picture a large reservoir of talent that can either grow or be depleted, and a series of sluices that deliver the talent to generator paddles. When the reservoir is too low, the talent cannot move the generator paddles at top speed, and therefore, power is not at its peak. When the reservoir is too high, talent spills over and is not used in the generation of productivity. And when this occurs, talent tends to become stagnant or is siphoned off to other organizations. In addition to managing talent levels, there is a second factor that decisively affects talent use and value: funneling that reservoir of talent in a way that generates power. When the sluices are closed, talent may just sit in the reservoir, becoming stagnant over time—think of these as skills that go unused or misdirected. When the sluices are open and the reservoir of talent is applied perfectly, we have both maximum power and a strong capacity for future power.[1]

This is what we are attempting to capture with ACE. When all three elements of ACE are high, we have tremendous capacity to deliver high productivity. When ACE is low, our potential is limited.

The Capabilities element of People Equity—the one containing talent competencies as it couples with information and resources to deliver value—is the most obvious place to spend our time in the Development chapter; there are important implications along the way, however, for how we develop leaders' competencies to Align and Engage talent in ways that enable the unit and its individuals to grow their value. In the Capabilities chapter, we addressed the impact of high Capabilities on important outcomes, creating and delivering customer value, in particular. Many of the drivers of value creation, and the role of the individual and teams, were covered in that chapter. In this chapter, we focus more on the role of talent leaders. More specifically, how ACE provides a framework to help organizations monitor and manage three important aspects of talent development:

1. Developing leaders who are capable of optimizing their talent
2. Planning for leader succession
3. Managing leader transitions

Developing Leader and Supervisory Capabilities

The People Equity model has the ability to help managers and supervisors understand how well they are executing the business strategy, especially those elements that are driven by and through people. Measures of People Equity (and its drivers) allow managers to identify and leverage people strengths, while reducing weaknesses. Leaders can apply the model to both themselves and to their direct reports who manage people. The model can serve as a guiding tool to help them increase their competencies to achieve high Alignment, Capabilities, and Engagement among their teams. Table 11.1 provides a list of some of the most important competencies needed by leaders to create a high People Equity environment.

Table 11.1

Leader Competencies Related to Optimizing Talent in Each of the Three People Equity Areas

Alignment

- Strategic and critical thinking to better understand issues related to organizational direction
  - Setting priorities, planning and decision making in a strategic context
- Communicating
  - Organizational direction
  - Organizational, departmental, and individual goals
  - Organizational values, such as ethics and safety
- Using performance measurement (for example, scorecards, team and individual measures) effectively
- Connecting rewards to performance
- Facilitating interdepartment cooperation
- Providing coaching and feedback that enables employees to improve performance and live the organizational values

Capabilities

- Matching the right talent (right competencies) with the right roles
- Providing or enabling the information needed to meet customer expectations
- Providing the right resources to meet customer expectations
- Supporting training that enables the employee to meet or exceed performance expectations
- Building effective teams
- Managing conflict
- Drawing on diverse resources that will create stronger solutions, better innovation

Engagement

- Motivating different types of employees
- Treating employees fairly

- Communicating and behaving in ways that create trust and feelings of respect
- Respecting employees with diverse backgrounds
- Providing reasonable flexibility to help employees balance work and family obligations
- Recognizing employees for their contributions in meaningful and motivational ways
- Helping employees learn and grow

The key point here is that managers need to be trained on all three legs of the ACE stool. It's not just about skills. A good example is ethics Alignment. After the Enron debacle and the consequent enactment of the Sarbanes-Oxley law, many realized that ethics understanding should not be assumed—values need to be espoused, trained for, and test driven. Another area of Alignment-related competencies is in training employees regarding the company direction, key priorities, and goals. With regard to Engagement, most managers are not born with all of the competencies to Engage employees—they learn sometimes painful lessons by trial and error or they have organizational training and experiences that help shape their strength in this area. Let's take a look at how this is applied.

Take Paul, a leader of a commercial banking business. Paul oversees Rod and Pam, both of whom are responsible for running the bank's local business in Chicago and Atlanta, respectively. The People Equity survey provided the bank's managers with valuable feedback on how to improve performance through better leveraging of human resources.

Pam's unit was doing reasonably well in a competitive marketplace, but the unit received low ratings from customers on responsiveness and customer knowledge. As a result, a number of key customers took their business to other providers. Pam's ACE scores shed light on this issue. Alignment and Engagement scores were high for the unit, but there were several Capabilities gaps that connected to the customer issues. Pam used the strengths in Alignment and Engagement to leverage this highly motivated group to achieve greater levels of customer service, and she used the Capabilities information to help the group gain additional skills to probe customer needs, improve their knowledge of commercial lending, and improve the speed with which they could deliver answers to customers. The People Equity feedback helped in two specific ways:

1. It helped Paul and Pam focus on the knowledge and processes that were inhibiting the unit from delighting customers.
2. It enabled Pam to evaluate herself and see gaps in her knowledge of commercial lending, especially within the textile industry, which was her key market segment. It also pinpointed for Pam the need to provide

more focused training for new customer reps, and it gave her the objective data to ultimately persuade Paul to provide greater financial support for the training.

Rod's group was different. It had the inverse profile—low in Alignment, high in Capabilities, and low in Engagement. The financial result of this was nearly disastrous. Paul's lack of personal understanding of the organization—he was recently recruited from outside the organization—led to serious misalignments with the home office around priorities, focus, and even values. Rod's arrival followed the retirement of a much-loved prior leader with far stronger interpersonal skills. Rod's loner style made him something of a cultural misfit, causing the people in his unit to become even further disengaged. The combination of new policy changes that Rod had introduced, mixed signals on priorities, and poor communication, led to labor troubles, diversity problems, and turnover of top performers.

The People Equity feedback was a wakeup call for Paul and Rod. For Paul, it alerted him to the realization that the region's performance was not simply an external market issue or a product problem. To a significant extent, the enemy was within. While gaining market share is never easy, it is an especially steep challenge when top performers are heading for the exit. The People Equity survey got Paul's attention and enabled him to engage Rod in serious discussion.

For Rod, the survey helped him diagnose the problem and hone in on where he and his unit were falling short. This enabled him to engage in a conversation with Paul regarding his regional funding and the level of visible support from the home office. He discussed with Paul issues about future direction, key priorities for his unit, and why the compensation payouts for the prior year sent all the wrong signals to his team.

By looking at the nine drivers and enablers of People Equity, Rod could quickly identify specific reasons why his unit's Alignment and Engagement scores relating to the manager and top management communications scores on the People Equity survey were so low. Subsequent focus groups added additional enlightenment, showing that his introverted style was interpreted by his team as uncaring, distant, and detached, when in fact Rod was highly concerned, but inherently shy. In the Alignment arena, his weak knowledge of the overall business became apparent, and he came to realize that he needed to deepen his business acumen so that he could convey a more confident and clear view of the organization and its direction.

Paul reviewed the survey data and decided Rod was a solid player who would benefit from coaching support, which Paul readily funded. The coach worked with Rod to improve his communications style and messaging—critical negatives for Rod—and his ability to interact with people more informally. This, coupled with clearer direction on priorities and direction, enabled him to improve.

People Equity information proved to be an important management development tool. It provided Paul with an early red flag and the information needed to prevent Rod from being buried by a serious financial collapse. Most importantly, it provided specific information that enabled Paul to choose targeted developmental actions—skills coaching, reinforcement of corporate values by Paul, speaking practice sessions, and some enhanced exposure to what more successful units in other cities were doing.

From Rod's perspective, the People Equity model helped him close key performance gaps and increase his staff's knowledge, and skills and therefore their value and future potential. And he did so with Paul's financial support and encouragement. It also averted an imminent departure for Rod because they caught these things early.

People Equity and Succession Planning

"Those who succeed do so by understanding *strategic future*. A critical element for our strategic future is planning for continuity, for who will want to perpetuate the firm," says Ed Guttenplan, managing shareholder of Wilkin & Guttenplan. The criticality of succession to executives was echoed again recently in a major study of more than 500 C-suite executives by the SHRM Foundation.[2]

Peter Cappelli argues that the old succession planning model didn't work.[3] It was too static and required organizations to be able to plan five or more years in advance. That model failed over time because the matches were poor, given the labor supply and the difficulty in predicting demand. People were either overtrained and underused—or the reverse. He contends, however, that talent does need to be assessed and developed, but perhaps in some different ways from the past. One of those ways is to provide broader, early skills training that is relevant to multiple job levels, and begin building an arsenal of developmental experiences that can be leveraged over time.

People Equity can be a helpful tool in both the assessment and skills targeting in this approach. More and more, it will be essential to promote leaders who can achieve superior performance through people. People Equity profiles can provide an important tool for evaluating who is ready for more challenging assignments and what areas of development are most important.

In Paul's case, which we described earlier, he had been recently promoted from a national product manager to a national operations leader. The People Equity survey provided Paul with an additional way to gauge his managers' potential for future growth and succession. Over time, the People Equity tool helped Paul move a number of his managers into senior individual contributor roles—senior analysts and senior credit officers—that were less dependent on their people skills. For others within Paul's area of responsibility, it was a major tool to validate potential for promotion. Managers with large spans of control must be able to create workforces that are high in A, C, and E. Paul realized that some of his regional managers would be ideal candidates for succession to his role and that these individuals would be able to coach other managers in how to most effectively leverage their talent.

Over time, the People Equity framework also enabled Paul to grow and develop his competencies for future promotion. He realized that the Alignment scores of his segment of the business could be far stronger, and that his close-to-the-vest, need-to-know style was, in part, responsible for the situation. The People Equity feedback across his organization suggested that he needed to share more with his managers, giving them the *whys* and not just the *whats*. He also began to realize that managing was a contact sport; his messages came to life when he connected with people face to face, so Paul decided to hit the road, visiting his various operating sites on a much more frequent basis.

Part of what held Paul back was a debilitating fear of public speaking. When he faced an audience, he invariably felt that "they were all staring at me, which makes me feel as if I am being evaluated on every word I say—so I don't say much." Paul retained a coach, and while he never developed the oratorical skills of Winston Churchill, he was able to reach out and touch those whom he addressed, leading to subsequent promotions.

People Equity and Leader Transition

Many firms face major knowledge challenges as experienced leaders (both people and technology leaders) transition out of their roles. A key challenge is how to most effectively determine in advance not only the intellectual content that must be replaced but also how to manage the relationships that are so valuable. Many of the stellar performers are not only knowledgeable about their subject area, but they have also often developed great relationships that they can quickly call on to obtain necessary information or support.

While People Equity is certainly a strong framework for ongoing management, it can also serve as a framework for the transitioning leader. In some of our coaching work, it has been helpful in working with planned changes of key leaders—often leaders who have been in a role for many years, with lots of informal knowledge that will be difficult to replace.

Alignment and Capabilities appear to be particularly crucial to successful transitions. We have found that it is possible to reduce the time it takes new leaders to get up to full speed by as much as 50 percent. One key element in achieving this is understanding, from multiple stakeholders, the knowledge that is embedded in that role—some of it ascribed to any incumbent in that role and some of it unique to the current role holder. Another key element is understanding how that role fits within a network of connected relationships (Alignment issues), both technical and personal, and how those connections will be replaced.

- Who does the current incumbent rely on most in regard to information, influence, or decision making?
- Who depends on this person's knowledge and networks? What type of knowledge is most difficult to replace?
- Does this person serve as a bridge or gatekeeper between two or more groups?
- How important is relationship knowledge and skills to being successful in the role?

These types of questions will help capture what is critical about the role beside simple knowledge, skills, and abilities.

A second powerful role of People Equity is in providing the new leader with a bird's-eye view of the organization and its effectiveness.

If used as part of a holistic assessment of the organization shortly after arrival, the People Equity framework and specific measures can give the new leader both broad and specific insights into the workings of the organization, and potential factors that may be inhibiting the unit from achieving higher performance. People Equity surveys can provide answers to important questions that the new leader must quickly find out. How strong are the managers? How engaged is the workforce? What are key capabilities gaps? Are people aligned with the broader organization's goals? Are interdependent units aligned with one another? What needs to change to add more value to customers?

Consider the alternative profiles of the East and Central regions displayed in Figure 11.1 that were initially described in Chapter 4. If you inherited Central, what would be your top priorities? What about the East? [Sorry, you cannot pick the West!]

If you inherited the Central, there are both systemic and unit issues that must be addressed before you can improve the organization. For example, Capabilities is clearly a problem across all groups and likely starts at the top of your chosen region. The survey should help to pinpoint whether it is talent, information, or resource gaps. If talent is the gap, is it likely a function of poor selection, formal or informal training, teamwork, or other issues. These profiles provide a quick look at managerial and supervisory strengths and weaknesses as they relate to talent management, and potentially identify future risks such as emerging labor relations, safety, or quality issues.

FIGURE 11.1   People Equity Profile

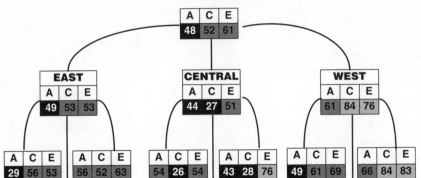

A = Alignment   C = Capabilities   E = Engagement

Weak: 0 – 49   Intermediate: 50 – 69   Strength: 70 – 100

If you inherited the East, while there are certainly some systemic actions you can take to perhaps increase Alignment, your challenge is more likely spot treatments of various units. One unit is quite low in Alignment (score of 29). Further investigation reveals that the manager who leads this unit has never distributed information about the strategy and goals or region scorecard. This information now enables the new leader to intervene and perhaps role-model and assist that manager with the first round of this type of communication. Such spot treatments allow you to conserve your limited resources and deploy your time and resources in the most effective way.

Another use of a People Equity survey assessment is in conducting pulse surveys—quick surveys on narrowly focused issues. The pulses can provide fast feedback on change that is occurring during the first six months of the new leader's tenure to enable more targeted communications, coaching of managers, and adjustment of priorities. We find such surveys especially useful during restructurings of all types—mergers, acquisitions, outsourcing, and resizing—because the leaders of the newly configured organizations are under enormous pressure to reorganize, optimize, and engage their talent in support of new goals or directions, often with a different set of organizational constraints. They provide the new leader with an important tool for inquiry and discussion. Why does the profile of the organization or unit look as it does? It is a compelling question that enables the leader to both engage her new team in focused, fact-based situation appraisal, and to make important judgments about the challenges and opportunities ahead.

Summary of Talent Development

This chapter is not intended to be a comprehensive review of talent development, but rather a look at how People Equity thinking can help with the important role of leader and talent development.

For more information on this topic, go to **reinventingtalentmanage ment.com.**

Summary of Key Learning Points

- Train for ACE—People Equity framework can be an effective tool for evaluating the effectiveness and developmental needs of leaders in optimizing their available talent.

- People Equity is a helpful framework for evaluating talent management practices throughout the organization, thereby enabling senior leaders to see the unique talent management strengths and weaknesses of their managers.

- People Equity is also useful in succession planning. More and more, it will be essential to promote leaders who can achieve superior performance through people. People Equity profiles can provide an important tool for evaluating who is ready for more challenging assignments and what areas of development are most important.

- The People Equity framework has also been used to accelerate leader transition. The organization can use the People Equity framework to assess the relational and knowledge capabilities that must be replaced. New leaders can also use People Equity surveys to provide quick feedback on their newly inherited organizations. How strong are their managers? How engaged is the workforce? What are key capabilities gaps? Are people aligned with the broader organization's goals? Are interdependent units aligned with one another? What needs to change so that more value can be added for customers?

Action Tips: What Can I Do Tomorrow?

- Are your employee development investments paying off? Here are a few ideas to answer this question.
  - Are the individuals in your company involved in continuous learning needed to remain market competitive?

- Is your organization committed to talent development during good as well as bad economic times?
- Is people development—including leadership—well connected to the vision and values, customer expectations, the unique strategy and competitive differentiators of the organization and the industry requirements?
- If your answers to these questions are "No" or "I'm not sure," what actions should you plan to address the situation?
- Do you currently have sufficient developmental opportunities in your organization? If not,
  - Think about employees' roles—especially your A-list players—and ways you may be able to change their roles.
    o Expanded roles
    o Swapping roles (or parts of roles) with someone else
    o Adjusting the old routine to provide varied experiences
  - Pilot a cross-training program in your department. Collaborate with employees to set up a schedule and a rotation plan.
- Limited budget? This does not mean you stop learning, thus risk losing customers and high potential employees.
  - Organize lunch and learns. You should lead the first one. Prepare to engage people in a learning tradition.
  - Lead by example. Attend conferences, lectures, and webinars, and invite others to join you.
  - Build learning processes into your organization. How are you compiling and organizing knowledge that will accelerate the learning of others? Are you using your existing technology to help people learn faster or more effectively?
  - Look for lower-cost public programs or community college programs that support your agenda. Caution must be exercised, however, to not simply throw learning at people; it must be relevant to their and your organization's goals.

12

Retaining Top Talent in Good Times and Bad

"Big challenge is keeping the top employees while being willing to let go of those who are not as effective."
—David Ulrich, professor of business at the University of Michigan

If you believe that talent retention waxes and wanes with the vagaries of economic cycles, think again. Most organizations are constantly faced with the challenge of holding on to top performers, especially in hard-to-staff roles. But as Davina Askin of the Girl Scouts, USA, has observed, "When the economy is in decline, people who should leave are holding on."

Retention is about making sure that an organization has enough A-list players at every level to make it fiercely competitive and is taking action to bring up the performance of the rest. As we have already seen, ACE is an important tool for revealing and managing differences in workforce productivity. The very same thinking can be applied to the retention issue.

Darcy is a sales manager for a health care organization. His sales force of 40 employees is achieving $125 million in sales annually. Kindra is a sales manager for another region with about the same number of sales reps. Four years ago, the two regions were created by splitting a larger region pretty much down the middle, with each new region generating about $150 million. Today, Kindra's sales are approaching $175 million, while Darcy's have slipped approximately 17 percent. What happened?

At first blush, you might think that one of them was dealt the premier territory. In fact, when the managers took those positions about four years ago, both regions were considered to be slow to no-growth regions based on their predecessor's results. When you dig past the minor demographic and structural differences, one primary factor that separates these two regions is their sales representative turnover. While other factors have some minor influence, when you look at the impact of turnover, it accounts for a significant portion of their results. Darcy has been plagued with 20 percent turnover while Kindra's is around 5 percent. Each of them inherited similar profiles of performers (see Figure 12.1), with their 10 bottom-quartile performers averaging about $2.2 million in sales and their 10 top-quartile performers averaging $5.5 million. From a performance standpoint, both managers began with very close performance.[1]

But Kindra has been stellar at retaining her top performers and replacing her bottom performers with higher-producing reps. While not all of her replacement reps were achieving the original top-quartile performance of $5.5 million, she certainly skewed the distribution in favor of higher performers (see Table 12.1 showing her distribution of reps after three years). In contrast, Darcy has lost many of his stars, and while his replacements were pretty well distributed over high and low performance, he continued to lose the best while hanging on to the weaker performers.

Table 12.1 shows the impact of such turnover over three years, and provides important insight about turnover.

FIGURE 12.1   High Variance in Sales Performance

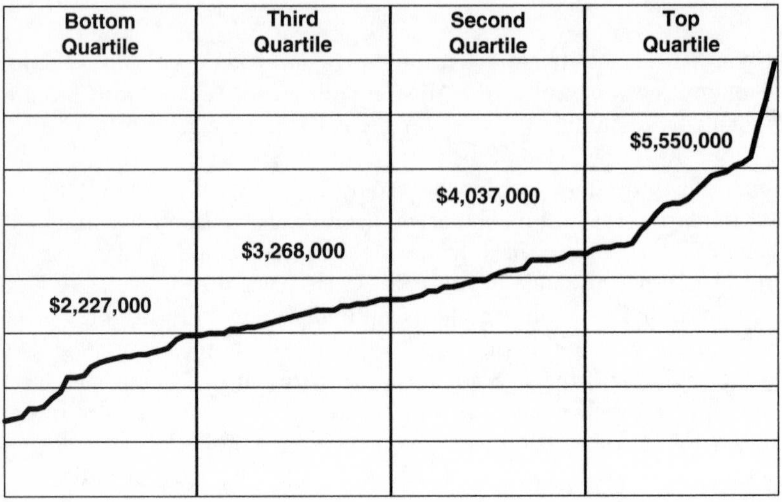

Bottom Quartile	Third Quartile	Second Quartile	Top Quartile
			$5,550,000
		$4,037,000	
	$3,268,000		
$2,227,000			

Table 12.1

Impact of Turnover on Two Nearly Identical Units

	Darcy	Kindra
Sales revenue three years ago	$150M	$150M
Total revenue after three years (without productivity gains)	$125M	$172M
Margin dollars gained/lost @ 20%	($25M)	$34.4M
Direct replacement costs @25K per representative	$600K	$300K
Productivity loss (in margin) during rep replacements	$9.2M	$4.6M
Total Impact	($34.8M)	$29.5M
Current Sales Rep Profile (annual sales):		
$2.2M	14	2
$3.3M	18	14
$4.0M	6	8
$5.5M	2	16

- Turnover has actually reduced Darcy's unit performance while increasing Kindra's.
- The net difference in bottom line cash was nearly $65 million ($35 million loss for Darcy against a nearly $30 million gain for Kindra) across the two groups.
- The replacement costs, while expensive, are relatively low compared to the productivity losses (in revenue and margin lost) while reps are being replaced.
- It is clear that by using turnover to reduce low performers and enhance top producers, Kindra now has a much higher-performing team going forward than does Darcy.

Even if we eliminated the impact of their differential performers and focused solely on replacement costs and productivity losses, Darcy has incurred nearly $5 million in higher costs than has Kindra as a result of this higher turnover (for full calculations, go to **reinventingtalentmanagement.com**).

Retain the Best; Lose the Rest

William Crouse, managing director of HealthCare Ventures LLC and former leader of major health care businesses for Johnson and Johnson, DuPont, Revlon, and others, attacks the performance issue directly. "It has always been my philosophy to pare out the bottom quartile. If they are still here, management is not doing its job." This philosophy, of course, assumes that there is a sizable gap in performance such as the one we just saw in our pharmaceutical example. It also assumes that management's approach to this does not create a culture of fear and competition that drains overall performance.

But the flip side is retaining top performers. As we saw in Darcy's case, one of the biggest killers of overall sales performance is losing top-quartile performers. If the overall organization with 100 reps (25 in each quartile of Figure 12.1) were to lose 20 percent, or 20 of their reps annually, it would certainly slow down revenue growth. Unfortunately, and not unexpectedly, such organizations typically lose more top performers than poor performers (who want to hang on as long as they can). Figure 12.2 shows the potential impact of losing just 10 reps in the top two quartiles. Unless you have perfect rep clones—same performance and customer intimacy—$47 million in sales revenue is at stake,[2] resulting in a lot of scrambling—and lost sleep.

Impact of the Economy

Of the 70 or so executives whom we interviewed for this book, about one-half saw retention as an important issue now and over the next two to three years;

FIGURE 12.2 High Performer Turnover Costs

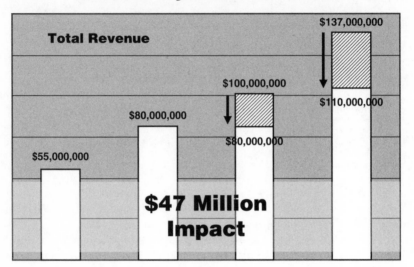

one out of five rated it their number one issue, despite the economic downturn. In my 30 or so years in this field, I have watched talent retention ebb and flow as an issue, most often tied to economic cycles. When unemployment is high, employers lose far fewer people. When unemployment is low, companies struggle to retain their best talent, and in some really competitive markets, to retain *any* talent. Regardless of the vagaries of the economy, the reality is that the same components of People Equity are operating during all cycles, with the distinction being that in some cycles people leave (mentally) while staying on the job. Of course, in robust labor markets, employees are tempted to head for greener pastures. Both of these situations spell reduced productivity for the organization.

So, while talent retention may be less of an issue during weak economic cycles, it is critical for organizations to understand and measure the same factors that drive retention or turnover during strong economic times. Many of the experts that we interviewed for the book have been through numerous economic downturns, and stated that how organizations manage their people during the recent economic malaise will be a major factor in retaining employees once the economy improves. As Dr. Richard Vosburgh, the former senior vice president for human resources of Mirage Resorts for MGM Mirage put it, "It is easy to turn the spigot off in non-people intensive functions, but to do so with people-intensive departments has a dramatic impact on culture." He describes the rapid downsizing of the 2001 recession and how hard it was to build back the necessary talent when conditions improved. Jeff Marcus, vice president and corporate controller, who has served in key roles in strategy, human resources, information technology and finance for the Federal Reserve Bank of Chicago, said, "The problem with cutting back too much is that it often puts at risk the future well-being of an organization."

Managing Retention

There are a number of factors that should be considered in any talent retention strategy in this new turbulent global economy. While there are myriad books and articles on the subject, this chapter focuses specifically on the role of People Equity in managing retention, especially for the pivotal roles and A-list players.

- What is the business impact of turnover?
- What level of retention is best for your organization? How much turnover is healthy?
- What are the drivers of retention—factors we can control?
- What is the cost-benefit of corrective action?
- How do we get good data to make decisions?
- What pre-emptive actions should we take—why wait for employees to leave?

Retention or Turnover?

Before proceeding further, we should address one commonly held myth.

Definition Myth

Turnover is the flip side of retention.

When viewed as how many stay rather than the inverse, how many leave, the concepts are not much different. Beyond that broad generalization, however, there are substantial differences in how they play out in our thinking, measurement, and decision making. Retention typically implies more about what is controllable and desirable, while turnover frequently mixes controllable and uncontrollable, desirable and undesirable. Retention is a more proactive concept, "How will we retain these people?" while turnover is more reactive, "Who left and why?" In the next sections, some of the implications will become more apparent.

The field has shifted from the gross management and measurement of turnover to more select management and measurement of retention. This shift allows for making finer distinctions about how successful an organization is at managing and retaining its most important talent. For a medical or pharmaceutical firm, a measure of the retention of Distinguished Scientists, a term reserved for their elite cadre of scientists, might be far more important than an overall measure of organizational, or even research and development, turnover.

The turnover-retention distinction leads us to think about retention in a more strategic way. What is the level of retention that is imperative to our business success for different job groups (or subgroups like the distinguished scientist) or even key individuals? Which job groups make or break the business model? Which job groups are most vulnerable to competition or scarcity? Even during bankruptcy, United Airlines carefully focused on the retention of its A players.[3]

Impact of Retention on Key Business Results

While we often think about turnover or retention as the final state in the employee life cycle, it should also be viewed as an important driver and leading indicator of important business outcomes. There are many studies that have demonstrated the link of turnover to customer satisfaction, quality, operating effectiveness, and financial performance.

These relationships are enhanced, and strategically even more important, in certain scenarios. While most customers expect to see changing faces at their local gas station, they are less comfortable with employee churn at their bank. They want loan officers, and even tellers, with whom they can establish a relationship. Even in highly transactional businesses, arguably with lower customer expectations, such as quick serve restaurants, retention influences customers. A study of Burger King revealed that high turnover led to longer wait times, lower sales, and lower profits.[4]

Retention also can be important in quality outcomes. More employee turnover often means quality gaps for a variety of reasons: lost knowledge of customer expectations, productivity disruption issues, or other factors that go into perfect order fulfillment. And in the growing service sector, people are the service delivery mechanism.

Not surprisingly, turnover has financial implications, some direct and some indirect. There are the direct costs of hiring and training replacement employees, but there are also the indirect costs and potential revenue that is compromised when relationships are broken or when quality glitches increase and productivity is lowered during such transitions. The true cost of turnover is rarely understood or even calculated in most organizations, but our analyses and case studies suggest that it is almost always substantially higher than what is believed. For more information, examples, and formulas for calculating the real cost of turnover and retention, see **reinventingtalentmanagement.com**.

What Level of Retention Is Appropriate?

What Goldilocks said in her fabled foray with the bears, "This is too much. This is too little. And this, is just right," may well be words of wisdom for today's executives. While most managers' knee-jerk reaction is to minimize turnover, zero turnover is both unhealthy and unrealistic. According to Professors Levin and Rosse,[5] even assuming the best selection techniques, organizations are still likely to have 20 percent or more error rates or misfits— for most organizations, it is closer to 40 percent or higher!

For firms operating in weak labor markets, turnover may be quite low and therefore ignored, but that may be a mistake! There are risks:

- Turnover can be too low, creating insular environments that are resistant to needed innovation, adaptability, and talent upgrades to remain competitive. Said one executive "We need new blood, whether we like it or not."
- High retention of the wrong players. We worked with an electric utility a number of years ago that prided itself on low turnover, yet the organization contained many weak performers and misaligned employees. While turnover costs were not high, lost productivity costs were significant.
- Victims of market blind spots. As one executive put it, "We believed our own messaging for too long; we were not receiving any disconfirming feedback through our high-tenured employees." There was an over-confidence of knowing what they needed.

Right Sizing Retention

Granted, some amount of turnover is healthy. The question is, how much? The answer depends on the strategy, the industry, and the geography. There are many sources of comparative turnover data by industry, geography, or job groups.[6] The Society for Human Resource Management, for example, provides data on annual voluntary turnover rates.

It may be useful, however, to go back to your business strategy and key issues raised throughout the book:

- What are your key roles? Who are your A-list players? For these roles, the focus on retention should most likely be far greater.
- How competitive is this talent market? When it is tight, you will need to redouble your efforts.
- Will a particular retention rate provide enough stability for knowledge transfer, inculcating core values of your culture in new hires, and meeting customer requirements?

- Will your turnover rate provide enough room for new talent and new views?
- How do your turnover rates compare to those competing for the same talent?

With a firmer understanding of what the strategic role of retention or turnover is, and its potential impact on your organization, let's turn to the factors that drive retention or turnover, so that it can be managed more effectively.

What are the Drivers of Retention and Turnover?

There has been considerable research done to identify the primary drivers of retention or turnover, well beyond the scope of this book. Peter Hom, Professor of Management at Arizona State University, a leading researcher in this area suggests some of the following predictors of retention or turnover based on the literature in this area:

- Overall job and work satisfaction
- Organization commitment
- Quality of the leader and member relationship
- Clarity of role
- Person-to-job fit—how well the individual's skills and interests are matched to the job requirements
- Level of conflict (this could be conflict within or across groups)
- The extent to which one is embedded in the community, such as social, religious, hobby, or political activities
- Job search intentions

Dr. Hom and others have also factored in the influence of available alternatives, which diminish in poor economic climates and increase in booming economies. The other key factor is the market perception cost of switching jobs. For example, frequent job changers might become less attractive, thus making it harder for them to move at a particular time. Some leaders, such as Dr. Vosburgh who has played a key HR role at organizations as different as MGM Mirage, Hewlett-Packard, and PepsiCo, tell us not to forget some of the fundamental tenets that date back to Maslow's needs hierarchy,[7] which identified some of the basic needs that people value. Dr. Vosburgh enumerated numerous retention drivers that "help keep them in the house":

- Job security
- A safe working environment
- Competitive compensation and benefits

- Culture and work unit that meets their affiliation needs
- Work flexibility
- Interesting work
- Decision-making opportunities
- Growth and ability to get ahead

Some of the research points to different causes based on job group, economy, or situation, but one theme comes through loud and clear: The supervisor or immediate manager is a major factor. It is often said that people join an organization but quit their manager, and that is supported by the research.

In the early 1980s, Morgan and Schiemann[8] pointed to the supervisor as a major driver of performance and retention based on a large employee database.[9] Many good, scientific studies[10] show that there are a variety of supervisory characteristics—many of them Engagement drivers—that seem to influence retention (see Table 12.2). Some of the research has discussed how these factors

Table 12.2
Frequent Drivers of Employee Turnover

Alignment	Capabilities	Engagement
• Fuzzy Future	• Lack of information or resources	• Job and organization satisfaction
• Supervisor-subordinate misalignment	• Talent mismatch: – Insufficient skills or training – Overqualified for role	• Organizational commitment
• Role ambiguity	• Shortage of employees or talent in unit	• Interesting and challenging work
• Reward mismatches	• Lack of innovation	• Low trust or respect
• Silo wars, often creating role conflict	• Insufficient management support	• Unfair or inconsistent treatment of employees
• Misalignment with customers and market	• Poor growth or learning opportunities	• Low tolerance for diversity
• Values and style misalignment		• Insufficient recognition
• Alignment of personal needs with organizational requirements (for example flexibility)		• Low job security or safety • Poor communication

cause the employee to withdraw from the workplace. Some employees leave mentally before they leave physically. Some never leave but essentially retire in place. As we discussed in an earlier chapter, many of these Engagement drivers not only affect retention, but also satisfaction, wellness, and productivity.

While Engagement—along with its drivers—is a dominant People Equity factor influencing retention, Alignment and Capabilities also play a role. Table 12.2 illustrates how there are other drivers besides Engagement that influence turnover.

The Alignment drivers of turnover often include:

- *Fuzzy future.* Company has no clear or understandable direction.
- *Supervisor-subordinate misalignment.* When reporting relationships are at odds, this leads to conflict, stress, inappropriate behaviors, and ultimately turnover.
- *Role ambiguity.* Lack of Alignment of organization direction with department or individual goals, often created by frequently changing goals or priorities or management conflict.
- *Reward mismatches.* When rewards are not connected to performance, or to some form of rational standards, employees lose faith that there is logic to how they will be rewarded.
- *Silo wars.* Interfunction conflict is debilitating over time, like a slow disease.
- *Misalignment with customers and market.* Sales and other customer contact people will quickly recognize areas in which the organization and its customers are out of sync. These employees will at first share their frustrations with many other employees, and ultimately depart out of frustration that the organization—and they—are unlikely to be successful.
- *Values and style differences.* When the gaps are too large to bridge, or the values so fundamentally different, employees tend to opt out. This is an area that should be vetted thoroughly in the hiring process.
- *Alignment of personal needs with organizational requirements.* Employees often need flexibility or schedules that allow them to meet other obligations, such as family care, education, or other matters. When these clash, and there are other alternatives available, an employee has a higher propensity to leave.

The Alignment retention drivers usually play a bigger role with more seasoned employees and rarely send people packing during their honeymoon period. Less-tenured employees may not have had time to become jaded, and will at first try to improve the situation, but if Alignment gaps are left unaddressed, these employees too will falter and depart.

The Capabilities dimension of People Equity is also a factor in controllable retention. Some of the Capabilities drivers that we see most frequently include:

- *Lack of information or resources.* One of the factors mentioned frequently in interviews with former and current employees is a lack of tools to be successful in their job. This can range from basic job tools to information promised to customers (internal stakeholders or external customers).
- *Insufficient training and skills.* While most employees will not say they didn't have the skills to succeed, they will point to factors that may indicate insufficient training or knowledge. Some of our interviews and surveys with former employees and current high-risk (of leaving) employees point to training programs that didn't provide sufficient product or market knowledge, or job know-how. Others say their departments did not have the abilities or training to meet customer expectations.
- *Shortage of employees or talent.* A frequent lament is "There are not enough employees." This is where we have found employee surveys to be very useful. Questions relating to having sufficient employees to get the work done effectively often receive relatively low endorsement scores; when we find units that are substantially below those norms, it is a cause for concern, and often a predictor of stress, work-family issues, and frustration, which can be drivers of turnover. The shortage lament may also be fomented by having insufficient talent—not people; it is not just quantity but quality of talent that can create this gap.
- *Lack of innovation.* While this driver does not come up frequently, it can play a key role in situations where employees have joined the company expecting a high innovation environment. In high technology firms or research and development units, for example, we find employees who have left because of poor technology or an environment that does not foster innovation—an important value for them.
- *Management support.* While this may seem Engagement related, when comments are directed at higher management or management in general, it often is a Capabilities issue. For example, in interviews with employees in the food industry, many employees described their departing co-workers as very frustrated with the lack of management support for the department, or the inability of their more immediate management to secure higher-level support for their operation. This situation is normally coupled with resources, tools, and staffing and other forms of shortage, but the root cause may be leaders who cannot effectively sell the units upstairs, or being in a unit that does not receive much support from higher leadership.

- *Poor growth or learning opportunities.* One reason employees move on is they feel they cannot continue to grow with their organization. Because of limited roles or lack of organizational support for the development of new skills, employees may feel that they are stagnating and need to move on.

The Capabilities area can affect both new and more tenured employees. Some simply get weary over time, while in other cases, recent hires quickly become disenchanted with what they see compared to their expectations at hire.

While the factors in Table 12.2 push people out the door when they fall below expectations, there are a smaller set of factors that create high inward pull. These are the factors that often keep people, even during difficult times:

- Alignment factors:
  - Strong affinity to the values or mission of the organization or an inspiring leader
  - Distinctly attractive rewards for good performance (particularly important for high-achievement employees and the A-list players).
- Capabilities factors:
  - Strong growth and learning opportunities, usually supported by strong training
  - Innovative or exciting work environment; exciting tools or technology to use (more so in high technology roles and organizations)
- Engagement factors:
  - Supervisor who gives recognition, is fair, communicates clearly, is ethical, and whom I can trust; someone who brings out the best in her subordinates
  - Particularly strong compensation and benefits (for example, health care that would be hard to replace in another organization)
  - Co-workers with whom I like to work (often described as a family)
  - Job security, especially for low risk individuals

Tools for Identifying the Drivers of Retention

Best Practice

The most effective tools to help understand and address retention-related issues with the current workforce include:

- Ongoing employee surveys of the entire workforce.

- Interim spot pulse surveys of targeted groups (for example, high performance groups undergoing disruption or economically risky areas such as those with low unemployment rates).
- Focus groups across job groups, especially the *A* roles discussed earlier.
- Interviews with samples of employees, especially targeted A-list players.
- Informal management–employee discussion sessions (for example, 10-on-1 breakfast meetings), where senior leaders get skip-level communication about issues that concern employees. These meetings often have the early warning indicators of future retention issues, if you read the tea leaves correctly.

An employee survey can identify those likely to stay or leave by asking about their intentions to leave—one of the best predictors of actual turnover. With a follow-up question on their reasons, it is possible to identify drivers of retention and turnover. In the example in Figure 12.3 from a study of 40 diverse companies, the top three reasons mentioned by those who said they plan to stay also includes the number one reason for leaving given by people who plan to leave: about 50 percent of each group cite their manager. That is a clear signal of variation in supervisory skill levels.

FIGURE 12.3   Reasons for Intentions to Stay or Leave an Organization

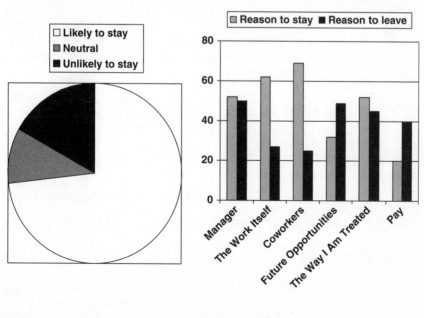

The determination or identification of the most powerful drivers requires some advanced modeling techniques, which is beyond the scope of this book.

What Is the Cost-Benefit of Fixing Retention or Turnover Gaps?

We now know what the risks of turnover are, including estimates of the cost impact, and we know the drivers that would need to be addressed to bring retention back in line with our strategic goals for particular job groups. But not all gaps are worth fixing.

For example (see Figure 12.4), in the high turnover quick-serve industry described earlier in this book (see Jack in the Box described in Chapter 6), we found a strong relationship between intentions to stay and actual turnover (−.54), and a moderately strong relationship between A, C, and E and intentions to stay (.37 to .45),[11] meaning that if you can improve your A, C, or E scores, you increase employees' intention to stay. If company executives were to improve the intention-to-stay ratings by 10 percentage points, the turnover rate would decrease by 5.4 percentage points, which translates to $1.9 million in annual savings just in direct replacement costs. Fully loaded with indirect and intangible costs, the savings would be significantly higher.

This organization then needs to determine how much it would be worth investing to reduce this cost. Perhaps a supervisory training program aimed at improving the C scores in units with the gaps would cost $100,000 and be expected to close one-half of the turnover gap—a savings of about $1 million in direct replacement costs alone. Depending on the cost of capital and other factors, the organization would need to decide if the $100,000 investment would be worth the return of at least a $1 million in savings.

FIGURE 12.4 Jack in the Box Linkage Analysis

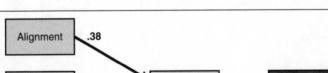

Getting Good Data

High-performance organizations often use more scientific approaches to identify the root causes of employee retention. This entails doing away with a common myth.

Exit Interview Myth:

Exit interviews provide us with the true causes of turnover.

Rarely do exit interviews provide the full picture and in many cases they mask the root causes, often diverting time and energy to Band-Aid solutions. The problem we find with exit interviews or other termination data-capturing mechanisms is that they are often 50 percent wrong. If you are like the majority of people that we have interviewed on the subject, you rarely burn bridges with prior employers and bosses. Where will your next references come from?

We have found far more accurate information instead from surveying and interviewing former employees. After the dust has settled, you are more likely to hear the real scoop. For example, Home Depot has found that about one-half of the losses of departing employees could have been avoided.[12]

Why Wait for Them to Leave?

While separated employees provide one important source of information, they may not represent the complete profile of what keeps many of your current employees.

Best Practice

A best practice step that strategic leaders are taking to understand retention or turnover drivers is to carefully assess their current workforce—especially the A-list players—for factors that both attract and repel them. The best tool for this is an employee retention-focused survey, coupled with in-depth interviews or focus groups with key players. In our surveys, we prefer to use the People Equity model coupled with some dedicated questions on retention issues, enabling us to identify 90 percent or more of the major issues that typically drive retention or turnover.

When coupled with the findings from prior employees, and analyzed by performance levels, this process is very powerful in identifying the primary retention (and productivity) risk factors.

Summary of Key Learning Points

- Turnover—especially top talent—is expensive. Period!
- Most firms underestimate the true costs of turnover in their organizations.
- Recessionary periods are dangerous because talent that is off-Alignment, Capabilities, and Engagement tends to remain in place.
- Treatment of people during down economies often sets the stage for who will remain when the next growth period occurs.
- Retention is not simply the inverse of turnover.
- The biggest risks are high retention of the wrong players and low retention of the right. Focus first on your top performers in A-list roles.
- Employee retention and turnover drive quality, customer loyalty, and financial performance.
- Beware of turnover that is too low!
- Exit interviews are notoriously inaccurate; opt to survey former employees.
- Capture and promote those aspects of the work environment that former employees regret losing.
- Carefully assess your current workforce—especially the A-list players—for factors that both attract and repel them.

Action Tips: What Can I Do Tomorrow?

- Assess the potential impact of turnover to your organization.
  - What is the impact on customers? Financial performance? Co-workers?
  - Have you translated the turnover into real cost numbers, including direct and indirect costs? Consider the following costs: Recruitment program costs; interviewing and testing; training; onboarding; managerial and peer time; productivity ramp-up.
  - Are talent-retention measures on your organization scorecard? Your HR scorecard?
- Determine your success in retaining A-list performers.
  - Do you know the turnover and retention rates of top performers? Among employees in pivotal roles?

- Has the organization been able to replace weak performers with high-producing individuals?
- Assess your turnover rate compared to the competition and the marketplace?
  - Search for your state and industry using Job Openings and Labor Turnover Survey (JOLTS) on the web site for the Bureau of Labor Statistics (bls.gov/jlt/).
  - Conduct more detailed research to gain a sharper comparison with companies having a similar strategy to your organization's strategy.
- Identify the causes of turnover in your organization. Here are immediate steps to take:
  - Don't rely only on the information gathered during the exit interviews. Find a neutral third party to interview former employees.
  - Conduct an employee-retention-focused survey to pinpoint actionable data.
  - For more qualitative information, have a third party conduct in-depth interviews or a focus group with the key players in the organization.
- Conduct cost-benefit analyses to determine which actions will have a positive payback.

The Road Ahead

Reinventing talent management is an urgent task for today's senior executives. In looking back at the preceding chapters, we distill five core principles from our research, which we hope will help you look ahead with greater confidence as you proceed to the talent reinvention task.

1. The People Equity framework—Alignment, Capabilities, and Engagement—is essential as a way of thinking about and measuring the reservoir of talent in organizations, evaluating the impact of our talent management practices, focusing human capital investments, enhancing leader capabilities in managing people, and increasing employee fulfillment.

2. Keep the talent management discussion strategically focused. Strategy is not only directional, defining where we are going, it also lays out a framework for getting there. Strategy is a holistic concept that guides interactions within an organization and makes possible Alignment to a larger set of goals. Functional groups such as Human Resources enhance their stature by thinking about the organization more strategically for how they best add value. In so doing, the talent plans that evolve become a central support for the organization's strategy and competitive advantage rather than peripheral to its future growth and success.

3. Contextualize your talent management plans. We started this book with a review of important trends that are taking place globally and locally. Many of these trends will affect the way we achieve the most value in our talent management practices. Talent management practices must match the world in which your organization operates. Otherwise, you will be unable to compete in the search for the talent goal or maintain the value of what you have in place.

4. Become measurement managed. It is impossible to manage talent without the right measures of key business outcomes, ACE, and the drivers and enablers of ACE. The right strategic talent measures will:
   - Create focus
   - Serve as leading indicators of important outcomes
   - Enable you to determine the level of impact of various investments
   - Provide the information for making important decisions
   - Help identify the controllable drivers of performance, retention, and customer and financial outcomes
   - Provide a shared language for communicating goals, workforce health, and other key talent imperatives
5. Develop talent plans that forge common ground between the goals of the organization and those of the individual. Win-win is the best outcome. Using the ACE model as a point of departure, ask:
   - Are organizational and personal goals aligned? If not, are they adjustable to find fit? Are we attracting talent that is likely to be aligned with our vision, values, and goals?
   - Are we investing in the talent growth of our people? Will that provide a payback to the organization? Will it create a more capable individual or team that is stronger in its talent than before they joined the organization? Did we help them build a better resume?
   - Are we finding ways to extract the best motivation of our people? Are they fully engaged in our mission? Are they excited to join their colleagues in the organizational quest each day? Do the vision, values, and policies excite them to go the extra mile?

These precepts are the basis for thinking about the various stages of talent management, even before new talent arrives and continuing after some talent is gone. We hope this framework has both provided some innovative thinking as well as some back-to-basics actions that are simply not getting implemented well.

Talent Management Challenge

With these principles firmly in mind, the question becomes: where to get started? Begin by taking the following Talent Management Challenge. We suggest assembling a team within your organization composed of the key players responsible for talent management. Use the questions posed here as the basis for the initial discussion of the quality and effectiveness of your organization's approach to managing talent. Based on your organization's maturity in this area, you may wish to select a subset of questions that will help stretch your organization to the next level. Incidentally, the questions presume that the overall business strategy and talent strategy are clear. If this is not the case, then strategy design and strategy mapping should be your first agenda item!

External Influences

1. How well are you balancing the close-to-home economic and industry challenges with the need to maintain worker knowledge and engagement in the near future?
2. How long will it be before the global shifts and challenges described in Chapter 1 affect your existing business model?
   - Which of the 10 trends are already affecting your organization?
   - Which of the trends may have the most significant long-term effect on your talent management strategy and plans?
   - How would you rate your organization currently in preparedness?

Staffing the *A* Positions

3. How well have you defined the pivotal or A-list positions—those roles that make or break your business strategy?
4. Will enough A-list talent be available to fill key roles within your strategic time horizon?
   - Are most A or pivotal roles currently staffed with A-list talent?
   - Is talent being developed internally so it will be ready when needed?
   - Does that talent know it is being groomed, so you don't lose it?
   - If talent will need to be secured in the marketplace, what will it cost in the next two years? In the next five years?

Performance Standards

5. Are roles designed in such a way that it is clear what high Alignment, Capabilities, and Engagement would look like?
   - What behaviors would you expect of high ACE employees? Of low ACE employees?
   - Are there clear ways to identify and measure A-list talent?
6. Are people held accountable for both the *What* and the *How* described in the book?
   - Are strong performers tolerated when they violate corporate or social norms, such as values statements or operating principles? Would most of your employees agree?

- Does the organization have an effective way to deal with chronic poor performers?

Measurement

7. Is the organization-measurement managed?
   - Do you know which employee drivers are most important in achieving financial, quality, or customer objectives?
   - Have you translated these measures into monetary value?
8. Is there a process for measuring how well talent has been optimized?
   - Do you have a way to measure the Alignment, Capabilities, and Engagement of your people? Does your employee survey capture Alignment, Capabilities, and Engagement dimensions, so that you can balance and prioritize actions that will have the greatest impact on people and performance?
   - Is the measurement linked to the organization's people and strategic (or balanced) scorecards?
9. Are there effective ways to measure the nine Drivers and Enablers of People Equity—the factors that you can control? Have you conducted linkage analyses to understand which Drivers and Enablers are most important?

Alignment

10. What percentage of talent is highly Aligned with your vision, mission, brand, goals, and customers?
    - Do employees understand and support the company strategy and direction? Are there good measures of this that can be tracked on a regular basis?
    - Are individual goals clear, specific, measurable, and accepted?
11. Do employees receive frequent feedback that helps them to improve their performance?
12. Are rewards directly connected to employee or organizational performance?

Capabilities

13. Are customers' (or stakeholders') requirements and expectations sufficiently understood? Are there measures in place to capture those expectations?
14. Does the organization have the right Capabilities—talent, information, and resources—to delight customers or stakeholders?

- Do employees have the knowledge, skills, experiences, and abilities to meet customers' expectations and increase perceived value?
- Do employees have the information—customer or product knowledge, process information, relevant databases—they need at the moment of truth to meet customer expectations?
- Do employees have sufficient resources—tools, equipment, working conditions—to meet customer expectations?

Engagement

15. What percentage of the workforce is highly Engaged in the mission of the organization?
    - What behaviors do they exhibit differently from lower Engaged people?
16. Is Engagement training provided for all new managers or coaches who have a responsibility for leading others?
17. Are managers held accountable for obtaining high Engagement (scores) in the units they manage?
18. If using other outsourced labor resources, do you measure the Engagement of those units?
19. Do employees rate your organization highly because it throws lots of benefits and perks at them or because your organization has created a two-way bond with them?

Talent Acquisition

20. Is the talent acquisition process effective in screening and selecting talent, especially A-list talent?
    - Is the talent selection process designed to screen out the improbable candidates early in the process?
    - Does the talent selection process put sufficient effort at screening for likely Alignment and Engagement of potential candidates?
    - Has your organization developed validated selection processes that can demonstrate the impact of using that process compared to random selection?

Acculturation

21. Does your organization do a great job of maximizing the fragile acculturation of the onboarding stage?
    - Are there frequent measures and planned interventions during the early stages of employment—day one, week one, month one, quarter one?

- Is there a clear process to intervene if the employee is signaling poor Alignment, Capabilities, or Engagement?
- Are managers trained to handle this fragile period effectively?

Development

22. Are development plans preloaded quickly after hire, or for *A* roles, perhaps even before Day One?
    - Are most employees aware of the development plans and their role in development?
    - Do supervisors or managers have clear expectations regarding their role in employee development?
    - How well they are executing against expectations?
23. Does your organization take leader development seriously?
    - Are there clear leader standards and competencies?
    - Is development in those competencies monitored?
    - Are leader development paths clear?

Retention

24. How good is your organization at keeping its A-list talent?
    - Do A players feel special in terms of how they are recognized, rewarded, and developed?
    - Are managers equipped to coach and accelerate A-list players into other roles?
25. Does your organization have clear definitions of what employee turnover or retention means?
    - Are there meaningful measures of turnover or retention that are tracked and reported regularly?
    - Are there clear retention targets for different roles and locations?
    - Are those targets and actual numbers broken out separately for A-list roles versus others?
26. Does your organization have effective processes to identify why talent stays or leaves?
    - Have you identified the major causes for turnover in your organization, especially in A-list roles?
    - Has your organization overcome the perennial problem of poor information from exit interviews? Do you assess former employees?
    - Have you calculated the cost of reducing key turnover or increasing the retention of high performers?

- Is this information linked to the ACE model in a way that enables you to prioritize improvements?

Resource Allocation

27. Do you have a process for strategically prioritizing the most important talent gaps in Alignment, Capabilities, or Engagement so that your resources are not diluted across too many initiatives?
28. Are initiatives linked with the element of the business or people strategy that they are intended to positively affect?

Technology

29. Has your organization leveraged technology as an effective tool for enhancing talent management?
30. Is data mining used as a way of understanding talent issues more effectively, such as the talent drivers of performance, retention, or customer loyalty?
    - Have you tried to mine the power of formal and informal work, professional, and social networks?
    - Has such information been used for identifying performance blockers, development needs, and succession requirements?
    - Has your organization been able to effectively leverage the time and capabilities of your talent through the use of virtual tools: meetings, educational sessions, interviews, orientation, and other virtual applications?

In Closing

There is a revolution around us. The world is surely different today from what it was even six months ago. Ultimately, people create change, which is why during times of churn and dislocation, effectively managing talent becomes an imperative of the highest strategic importance. These changes are exciting and bode well for those who survive in this new marketplace. It will place people squarely in the center of profitability and mission, and those who can grasp a role in shaping, guiding, or leading talent have an opportunity to not only make a major difference (my idea of fun and reward!), but they will also have a premier role to play in the organization of the future.

There is an urgent need to get started. Why not do so now? With the ACE model firmly in hand, begin to assess, measure, and deploy your human resources so that you maximize Alignment, Capabilities, and Engagement. Do so, and you bring maximum value to your organization and the customers it serves.

Appendix

EXERCISE: IMPACT OF TRENDS ON YOUR TALENT MANAGEMENT

Please review the following 10 trends that are influencing talent decisions in organizations. For each trend, use the worksheet template to identify which trends are having an impact on your organization, the likely impact, and potential actions that may prove helpful in preparing for or addressing the impact of the particular trend.

Trend 1. Global Competition. With global barriers coming down and technological reach expanding, there are far more suppliers offering more products than customers can consume. Many businesses will depend on their ability to find a unique value they can provide and sustain in a marketplace characterized by new forms of competition and a far greater number of competitors.

Trend 2. A Change in Labor Supply and Demand. In 2005, labor supply and demand curves have crossed. In aggregate, there was an insufficient number of people to fill the number of jobs that were required to fuel current needs, not to mention future growth. In 2008, a recession led to the downsizing of workers in many areas, creating other imbalances. Nonetheless, there continue to be shortages in certain occupations, industries, and locales.

Trend 3. Uneven Distribution of Talent. Niche shortages are likely to appear in the near term. In some places, like Hawaii, jobs such as nursing, and industries like high tech and energy have been struggling to find the right talent for many years. Emerging industries like green technology are desperately seeking talent in fields like wind and solar power, bioecology, marine food harvesting, and clean energy.

Trend 4. Managing diverse workforces in diverse places. Demographic trends also will change substantially the look and behavior of our workforce. Organizations progressively employ individuals all over the world (various religions, languages, nationalities, races, and so on). Generational differences are a specific form of diversity that will challenge current and future leaders.

Trend 5. Skill and Mind Shifts. Skilled jobs are being automated or deployed to lower-cost locations, and critical remaining ones will need to be staffed and managed in different ways. A large number of emerging job opportunities will include roles and tasks that are not capable of being reengineered or outsourced abroad—tasks requiring innovation, artistry, complex decision making, in-person services, and so forth.

Trend 6. Technology. Much progress has taken place over the past decade in the development of better human resources databases that allow organizations for the first time to connect demographic information with performance data, customer ratings, benefit preferences, safety, and a host of other important information.

Trend 7. Leadership Succession Gaps. Many organizations are already suffering from a lack of top leadership talent, and this gap will only increase in the upcoming years. The heightened level of competition for talent will be a great advantage for free agents, but will prove increasingly cost prohibitive for organizations and their shareholders.

Trend 8. The costs of talent mistakes are growing. As strategic talent becomes scarcer in many industries and jobs, and as human capital becomes a larger portion of overall corporate assets in many industries, the cost of talent mistakes is more important to the bottom line. The quality of selection processes, onboarding, training, developing, and coaching talent will be crucial to retaining it.

Trend 9. Paucity of Human Capital Measures. Many organizations are lacking the people measures on their balance sheets. Measures that do exist for an organization's talent are often tactical and rearview metrics that do not adequately capture the value of the workforce. To manage talent well, leaders will need to understand how to measure it.

Trend 10. Low Readiness for Change. Few organizations are prepared for the talent gaps (and in some cases gluts) that are around the corner, and fewer still have carefully determined which jobs are strategically critical.

Worksheet

This worksheet is also available online at reinventingtalentmanagement.com.

Definitions

Likelihood. Please indicate the likelihood that the trend is having an impact on your organization.

1 = Very Unlikely

2 = Somewhat Unlikely

3 = Somewhat Likely

4 = Very Likely

Affected job categories. Please list departments, business units, or job categories that are most likely to be affected by this trend.

Impact on organization. What would be the likely impact on your organization? Examples: loss of top performers, hard-to-find replacement talent, low productivity, customer dissatisfaction.

Action and resources. What action can you take now to prepare for or to respond to this trend?

- Whose buy-in will be needed to take actions?
- What resources are needed to address this issue? (departments, key players, and tools you will need to reach a solution)

IMPACT OF CURRENT TRENDS

Trend	Likelihood	Affected Job Categories	Impact on Organization	Action and Resources
1. Global competition				
2. Change in labor supply and demand				
3. Uneven distribution of talent				
4. Managing diverse workforces in diverse places				
5. Skill and mind shifts				
6. Technology shifts				
7. Leadership succession gaps				
8. Growing costs of talent mistakes				
9. Paucity of human capital measures				
10. Low readiness for change				

Notes

Chapter 1

1. The company and employees names have been disguised to protect confidentiality.
2. *Wall Street Journal* (2009). "GM Sales Fell 11% in '08; Toyota Takes Crown," January 22, 2009.
3. Erickson, Tamara J. (2005) "Engaging Both Heart and Mind: The Coming Crisis of the Changing Workforce," presented at the SHRM Foundation Thought Leaders Retreat, September 2005.
4. Pink, Daniel H. (2005). *A Whole New Mind*. New York: The Penguin Group.
5. Schiemann, William (2007). "Measuring and Managing the ROI of Human Capital," *Cost Management*, July/August 2007.
6. Rust, Roland T., Katherine N. Lemon and Valarie A. Zeithaml (2001). "Driving Customer Equity: Linking Customer Lifetime Value to Strategic Marketing Decisions," *Marketing Science Institute Working Paper Series*, No. 01-108.
7. Gale, Bradley T. (1994) *Managing Customer Value: Creating Quality and Service That Customers Can See*, New York: The Free Press.
8. We actually found scores of employee variables that had been demonstrated to connect to outcomes such as turnover, productivity, quality, and customer satisfaction. However, in reviewing many of those employee predictor variables, it appears that the way in which they predict is to increase Alignment, Capabilities and Engagement of employees, which then in turn drive the important outcomes such as customer satisfaction.
9. Schiemann, William (2006), "People Equity: A New Paradigm for Measuring and Managing Human Capital," *Human Resource Planning*, 29.1, April 2006.
10. Schiemann, William (2005), "Measuring Return on Human Capital: Build the Equity of Your People," *Leadership Excellence*, Volume 22, No. 8, August 2005, p. 19.

Chapter 2

1. As quoted in Ram Charan and Geoffrey Colvin, "Why CEOs Fail," *Fortune Magazine*, (June 21, 1999), 69.

251

2. As quoted in J. H. Stronge, H. B. Richard, and N. Catano, *Qualities of Effective Principals* (Alexandria, Va.: Association for Supervision and Curriculum Development, 2008).
3. Edward E. Lawler III, *Talent: Making People Your Competitive Advantage* (San Francisco: John Wiley & Sons, Inc., 2008).
4. In this book, we will usually refer to them as *stakeholders*, as some critics are concerned that the use of *customer* will distract people from the true external customer who pays the bills.
5. J. T. Kostman and William Schiemann, "People Equity: The Hidden Driver of Quality," *Quality Progress*, (May 2005), 37–42.
6. Jerry Seibert and John Lingle, "Internal Customer Service: Has It Improved?" *Quality Progress*, (March 2007), 35–40.
7. William J. Feuss, Joel Harmon, Jeana Wirtenberg, and Jeffrey W. Wides, "Linking Employees, Customers, and Financial Performance in Organizations," *Cost Management*, 19(2) (January/February 2004): 12–22.
8. Roland T. Rust, Katherine N. Lemon, and Valarie A. Zeithaml, op. cit.
9. Actually, the number of profiles depends on whether you simply rate each dimension high or low. In practice, it often is more informative to divide scores into high, medium, and low, which results in 27 different profiles. The high profiles are the most telling in terms of strengths and weaknesses, as will be described in Chapter 4.

Chapter 3

1. Michael Treacy and Fred Wiersema, *The Discipline of Market Leaders* (Reading, Mass.: Addison-Wesley Publishing Company, 1995).
2. It is unclear whether the three that are articulated are the only major differentiators, but clearly there are a number of factors that appear to differentiate successful businesses within the same industry.
3. It should be noted that firms rarely have a "pure" version of any single strategy; rather, most use a combination of strategies or have different divisions or product groups that may have purer versions of a single differentiating strategy.
4. As explicated by:

   Brian Morgan and William Schiemann, *Supervision in the '80s: Trends in Corporate America, A Human Resource Strategy Report*, Opinion Research Corporation (1984).

   Marcus Buckingham and Curt Coffman, *First, Break All the Rules: What the World's Greatest Managers Do Differently* (New York: Simon and Schuster, 1999).

   James K. Harter, Frank L. Schmidt, and Theodore L. Hayes, "Business-Unit Level Relationship Between Employee Satisfaction, Employee Engagement and Business Outcomes: A Meta-Analysis," *Journal of Applied Psychology* 8 (2) (2002): 268–279.
5. Some organizations are beginning to refer to this role as a coach, and using a coaching model for their managers.

Chapter 4

1. William Schiemann, "Measuring and Managing the ROI of Human Capital," op. cit.

2. Bradley T. Gale, op. cit.
3. Such as the Kuder Occupational Interest Inventory (KOIS) and Strong Campbell Interest and Skill Survey (CISS).
4. Actually, a short form can capture People Equity and many of the drivers and enablers with fewer than 25 items.
5. The scores represent the percentage of employees who have given a particular factor (A, C, or E) a favorable rating (Strongly Agree or Agree).
6. *Strategic Research on Human Capital Challenges* (Alexandria, Va.: Society for Human Resource Management Foundation Human Capital Challenges Report, October 2007).

Section III: Optimizing Talent

1. David Ulrich and Wayne Brockbank, *The HR Value Proposition* (Boston: Harvard Business School Publishing, 2005).
2. On a scale of 1 to 100.
3. Peter Cappelli, *Talent on Demand: Managing Talent in an Age of Uncertainty* (Boston: Harvard Business School Press, 2008).

Chapter 6

1. Adapted from Schiemann, William, "Aligning Performance Management with Organizational Strategy, Values, and Goals," in *Performance Management: Putting Research into Practice*, Jim Smithers and Manny London, eds.
2. Or stakeholders if you are a non-profit.
3. As reported:
   Tom Ehrenfeld, "Drama is in the Details of HP-Compaq Merger Battle," *The Boston Globe*, March 2, 2003.
   Matthew Fordahl, "HP's Tech Record Mixed During Fiorina Years," *AP Worldstream*, February 10, 2005.
   "Fatal Error at HP," International Herald Tribune, February 12, 2005.
   "Exit Carly: Hewlett-Packard," *The Economist* (U.S.), February 12, 2005.
4. Andrew Martin, "The Happiest Meal: Hot Profits," *The New York Times*, January 11, 2009, 8.
5. Andrew Martin, ibid.
6. J. T. Kostman and William Schiemann, op. cit.
7. This is a shorter standard set of questions in the Alignment area to provide insights into the types of topics that comprise the Alignment dimension of People Equity. In practice, it is best to customize more specific questions to reflect the unique strategy and culture of that organization.
8. Sooksan Kantabutra, "Identifying Vision Realization Factors in Apparel Stores: Empirical Evidence from Australia," *International Journal of Business* 12 (4) (Fall 2007): 445–460.
9. For an elaboration of this point, see *Bullseye! Hitting Your Strategic Targets through High-Impact Measurement* (New York: The Free Press, 1999).
10. William Schiemann and John Lingle, *Bullseye! Hitting Your Strategic Targets through High-Impact Measurement* (New York: The Free Press, 1999).

Robert S. Kaplan and David P. Norton, *The Balanced Scorecard: Translating Strategy into Action* (Boston: Harvard Business School Press, 1996).

11. Mark Smith, "Sales and Operations Planning: Making BPM Work," *Business Performance Management Magazine* 6 (1) (March 2008): 4–8.

12. Elaine D. Pulakos, *Performance Management* (Alexandria, Va.: Society for Human Resource Management Foundation, Effective Practices Guidelines Series, 2004).

13. Charlie Nordblom, "Taking Measurement a Step Further at Volvo Group," *Strategic Communication Management* 12 (2) (Feb/Mar 2008): 20–23.

14. E. A. Locke and G. P. Latham, *A Theory of Goal Setting and Task Performance* (Englewood Cliffs, N.J.: Prentice-Hall, 1990).

15. David Clutterbuck, "Are You a Goal Junkie?" *Training Journal*, May 2008, 43–46.

16. Jeremy Hope and Robin Fraser, *Beyond Budgeting: How Managers Can Break Free from the Annual Performance Trap* (Boston: Harvard Business School Press, 2003).

17. Edward Liddy, "Driving Better Talent Decisions . . . That's Allstate's Stand," presented at the Human Resource Planning Society Annual Global Conference, Fort Lauderdale, Fla., April 15-18, 2007.

18. E. A. Locke and G. P. Latham, op. cit.
Manuel London, *Job Feedback* 2nd ed. (Mahwah, N.J.: Erlbaum, 2002).

19. Jerry Seibert and John Lingle, op. cit.

20. William Fitzgerald, "Forget the Form in Performance Appraisals," *HR Magazine*, 40 (12) (1995): 134–136.

21. William Schiemann and John Lingle, op. cit.

22. Robert S. Kaplan and David P. Norton, op. cit.

23. William Schiemann and John Lingle, op. cit.

24. Schiemann and Lingle discuss the process and roles of consultants and leadership teams in creating such maps *in Bullseye! Hitting Your Strategic Targets through High-Impact Measurement*.

25. Gordon Bethune, *From Worst to First: Behind the Scenes of Continental's Remarkable Comeback* (New York: John Wiley & Sons, Inc., 1999).

26. Continental Airlines had recently merged with the failing Eastern Airlines whereas Southwest Airlines started with a non-traditional approach to airline management from its inception.

27. Originally top five.

28. Since those halcyon days, Bethune has retired and Continental has slipped somewhat in on-time performance.

29. Scott McCartney, "How US Airways Vaulted to First Place," *Wall Street Journal*, July 22, 2008, D3.

Chapter 7

1. Edward E. Lawler III, op. cit.

2. James L. Heskitt, W. Earl Sasser, Jr., and Leonard A. Schlesinger, *The Service Profit Chain: How Leading Companies Link Profit and Growth to Loyalty, Satisfaction, and Value* (New York: The Free Press, 1997).

3. This is a subset of the questions in the Capabilities area to provide insights into the type of topics that comprise the Capabilities dimension of People Equity.

4. Michael Webb with Tom Gorman, *Sales and Marketing the Six Sigma Way* (New York: Kaplan Publishing, 2006).
5. John W. Boudreau and Peter M. Ramstad, *Beyond HR: The New Science of Human Capital* (Boston: Harvard Business School Press, 2007).
6. James Surowiecki, *The Wisdom of Crowds* (New York: Doubleday, 2004).
7. Edward E. Lawler III, op. cit.
8. Ibid.
9. Ibid.
10. Ibid.
11. Jack Stack and Bo Burlingham, *The Great Game of Business* (New York: Broadway Business, 1994).
12. John W. Boudreau and Peter M. Ramstad, op. cit.

Chapter 8

1. Yahoo! HotJobs, "Nearly Half of U.S. Workers are Expected to Search for a New Job in 2007," *Yahoo! HotJobs Job Satisfaction Survey,* January 3, 2007.
2. Judith Bardwick, "The Financial Case for Making a Commitment to Employees," presented at a meeting of the New York Human Resource Planning Society, October 2005.
3. Society for Human Resource Management and the *Wall Street Journal*'s CareerJournal.com, *2006 U.S. Job Retention Poll,* December 19, 2006.
4. "Understanding What Drives Employee Engagement," Towers Perrin Talent Report, (2003).
5. J. T. Kostman and William Schiemann, op. cit.
6. Towers Perrin Global Workforce Study, "2007–2008 Towers Perrin Global Workforce Study."
7. Society for Human Resource Management Foundation, "Employee Engagement and Commitment," Effective Practice Guidelines Series, 2006.
8. Society for Human Resource Management Foundation, ibid.
9. Society for Human Resource Management Foundation, ibid.
10. William H. Macey and Benjamin Schneider, "The Meaning of Employee Engagement," *Industrial and Organizational Psychology: Perspectives on Science and Practice* 1 (1) (2008): 3–30.
11. Macey and Schneider do not include satisfaction in their definition because they argue that individuals can be satiated without being energized. However, we include it as a component for several reasons. First, the two concepts are frequently highly correlated in our analyses of many organizations. Second, we have found that the absence of organizational satisfaction is a limiting factor that automatically inhibits Engagement, and while we could technically include it as a driver of Engagement, we find it more valuable for practical decision-making to include it with commitment and advocacy as a grouping of closely related concepts that are similarly predictive of important outcomes.
12. Frederick Herzberg, B. Mausner, and B. B. Snyderman, *The Motivation to Work* (New York: John Wiley & Sons, Inc., 1959).
13. J. R. Hackman and Edward E. Lawler III, "Employee Reactions to Job Characteristics," *Journal of Applied Psychology Monograph* 55 (1971): 259–286.

14. William H. Macey and Benjamin Schneider, op. cit.
15. This is a subset of the questions in the Engagement area to provide insights into the types of topics that comprise the Engagement dimension of People Equity.
16. David Sirota, Louis Mischkind, and Michael Meltzer, *The Enthusiastic Employee: How Companies Profit by Giving Workers What They Want* (Philadelphia: Wharton School of Business Publishing, 2005).
17. David Sirota, Louis Mischkind, and Michael Meltzer, ibid.

Section IV Managing the Talent Life Cycle

1. M. Huselid, B. Becker, and R. Beatty, *The Workforce Scorecard: Managing Human Capital to Execute Strategy* (Boston: Harvard Business School Press, 2005).
2. John W. Boudreau and Peter M. Ramstad, op. cit.

Chapter 9

1. Personal communication with John Dooney, December 2008.
2. Karl Ahlrichs, "Uncommon Knowledge: Align Your Strategy with Applicant Values Before They're Hired," Society for Human Resource Management, Strategy Conference, October 2007.
3. S. Zaccaro, "Executive Talent Assessment and Selection: A Literature Review," Society for Human Resource Management Foundation, Commissioned Literature Review, October 2008.
4. Organizations need to review their relevant laws to ensure that each of these practices is allowed locally.
5. Eric Greitens, Strength & Compassion (Washington, D.C.: Leading Authorities Press, 2008).

   Eric Greitens, Keynote Session of the Society for Human Resource Management, Strategy Conference, Palm Springs, Calif., September 2008.

Chapter 10

1. A. Demarais and V. White, *First Impressions: What You Don't Know About How Others See You* (New York: Bantam, 2004).

   T. W. Dougherty, T. B. Turban, and J. C. Callender, "Confirming First Impressions in the Employment Interview: A Field Study of Interviewer Behavior," *Journal of Applied Psychology* 79 (5) (1994): 659–665.

   L. K. Kammrath, D. R. Ames, and A. A. Scholer, "Keeping up Impressions: Inferential Rules for Impression Change Across the Big Five," *Journal of Experimental and Social Psychology* 43 (3) (2007): 450–457.
2. John D. Kammeyer-Mueller and Connie R. Wanberg. "Unwrapping the Organizational Entry Process: Disentangling Multiple Antecedents and Their Pathways to Adjustment," *Journal of Applied Psychology* 88 (5) (2003): 779–794.

   R. T. Mowday, L. W. Porter, and R. M. Steers, *Employee–Organization Linkages* (San Francisco: Academic Press, 1982).

   C. L. Adkins, "Previous Work Experience and Organizational Socialization: A Longitudinal Investigation," *Academy of Management Journal* 38 (1995): 839–862.

C. Filstad, "How newcomers use role models in organizational socialization," *Journal of Workplace Learning* 16 (7) (2004): 396–409.

J. P. Wanous, *Organizational Entry: Recruitment, Selection, Orientation, and Socialization of Newcomers* (Reading, Mass.: Addison-Wesley Publishing Company, 1992).

3. On a scale of 1 (low) to 100 (high).
4. Daniel Katz and Robert Kahn, *Social Psychology of Organizations* (New York: John Wiley & Sons, Inc., 1966).
5. F. Dansereau, J. Cashman, and G. Graen, "Instrumentality Theory and Equity Theory as Complementary Approaches in Predicting the Relationship of Leadership and Turnover among Managers," *Organizational Behavior and Human Performance* 10 (1973): 184–200.
6. Robert C. Liden, B. Erdogan, and T. N. Bauer, "The Early Development of Leader-Member Exchange: A Longitudinal Investigation," presented as part of a symposium at the national meetings of the Academy of Management, Atlanta, Ga., August 2006.

Chapter 11

1. Robert Levin and Joseph Rosse have also used water to describe talent flow as something that passes in and out of an organization like a river running by, in which you can control some elements and not others.
2. S. Fegley, "Society for Human Resource Management 2006 Succession Planning Survey Report," Alexandria, Va.: Society for Human Resource Management (2006).
3. Peter Cappelli, op. cit.

Chapter 12

1. For this example, I have removed the impact of their actual productivity improvements, as they are similar.
2. This is the amount of sales generated by five reps in each of the top two quartiles.
3. Peter W. Hom, "Organizational Exits," (in press), in S. Zedeck, H. Aguinis, W. Cascio, M. Glefan, K. Leung, S. Parker, and J. Zhou (eds.), *Handbook of Industrial and Organizational Psychology* 2, Washington D.C.: American Psychological Association.
4. M. K. Kacmar, M. C. Andrews, D. L. Van Rooy, R. C. Steilberg, and S. Cerrone, "Sure Everyone Can Be Replaced . . . But at What Cost? Turnover as a Predictor of Unit-Level Performance," *Academy of Management Journal* 49, (2006): 133–144.
5. R. Levin and J. Rosse, *Talent Flow: A Strategic Approach to Keeping Good Employees, Helping Them Grow, and Letting Them Go* (San Francisco: Jossey-Bass, 2001).
6. Office for National Statistics (ONS) provides this information for the United Kingdom. Web site: statistics.gov.uk/.

Statistics Bureau and the Director-General for Policy Planning (Statistical Standards) provide turnover information for Japan. Web site: stat.go.jp/english/.

Statistics Norway provides this information for Norway. Web site: http://ssb .no/en/.

7. Abraham Maslow, "A Theory of Human Motivation," *Psychological Review* 50 (1943): 370–396.

8. Brian Morgan and William Schiemann, op. cit.

9. The database contains hundreds of companies and thousands of employee survey participants.

10. G. S. Benson, D. Finegold, and S. A. Mohrman, "You Paid for the Skills, Now Keep Them: Tuition Reimbursement and Voluntary Turnover," *Academy of Management Journal* 4 (3) (2004): 315–333.

Leigh Branham, *The 7 Hidden Reasons Employees Leave: How to Recognize the Subtle Signs and Act Before It's Too Late* (New York: American Management Association Communications, 2005).

Peter W. Hom and Angelo J. Kinicki, "Towards a Greater Understanding of How Dissatisfaction Drives Employee Turnover," *Academy of Management Journal* 44 (2001): 975–987.

John D. Kammeyer-Mueller and Connie R. Wanberg, op. cit.

John D. Kammeyer-Mueller, Connie R. Wanberg, Theresa M. Glomb, and Dennis Ahlburg, "The Role of Temporal Shifts in Turnover Processes: It's About Time," *Journal of Applied Psychology* 90 (4) (2005): 644–658.

T. R. Michell, B. C. Holtom, T. W. Lee, C. J. Sablynski, and M. Erez, "Why People Stay: Using Job Embeddedness to Predict Voluntary Turnover," *Academy of Management Journal* 44 (2001): 1102–1122.

C. A. O'Reilly III, J. Chatman, and D. F. Caldwell, "People and Organizational Culture: A Profile Comparison Approach to Assessing Person-Organization Fit," *Academy of Management Journal* 34 (1991): 487–516.

Charlie Trevor, "Interactive Effects Among Actual Ease of Movement Determinants and Job Satisfaction in the Prediction of Voluntary Turnover," *Academy of Management Journal* 44 (2001): 621–638.

Ryan Zimmerman, "Understanding the Impact of Personality Traits on Individuals' Turnover Decisions: A Meta-Analytic Path Model," *Personnel Psychology* 61 (2008): 309–348.

11. For purposes of this illustration, these are correlations, although more advanced statistical analyses were done.

12. Peter W. Hom, (in press), op. cit.

Index